Moncure Daniel Conway

**Pine And Palm**

A Novel

Moncure Daniel Conway

**Pine And Palm**
*A Novel*

ISBN/EAN: 9783337029364

Printed in Europe, USA, Canada, Australia, Japan

Cover: Foto ©Thomas Meinert / pixelio.de

More available books at **www.hansebooks.com**

*LEISURE HOUR SERIES.—No. 207.*

# PINE AND PALM

*A NOVEL*

BY
MONCURE D. CONWAY

NEW YORK
HENRY HOLT AND COMPANY
1887.

BY
HENRY HOLT & CO.

Press W. L. Mershon & Co.,
Rahway, N. J.

# PINE AND PALM.

## CHAPTER I.

### THE COURT IN DANE HALL.

AMERICANS whose memories stretch vividly across one generation bear with them the impress of a period when the United States Senate was aglow with splendors of eloquence since visible as writings of flame on its walls. As the century neared its noon the agitation which had burthened every hour of its history was rapidly reaching its crisis. Northern Abraham and Southern Lot were awaiting the stroke of an hour which must part them, because "the land was not able to bear them that they might dwell together." But between the two stood certain Senators, grown gray in defense of the Union, to whom it had become an idol. They were so willing to sacrifice themselves before it that they could not conceive how any interest or sentiment should be raised above its priceless integrity. On that altar Webster was laying enthusiasms of Young Massachusetts ; and Clay tottered up the steps of the Capitol to utter those seventy speeches which summoned the country to the last compromise that consoled his dying eyes with its delusive victory.

It was not many years after this debate that the irrepressible question was causing excitement in the small world of Harvard University. However small this scholastic arena, a political prophet might watch the discussions among young men unawed by constituencies with keener anxiety than the debates at Washington; for these were senators of the future, and issues of their dispute studies of to-morrow's history.

In the Moot Court, where fledgling lawyers plumed their casuistic wings on the interminable issues 'twixt John Doe and Richard Roe, political questions had been avoided; but on one occasion, in the absence of the vigilant head of the school, Judge Minott, a case in constitutional law led to a point affecting slavery, and a perilous controversy was sprung on the assembly.

The ablest southerner in the law school was Randolph Stirling of Virginia. His father, Judge Stirling, had scandalized some of his neighbors by intrusting his son to a northern university; and indeed the judge himself, though he had not with the younger generation outgrown the anti-slavery traditions of Virginia, sometimes wondered at his own eccentricity in this matter. His misgivings had always ended in reverie over an episode in his life remembered with a satisfaction almost poetic. A good many years before, Richard Stirling, recognized head of the Fauquier Bar, while examining certain documents of the Supreme Court at Washington, met there Mr. Russell Minott of Msasachusetts, similarly employed. So many pleasant conversations passed between these two gentlemen that they fairly fell in love with each other. They secured adjacent rooms, walked arm-in-arm to the library of the court, and passed their evenings in the same sitting-room. The Boston lawyer listened with delight while the Virginian evoked from southern court rooms, barbacues, and the like, a procession of droll and pathetic figures; the Virginian laughed, till waiters paused in the corridor, or again he listened like a spellbound child, as this new friend told his stories of "down east." Fine law points were discussed between them, and valuable suggestions interchanged concerning the cases that had brought them to Washington. When at length they had to part, two facts remained thenceforth established—that Richard Stirling was "the truest gentleman in the world," and Russell Minott "the finest legal mind in the United States, yes, sir, the very finest."

But neither of these simple-hearted gentlemen knew how much provincialism had slipped away from him during that brief sojourn together. For the Virginian especially the experience was fruitful. It must be admitted that hitherto Richard Stirling's map of his country had held a small Arctic space called "Yankeeland" marked with chimeras bearing the names of violent disunionists; but now that region was populous with Minotts; and when his old friend became Dean of Harvard Law School he resolved to send to that institution his eldest son, just graduated at the University of Virginia. Neighbors shook their heads, but the judge stuck to his argument—"I know the head of that school, and he is the finest legal mind in the United States, yes, sir, the very finest."

"But what if Randolph should become an abolitionist?"

"I know my boy, sir: he may have faults, but disloyalty is not among them; nor is idleness, and Randolph will have enough to occupy him without attending to crack-brained fanatics."

So one day Randolph left the Palms, his Fauquier home; left his brother Douglas, grave and anxious, beside their two weeping sisters, Gisela and Penelope, and his father gazing into the fire where a tender face shaped itself as he asked, "What would she have said?"

Judge Minott was touched by his friend's confidence, and when he first looked upon Randolph his heart went out to him. The youth was large of frame and strong, but of a sensibility almost feminine, no doubt increased by care for his sisters since their mother's death; in his speech was that sweetness which is the natural accent of simplicity and humility. He had known the friendship of his father; he had never been without a true and wise man to look up to; and now he sat blushing and happy before a man to whom his father looked up. When Mrs. Minott presently wondered that so prudent a man as her husband could insist on having a stranger in the house for a week, the judge confessed he had been bewitched by the youth, and only begged that his further reproof might be deferred. The reproof never came. The guest was soon taken to the wise lady's heart.

There Stirling first met a law-student regarded as a son in that household. This was Walter Wentworth, the only representative of an old Boston family. His mother had died by an accident, and his father, a dry business man, had soon followed her to the grave, broken-hearted. Walter, too young to know his bereavement, was left to the charge of his maternal grandmother, and to Judge Minott the guardianship of his substantial inheritance. The grandmother was a learned lady; she had herself, mainly, prepared him for college. She lived to witness his honorable graduation, at Harvard College, but died the same year; and when Walter entered the law school he would have been homeless but for the affectionate welcome always extended to him by the Minotts—themselves childless. He had the gravity usual in young men brought up among elderly and literary people. Though not deficient in humor, he smiled rather with his eyes than his mouth, whose firmness suggested a certain retractile element in his generally equable character. There had been through his undergraduate years a sort of "Wentworth cult" in the college; when he was speaking his young admirers saw laurels crowning the fine curve of his head. His reputation as "a thinker" was transmitted to the law school, and he had long been accorded the palm for oratory. The Virginian orators had not prepared Stirling for this new variety of eloquence, at once passionate and restrained. He was carried away by the first speech he heard from the Bostonian, and, taking his hand, silently beamed his delight. Wentworth became his hero.

Stirling also had a reputation. "He is a man of genius," said Wentworth one day, and his opinion gained currency. When Stirling was counsel, the court in Dane Hall was sure to be crowded. His speech was unique; he so merged himself in his theory that his gestures became quaintly expressive, and had they not been so few would have verged on the grotesque. His voice was melodious, and it used to be said that Stirling could draw tears for the basest of sham criminals.

One day when Mr. Webster visited Cambridge, and was walking through the Yard with Judge Minott, this proud professor pointed to his two distinguished students, moving arm-in-arm, and pleasantly remarked that when those young men entered the political arena the greatest senators would have to look to their laurels. Stirling and Wentworth had formed a warm friendship, but one subject was suppressed between them. Wentworth knew that his friend's family were slaveholders, and, though he himself represented the awakening of the university to the new radical age, was careful not to say any thing to Randolph on that subject. Perhaps it had been better if these friends had at once joined issue on the question and had it out, for the burning question could not be repressed, and at length blazed up between them with consuming intensity.

On this memorable occasion Stirling had submitted a vigorous argument in affirmation of the national character of slavery, and carried the sympathies of a majority of his audience. This success tempted him to lapse into something like a stump-speech, in which he denounced as "pseud-philanthropy," the spirit of "those who, overlooking the evils of northern society —serfdom of labor without the parental care enjoyed by the slave—must needs wander South and mourn over the sins of other people." When Wentworth rose to reply he felt that if his cause were not upheld by him there it would not be upheld at all,—for anti-slavery views had not yet made much progress in the university. But he had not realized how much he was stung by that phrase " pseud-philanthropy," until it caused his artistic instinct to fail him. He began where he should have ended,—dealing at once with Stirling's stump peroration instead of with his argument. For this he never forgave himself. Until his unfortunate retort was irrevocable, Wentworth never suspected the stormy susceptibilities that lay beneath his own equability, and his admirers were amazed by the lightning that darted from the eye of their calm Apollo. "If," he said, with an unreal appearance of deliberation, "there is such a thing as pseud-philanthropy, there is also such a thing as lying inhumanity, and it seems exemplified by those who, after living North, can compare the lot of its free laborer with that of the slave who sees his wife and child sold like cattle."

On the utterance of these words a Carolinian sprang up and cried—"Men of northern manners do not know that among gentlemen the lie is equal to a blow." Then the whole court lost its calmness; there was vociferation on all sides. Wentworth stood still, and had already framed an apology, when the terrified chairman arose and declared the court closed. Unable in the hubbub to utter his apology, Wentworth hastened to Stirling and offered his hand, but the hand was thrust away—it was almost a blow—and Stirling walked out of the room followed by a train of excited " Southrons."

That evening Wentworth sat in his room revolving, as it were a wheel of torment, the thought : He saw my regret, the apology on my lips, my hand stretched out ; he fairly struck it, and turned on his heel. Then memories of their friendship moved him. He went to his window and looked toward that of Stirling ; it was near midnight, but a light was burning there, and shadows moved on the curtain. He descended the stairway, went over to the door and gave his well-known knock. There was enough movement within to add a sting to the silence with which his knock was received, and he returned to a painful pillow.

At Wentworth's knock Stirling had started, and had he followed his impulse would have opened his door and his heart ; but with him were several " Southrons," and behind them a cloud of witnesses demanding that he should uphold the honor of his family, of his State, of the South. Innumerable voices commanded—challenge him, or never return to Virginia !

" Well," said the confused youth, " I suppose it must be so, but——"

" Suppose ! " shouted Montgomery of Charleston ; " are we who patronize northern colleges working on a plantation with Yankee whips cracking over us ? "

"Come now, Montgomery," said Stirling, "considering the region we come from, the less said about cracking whips the better. However, fellows, I put myself in your hands; write what you all think necessary, I'll copy and sign it."

"Of course he'll not accept," said Armistead of Richmond.

"You do not know Wentworth if you think him wanting in courage," said Stirling.

While four southerners were framing the challenge Stirling lay on a sofa, still, but torn with conflicting emotions. At length the conventional challenge was completed. Stirling copied it without criticism—silently and mechanically—but the signature was marred with a blot.

Stirling vainly tried to sleep; whenever he was about sinking into slumber he heard three familiar taps at his door, and started up crying—"Come in, Wentworth!"

## CHAPTER II.

### CHANGELINGS.

ON the morrow of the scene in Dane Hall a council of northern students sat in Wentworth's room. Some were for refusal of the challenge on moral and legal grounds; others for meeting it with a proposal for arbitration; but the majority were for acceptance. It was not the first time, these urged, that northern students had been bullied at their own doors. If, as the South believed, there is no fight in a Yankee, let the fact be frankly acknowledged and southerners recognized as their natural masters; if the fact be otherwise, the sooner that is known the better. Had the challenge said any thing about apology or arbitration that would be another matter, but it simply demanded a fight. Let them have it!

Had Wentworth been able to postpone the decision for a few days his advisers might have reflected that the true victory, in such situation, were to maintain their civilization against relapse into the barbarism of single combat. But he had not time to consider the novel affair in all its bearings. In the interest of Stirling and himself he took the precaution to return the challenge, saying that he must decline to receive it in Massachusetts, and naming an evening when he would be at the Queen's Hotel, Montreal, to consider any communication that might be sent.

When Burgess of Rhode Island handed back to Stirling his challenge, it was dashed on the floor. It flashed through the Virginian's mind that his friend was greater than he thought, that he had bravely declined, and so saved them both from these agonizing coils. When Wentworth's verbal reply was delivered the messenger remarked the look of disappointment on Stirling's face. "There was no trace of fear, but a look as if he had heard of his best friend's death." Poor Stirling had indeed lost his hero.

Then he began to "set his house in order." He wrote to his father informing him of the circumstances under which he was about to meet a student who had insulted himself and the South. He should inclose this letter, he said, with souvenirs for his sisters, in one to Judge Minott; and though he could not in honor allow that dear friend and teacher—now absent from home—to hear of this unhappy affair for a few days, he had written to him some expression of his affection. Had Stirling, while writing this, known how Wentworth was occupied at the same moment, this affair might have been brought to an abrupt end. With no near relatives of his own to consider, Wentworth had been thinking about those of Stirling, and wrote to Judge Stirling a letter of the most considerate and handsome character, to be posted at some sufficiently distant point on the northward journey. With such feelings deep in their hearts, these excellent fellows started for Canadian snows, there to exchange shots instead of their usual kindnesses.

The parties took their seats in different cars to be

borne by wings of civilization to their medieval ordeal. After passing Lowell, Stirling slipped away from his two friends and sat alone in the adjoining car. There, in gloomy reverie, he gazed on the panorama through which he was passing. The snow-marbled hills, the trees silvered with hoar frost, the bright houses, the crystal ponds and the shining Merrimac, the merry skaters, how beautiful they all might have been— but, ah, how frequent seemed the village cemeteries along that road! Near one station—it was Enfield —Stirling remarked a pretty group of girls and children descending the steps of a terrace with a lovely maiden; she kissed them and hurried to gain the forward car. The unhappy youth soon forgot the maiden and her little friends.

Nevertheless it was into the hand of that casual maid that Stirling's fate quietly passed the thread of his destiny. She happened to take her seat immediately behind his seconds—no other being near— and those two were exchanging excited whispers which she could not help hearing, and which filled her with terror.

"Stirling will never return from this Montreal journey alive. Wentworth is a sure shot and will certainly kill him."

"My God, I'm afraid it's so. I almost wish the train would smash. I can see that Stirling feels himself in the wrong about this duel too. He hates the whole thing."

There were more of these half whispers, and they smote the girl's ear like thunder. She felt that she ought to do something. The responsibility of sounding an alarm was too heavy for her. Should she speak to the conductor there might be a fight, perhaps shots; or these gentlemen might be imprisoned. In twenty minutes they would reach White River Junction, where she must leave the train. She would hardly be able to consult her father, keeper of the hotel there, who would be occupied in serving the passengers with dinner. Usually she was the accountant in the Junction restaurant, and she remembered a device by which she and her father had detained a fugitive defaulter until his train had gone. But here she was single-handed, ignorant of the circumstances. She had nearly made up her mind that she could do nothing, when there approached the finest looking man she had ever seen.

"Well, Stirling, I reckon you're tired," said one of the youths, trying to smile.

"Not very. We are coming to White River Junction now. You fellows will dine with me. I shall be offended if either of you pays any bill on this trip, unless it has to be when you're coming back."

Stirling smiled faintly as he said this. The girl was moved with pity and horror; there rose before her a vision of the noble youth stretched stark and dead on the Canadian snow. Surely he must be saved. The train had slackened speed at West Lebanon; it was moving slowly over the Connecticut. The first to leap from it was the pretty accountant. When her father met her she whispered in his ear: she hurried from the embrace of her sister into the dining-room. There she assumed her place at a desk, and, while the passengers were making the most of their twenty minutes, a council of three was in close consultation.

Wentworth and Stirling almost met when posting their letters, written before starting. They sat with their respective friends in the dining-room. The seconds had appetites, and those of Stirling were nearly the last to rise.

And now occurred a singular and irritating incident. Stirling handed five dollars to a collector at the door, to pay for his party, and was requested to wait for the change. After waiting until the last diner had disappeared from the saloon, he called to the collector.

"If you can't give me my change I must go without it."

"Just a moment, sir,—plenty of time," said the man, rushing to the bar; whence, however, he presently returned with his superior.

"This is a counterfeit, sir."

"Then here is another," said Stirling.

"But that won't do; a man can't go about offering bad money and then slip off when he's caught."

"I have friends on the train to answer for me, but don't detain me. You can point me out to the conductor and tell him about it."

The saloon men rushed wildly about calling for the conductor, wherever he was least likely to be, while Stirling tugged madly at the locked door. Only as the engine gave its parting cry was the door opened. Had he been on the way to his wedding instead of his possible grave, Stirling could not have been more dismayed. He had lost the only train that could bring him to the rendezvous at the appointed time; he already saw the sneering faces of his "Southrons." That the honor of Virginia should be trailed in the dust, that the Yankees should wag their heads, all on account of a beggarly beefsteak, was too much for his equanimity; he straightway collared the collector and began shoving him furiously among the chairs.

"Don't, sir; don't!" shouted that alarmed functionary. "It's all right, sir!"

"All right! What do you mean, you scoundrel!"

"It's all right—"

"I tell you it's all wrong," cried the infuriated Virginian.

"I mean the money, sir; that counterfeit wasn't yours after all, and I humbly apologize."

"Apologize! Idiot! When you've made me lose my train, and—"

Stirling again clutched at the man, who ran calling for help, and the master of the establishment intervened.

"Come, sir; don't be angry; accidents will happen sometimes, and that stupid fellow shall be punished. There's a midnight express, or if you'd rather travel by day you shall have the best accommodation my house can afford, gratis. Very sorry sir; but it can't be helped now, you know, and the best way's to put as good a face on it as you can."

"Is there a telegraph office in this infernal hole?" asked Stirling.

"Just there at the corner, sir."

Stirling at once sent a telegram, addressed to the care of the conductor on the lost train for delivery to his friends. These were in the utmost dismay. They had supposed their principal was seeking solitude somewhere on the train, but at length one of them, becoming uneasy, strolled through the cars to return with the astounding report that Stirling was not to be found. Wentworth turned pale; a suspicion of suicide flashed through his mind. The conductor was summoned, and promised to telegraph an inquiry to White River Junction.

As Wentworth's friends were presently leaving him, for a consultation requested by the others, he beckoned them back for a moment.

"Remember," he said, "nothing will be said by any man who respects me disparaging to the honor of Stirling."

The Virginian's seconds were not quite so confident in their principal, and had to suffer some shame for their misgivings when the conductor brought Stirling's telegram stating that he had been detained on a ridiculous charge and would follow them by the next express.

But Stirling did not follow, either by the night or the next day's express. Wentworth and his friends were relieved, the southerners annoyed and angry. They were all weary, and with one exception slept through the night on their way back to Boston. When their train stopped for a moment, about three in the night, at the Junction, Wentworth peered out into the darkness, but saw no one.

After Stirling had been left by his train he paced the depot till the cold drove him into the restaurant; there he strode up and down the dining hall, angrily refusing the proprietor's solicitations that he would take food. Fatigue and worry overcame him at last, and when the hotel-keeper begged him to cross the street to his hotel, where a room was prepared for him—" and no expense, sir, if that may be mentioned" —he yielded. He was conciliated by the persistent good-nature of the man through all repulses. "Why should I be angry with this simple-hearted Yankee, so eager to serve me? If Gisela and Pen were here they would throw their arms around his neck for making me miss my train." The kindly host, as he left him in the neat apartment with its bright fire, said, "You'll be entirely alone."

Alone indeed. The wild wind was the only voice he heard. How far that dear home in Virginia! One friend he had found in this northern clime, tender as his brother, but this friend's familiar knock had been refused, and he had compelled him to become an enemy. While gazing into the fire with dim eyes he started at a gentle knock on his door—had it only been Wentworth's once more! A comely young woman brought in a dainty repast. Stiriing had a confused sense of having seen her face before.

"My father hopes you will eat something," she said, with friendly tone.

"Your father is kind,—I suppose it is he who invited me in here. I've been rude to him and ask his pardon. But I do not feel like eating, thank you."

"Try, sir; father says you have eaten nothing. He is not vexed at any thing you said; it was quite natural; we hope you will let us make up for the trouble caused you with this little dinner and a comfortable bedroom."

There are circumstances under which any woman with kindly look and voice may represent all beloved women. In his loneliness Stirling saw beside this maid, so delicately ministering to his need, the faces of his sisters.

"I will eat because you are good enough to wish it," he said rising ; but the next moment he sank back in his chair and buried his face in his hands. Since his excited speech in Dane Hall the poor youth, naturally emotional, had passed two sleepless nights and hardly tasted food. And now this tender voice brought Wentworth's gentle unanswered knock thundering again at his heart, and breaking it.

The roses faded from the cheek of the young hostess, her eyes grew large and soft, as she looked on this strong youth bowed down with anguish of mind. A deep sympathy was in her voice when she spoke.

"What can I do for you, sir? I can not know what distresses you, but if the loss of your train means some other loss, we would all be very sorry and will do all we can to make it good."

Her tones were a balm, but Stirling had not quite caught what she said and made no answer.

"Cheer up, sir," she continued, after some moments' silence ; "many things that seem hard come right in the end. Perhaps it may be all for the best that you cannot go on."

"Cannot!" cried Stirling, raising his eyes—"I must! I must go on this night, though I had rather die this moment." Again his head was bent in his hands, over which was a burning forehead.

Her word "cannot" was artful; it might mean only that no northward train was at hand; but his ominous words, their undertone of horror if not of guilt, withheld her from changing what she had spoken. Here was a noble youth on his way to something worse than death. He should not go! No friend was near him, and she must do her best.

The fatal hours flew swiftly to midnight, soon after which the train would arrive. The gracious hostess had brought Stirling a good supper, and taken it away,—like the dinner, scarce tasted. She had brought him books also, but he could not read. He passed the evening smoking and walking the floor. About midnight there was a knock, and again the young hotel dame appeared.

"Did you ring, sir?" she asked, with a blush at the pretense.

"No, but I am glad you have come. I would like to settle."

"There is nothing to pay. We shall certainly take no money."

"Not even for my wine to-day?"

"Not for the wine."

"Well, you are carrying your compensation very far. I am much obliged. Has my train been signaled?"

"No, sir; and it will not be. You can not go on to-night."

"What, has any thing happened?"

"Yes; I have had a warning which leads me—

leads me—Oh, sir; do not try to leave here this night!"

"Who has warned you? What do you know?" demanded Stirling, sharply.

"What do I need more than your own anguish and tears! You said you'd rather die. That's enough. Your heart says no, and you can not go on."

"Your feeling is kind, and I ought not to have troubled you with my worries. I must go on—there is no help for it."

"There is help for it. Forgive my boldness, but you are in trouble—not mere worry—and I can't leave you so. You said it was worse than death. I'm afraid it's something wrong."

Again that knock of Wentworth at his door sounded through his brain,—gentle, appealing. His face was suffused with shame; his head began to swim, but no tears relieved his burning eyes. He shook his head silently and arose to take his hat. But in his way stood no compliant hostess; he was confronted by a pale compassionate Fate.

"Somewhere in the world there are women who love you; I am speaking for them; you will surely go no step further towards what is unworthy of you, and would bring them grief and shame."

She had spoken like one inspired, had thrilled him by her authentic voice, but only now had touched the quick. He was indeed standing between love and friendship on one hand, grief and shame on the other. Stirling closed his eyes and sat still before the alarmed girl for almost a minute; then he started up with a look of determination, and words leaped from his lips.

"I will not! I'll not go a step further in this damned baseness—never, by God!"

"You have now given your word to God," said the girl.

"And I give it to you. I don't care who sneers. I'll be a man. I'll tell you the whole story—I love one man above all men and have forced him to—"

At that moment the scream of an approaching train was heard, and Stirling rushed to the door.

# CHAPTER III.

### THE MEETING.

THE secret of the proposed duel had been well kept at Harvard. The two councils in which it was arranged had sworn secrecy; the whole thing was too incredible to circulate swiftly. When Wentworth was soon after seen walking about as usual all might have blown over, but for the non-appearance of Stirling. When it was observed that the Virginian had not appeared at Miss Upham's boarding-house for several days, rumor took a bold flight; it whispered that the Bostonian had left his man dead in the field. This rumor was presently confirmed by the sudden flight—so it was construed—of Wentworth himself. He had remained in Cambridge two or three days after his return from the north, but after that did not appear at the law school, and knocks at his door were unanswered.

Wentworth had returned to Cambridge fully expecting to find Stirling there. Having ascertained that he had not been seen since he started for Canada, the Boston "principal" became uneasy about the Virginian, and sent a dispatch to the landlord at White River Junction, the reply to which had caused his sudden departure.

When Stirling, on the point of telling the burden

on his mind, rushed to the door, as we have seen, he found it locked, the sympathetic young hostess having quietly fortified that point. Turning round she saw Stirling fall. She called, but the noisy train drowned her voice. She saw that he had fainted, and bathed his forehead, but he did not at once recover and she ran for her father.

Between the two—Emanuel and Emanuella Rhodes—a brief interchange of theories then occurred.

"Father, it's a great trouble."

"Child, it's starvation."

"Father!"

"Don't tell me! I've watched that young man like a hawk, ever since he lost his train; he hasn't had as much as a mouthful, and how far mayn't he have come?"

Nuella looked reproachfully at her prosaic father, but remembered with misgivings the untasted food, with a pang of regret that she had not managed to have the poor man eat something before pleading with him. She summoned waiters to put him to bed. After he had been carried thither, Nuella again entered; he was breathing gently, as if in sleep. After a silent hour, in which she watched some covered dishes set near the fire, the young man moaned as if trying to say something; she listened and heard him breathing heavily. Emanuel looked in from time to time and at length read an unfavorable bulletin on his daughter's face. Thoroughly alarmed about the day's transactions now ending so seriously, he sent for the doctor; but the only one in the place had gone to a patient several miles away. The long sleigh drive after him was undertaken by Emanuel, and Nuella watched through the painful night. Once Stirling started and sat up in bed, and she managed to have him swallow a little broth ; but he did not appear conscious, and it was a great relief to the anxious hostess when, about daybreak, the doctor arrived.

Wentworth when he arrived at once had a consultation with Dr. Chase, who said the patient had a severe fever; he would not like to have three more beats per minute added to his pulse : but he had a good constitution and it would probably parry the blow. Constant care would be required, and no opportunity for nourishment lost. Nuella had a sister of seventeen years competent to relieve her of many duties in the hotel, so that she could devote her attention to the invalid. A room adjoining that of Stirling was assigned to Wentworth, with whom Nuella now shared the care which for the larger part of the week she had borne almost alone. To Wentworth alone she confided all that had passed between Stirling and herself, and from him learned that this youth was far from his southern home and that he was worthy of the kindness she had bestowed, and that, though the purpose of his journey involved no moral baseness, she had done good service in preventing it.

Wentworth and Nuella took their needful rest by relays. It was under her watch that the patient's formidable fever began to abate. On the second morning after Wentworth's arrival she brought the happy tidings to his door.

"I'll be with you in a moment," he said,

"I think you had better wait till I call you; he is very weak and should eat before talking."

That monarch for whom, when near his end, all manner of meats were kept turning on spits in case his majesty might desire some particular dainty, was not more cared for than Stirling, for whose possible need Nuella kept things always simmering and ready. Her answer to Stirling's first intelligent question was a plate of broth.

"Not until you have eaten something," she said; "I'll tell you every thing then. The doctor says you need food, and must obey me in every thing." She blushed a little, but reflected that the doctor ought to have said this.

Stirling began to eat feebly but proceeded ravenously; and when, with some misgivings as to what the doctor might think, Nuella suggested "perhaps that may do for a little time," he smiled; to this smile, the first she had seen on that pathetic face, Nuella responded with a laugh—an audible laugh, with which she glided out of the room and burst into tears.

"What is the matter?" asked Wentworth, approaching at the moment, "Has any thing happened?"

"Oh no, sir, he is better, I am happy."

"Miss Rhodes, you have had no rest, no sleep—you are broken down—you must—"

"Don't think of me—it is nothing—go to him!"

"But stay," she whispered, "I wonder if that would be best before the doctor has seen him."

Dr. Chase was soon brought by Wentworth, and after seeing the patient hinted that a friend had arrived.

"It is Wentworth," said Stirling; "let me see him."

Wentworth had been alive to the danger of suddenly meeting Stirling, and had kept out of the way of his eyes when they were open. He meant to be prudent now, but could not refrain from bending over to kiss the pale forehead, making it burn again. Stirling was nevertheless sore of spirit, and, so soon as his recovery was assured, Wentworth left for Cambridge for fear of an agitating conversation arising concerning their unsettled misunderstanding. Before leaving he warmly expressed his gratitude to Nuella.

"You have saved him and me from a calamity; you have carried through his illness as noble a man as ever breathed; to have done that is all the reward you want, I know: but I beg you keep this address, and if, in all your life, you should want a friend, be sure you can count on me if I am alive."

Nuella answered with a few deprecatory words and went off with throbbing temples: she was overwhelmed by finding her little life surrounded with strange events. Stirling remained nearly a week after Wentworth had gone. During his convalescence Nuella often read to him, and they became good friends. Stirling could not know all she had done for him, but he remembered her oracular "cannot," when on his way to a hostile meeting with his friend, and attributed to Nuella mysterious insight. Her time went on with happy hours until Stirling left.

Emanuel received compensation, but no one ventured to approach Nuella with money. She parted from Stirling silently and withdrew to her room, whither we will not follow her. Manuel did, indeed, presently follow her there, and came out with face much less merry than usual. He called to his other daughter, Ruth, who, after a few words had passed between them, undertook the affairs of the house for the rest of the day.

One encounter no Nuella could prevent. Stirling and Wentworth, notwithstanding their meeting at White River Junction, had felt a certain shyness since their return to Cambridge about being seen with each other. None had formed any definite theory to explain why the affair of honor did not come off in consistency with the essential postulate that both men had behaved with absolute honor and courage. After a few days of oppressive silence on the part of every body concerning what was uppermost in every body's mind, Stirling began to feel somewhat sore that Wentworth suggested no apology or other settlement, while the latter wondered why the challenge was not withdrawn. Probably both of them were restrained from taking any immediate step by a feeling that they would have to meet in the presence of the college authorities. This was a suspended sword over them that must soon fall. Judge Minott, however, had persuaded the authorities to ignore the incident, leaving its due treatment to himself. When notified of his desire to see them in his library both youths felt a certain relief; but when they actually met they found it sufficiently embarrassing, and stood silent, flushed, perhaps a little irritated.

"Your meeting here," said the judge, "may be vexatious, but less so than if it were before a magistrate—as it might have been. I have not brought you together for a scene, but some painful words must be spoken. As a teacher of law I have the right to expect that differences between our students shall be settled by other means than those declared criminal alike by the laws of Virginia and Massachusetts. I might add, settled by other weapons than those with which any bully could triumph over the wisest man in the country; that blackguard, for instance, who lately challenged Webster. As a friend I might have expected that my arbitration might have been sought——"

The young men started forward simultaneously, as if to grasp the hand of their friend, but he proceeded as if their movement had been unobserved.

"Well—let it be that I am nothing to men whose fathers trusted me; I abdicate; but reason does not abdicate. I hear that the trouble began with some personal remark by you, Walter?"

"It is true. The moment after I realized what I had done, and had not the court been foolishly broken up would have tendered an apology; as it was I went to Stirling to apologize."

"Of course," said the judge, "a hand offered in private is no apology for an insult in public. But somehow I can not recognize either of you in these transactions. As you were friends, I assume that all efforts to reach an understanding were exhausted."

Stirling began to feel uneasy; it dawned upon him that he had surrendered himself too fully to his "Southrons" in the framing of his challenge.

"Of course, Randolph," said the judge, "you demanded that he should apologize or fight?"

Stirling's face reddened; he made no reply.

"I am glad to conclude that it wasn't you, Randolph, who wrote that challenge, though sorry you should have surrendered yourself to a set of braggarts spoiling for a fight by proxy, and fancying themselves defenders of southern honor."

"But I have done worse, sir," cried Wentworth; "I gave myself to bad advisers in a region, unlike Stirling's, whose public sentiment would approve a refusal to fight. After insulting my friend I consented to shoot him——"

"Walter," interrupted the judge, "let us stick to the truth. Randolph, I received a letter from your father the other day, with an inclosure that may interest you."

Stirling read as follows:—" Hon. Richard Stirling, —Dear Sir,—It has been my misfortune to utter words which, being generally deemed insulting to your son, have caused him to demand satisfaction. It may be that some rumor of our leaving Cambridge for a hostile meeting may cause anxiety to yourself and family; I therefore beg that you will be under no apprehension; nothing could induce me to harm your son. The only danger under which he stands is that of burthening his memory with a regret, and I rely on your affection never to add to that regret by revealing the contents of this note. I am, sir, your obedient servant, W. Wentworth."

"Oh, Wentworth," said Stirling, with a great pain in his voice.

"It wasn't fair to give him that note," said Wentworth.

"Hush, Wentworth," said Stirling; "we have had our meeting; you have conquered; the man who challenged you is dead."

"The man who accepted can not survive," said Wentworth, taking his friend's hand.

Judge Minott touched a bell, and soon after Mrs. Minott appeared. The young men passed out to dinner, leaving their changeling selves dead in the library. As Stirling preceded with Mrs. Minott the judge moved slowly enough to whisper to Wentworth —"It is probable that your duty to North and South would hardly have been fulfilled in the eyes of your seconds. I happen to know that Stirling also had resolved to be shot without shooting. What fine stage assassins you two would make!"

## CHAPTER IV.

### THE JUDGE PROPOSES AN AFFAIR OF HONOR.

THE reconciliation just described did not terminate the Wentworth-Stirling incident so completely as that little dinner company may have hoped. The partisan feelings excited could not subside at once. When Stirling said to his friend "the man who challenged you is dead," the words were truer than he thought. He showed coolness towards the framers of his challenge, without concealing from himself his own fault in that matter. Knowing now Wentworth's unbroken loyalty, he felt so guilty that he must needs do penance, and refrained from assuring his friend that he also had resolved not to fire at him. Wentworth, as we know, had been informed of this by Judge Minott, to whom Stirling had said it in a note to be delivered after the hostile encounter, but this he did not suspect, and felt that it was only what he deserved if Wentworth should continue to believe he really meant to kill him. On the other hand Wentworth also had been running up an account against himself for not having refused a friend's challenge compelled by southern sentiment.

When these principals, at a time when one or both should have been duly lying stark on Canadian snow, were distinctly observed walking arm-in-arm once more, the sight was not regarded with universal satisfaction. In the Harvard republic two camps had been formed, and each feared its champion had shown the white feather. Naturally, the chief cloud of suspicion gathered around Stirling. It was all so transparent—that loss of a train and supplementary illness! Such innuendoes reaching Wentworth just before a meeting of the court in Dane Hall gave a certain impressiveness to an apology he had prepared. He "humbly apologized" to the Court, and to its distinguished member Mr. Randolph Stirling, for a hasty and injurious phrase uttered on an unhappily notorious occasion. His words, he acknowledged, were " susceptible of an insulting application, and he could never sufficiently regret having wronged a gentleman of truth, honor, and courage, who had, with characteristic magnanimity, forgiven him, and whom he was proud to call his friend."

The mean view of this incident was the first to make itself heard. It was all a "plant." The two had their private understanding all along; one was to miss reaching the rendezvous, the other to proclaim him the soul of honor. Such posings were too thin. But the theory which gradually prevailed was that Stirling, disappointed at finding a Yankee who would fight, had backed down as plausibly as he could, and Wentworth had compassionately covered his old friend's retreat with an apology. Such was the form in which the gossip presently reached Stirling. He did not feel humiliated, but even experienced a certain satisfaction in such completeness of his penance. He was now about "square" with Wentworth, who had got ahead of him in chivalry by that public apology, to which he had only been able to reply with a low bow. But Wentworth would not regard it as "square"; on the contrary he was furious. It was even asserted that when the charges against Stirling were last mentioned in his hearing he uttered an oath big enough to embarrass the recording angel. He did not rest until he had submitted all the facts,—as known to him through Manuel, Nuella, and the physician,— before a company of leading law-students, northern and southern. Stirling did not know of this conclave for some time, but he began to perceive that this Bostonian was more jealous for his honor than any southerner. The atmosphere around him became less sultry with suspicion, and presently cleared altogether; but a change had been wrought in him greater than he could realize. It had come about that his ideal gentleman was now a Yankee abolitionist.

It was equally impossible for these experiences to leave Wentworth just where he was before. This slaveholding southerner, so sensitive about his honor yet so patient under calumny, so eager to take more than his share of the disgrace consequent on their joint folly, raised the whole South in his estimation. Could such a man, or the community which produced such, be cruel toward helpless negroes? Thus these youths were somewhat withdrawn from the camps they had done so much to form, and alarmed their followers with conciliatory sentiments.

Judge Minott perceived that a fictitious affair of honor between his young friends had been succeeded by a real one. They were contending in the presence of partisans, for the honor of surpassing each other in magnanimity. In that competition both had conquered, and it set the judge to dreaming. What if the South and North could similarly end their dissensions, come close to each other's heart, and vanquish each other with generosity! And why might not these two noble leaders in the university become leaders in the nation, and help to bring about the happier era? It is easy to be philosophical after the fact, but in those days many were the straws floating on the flood which to their discoverers appeared material for an ark. The judge's dream was that of a man accustomed to consider both sides of every question, also of an optimistic temperament. He was awakened from his dream by the sound of a shell bursting on Fort Sumter; but meanwhile that dream had not been without its effect on the lives of the two young men with whom it was associated.

Wentworth and Stirling also had their dreams, and, as their graduation drew near, one vision acquired the consistency of a purpose: they would pass together a year in Europe. Stirling's sisters did not quite like this; and Penelope pouted through the longest letter she ever wrote. Judge Stirling had enjoyed too few similar opportunities in his youth to deny his son any he had power to give; so he wrote Randolph a cheerful consent, with tears in his eyes. But when the friends visited Judge Minott one Sunday afternoon to talk over their plan, they perceived with dismay that it was unwelcome. Very soon he was pleading against the European tour with unwonted warmth. Had they not better know more of their own country before wandering abroad? Northern and southern men in the West were beginning a war which might spread from Kansas over the whole country; and what else could be expected when even northern and southern scholars can not discuss the constitution of their country without a proposal to exchange shots in Canada? What do those rude combatants in the West know of each other? An educated northern student describes the South, and his best friend, who has lived there, is amazed at the picture. An educated southern student characterizes the North, and his best friend, a northerner, is aghast at the description. Not realizing that this kind of misunderstanding is bringing on a struggle between millions, faintly foreshadowed by their own abortive combat, these scholars repair to classic lands. They return perfectly agreed on measurements of the Parthenon, and relative merits of Florentine and Venetian schools, but sundered like repellent poles on a vital issue they dare not name to each other, and which will surely shatter their friendship as it is shattering their country. Europe would keep. Whether their own country would, was becoming doubtful. They had been able to form hostile camps in the university; if they had to do all over again they would try to make those camps friendly; they might at least try to do that in the nation. But they could only help bring warring sections to some common ground if they first get there themselves. "You will never be true friends until that old issue, suppressed between you, is honestly fought out and settled. Your hearts warned you it could not be settled by proving which is the best shot ; you both found that to be an affair of dishonor, and resolved not to shoot. Now let me propose an affair of honor : instead of shots, exchange residences for a time ! Let the southerner explore the North, the northerner the South. Let the year be devoted to study of the social conditions which each is believed by his best friend to misunderstand. Then meet, and God save the right !"

The friends went off in disappointment ; but that evening they had their first conversation on the slavery question and, though they could not agree, they talked quietly and parted as friends.

"What goody-goodies you are making these college heroes of yours !"

Very true, O piquant reader ! I look through my diary of those days, search my memories, and find these two youths steadily appearing and reappearing through rainbow archways, with morning-glories about their brows. No doubt it was absurd. Possibly, were I there now with the same fellows, I might decribe Wentworth as priggish and Stirling as quixotic. But the most democratic man is a blind loyalist at college ; he will have his king and hold that His Majesty can do no wrong. When lately I walked the Yard with a comrade of those years we met ourselves, and smiled to see what ridiculous devotees we were; may-be, had we lingered longer, we should have met our young gods wearing gilt aureoles. But these realities—granting them such—do not give one so much pleasure as illusions of the earlier time. So pray indulge me, for the present, by accepting the images left by our heroes in our foolish hearts. For their college days are ended. They must now win or lose their haloes from your cynical self. I can only add that to the last we were all fools about those two boys. Why, on the evening after Class Day, when Walter and Randolph gave their friends a supper in Boston, the northern and southern camps were so demoralized that they touched glasses, vowed eternal friendship, and supported each other in a movement on Cambridge. We beheld the great sectional discords ended then and there. Is it to be supposed that all this milk was poured out of a champagne-bottle? It may have been so in one or two cases,—I fear that Biglow of South Carolina and Calhoun of Rhode Island would never have spoken to each other but for that last Mumm,—but in truth these fellows could never have been brought together by any except Walter and Randolph: but for their magic the champagne would have turned to vitriol.

# CHAPTER V.

## THE WORM OF SPINDLETON.

ON a soft Sunday morning of early autumn a working-man strolled along one of the rural lanes where virginal nature is not yet devoured by the fire-breathing jaws of Spindleton. She knows that her time must come; the monster is not of the classic kind that guarded pretty gardens, but of the modern virgin-devouring kind; and King Cotton, who ruled in Spindleton, had ne'er a knight at his court inclined to defend any beauty from such fate. Out here, however, where the workman strolled, was a beautiful retreat. The hills were already putting on their purple and gold; the air was warm, and a mystical mist softened like gauze the autumnal tableaux. The sun had just come forth from his tent, but not as a strong man to run a race, rather as one shorn of his locks in the lap of dusky Delilah, and to be looked at without fear. Over the tall chimneys of Spindleton remained a canopy of smoke, the ever-ascending smoke of its toilers' torment, shutting off the blue-and-gold day. Far over it floated a mass of white cloud which seemed now a Madonna looking down with pity, now an eagle with spread wings and curved beak.

Presently church-bells sounded across the distance; suggestions above the smoke-roof, fairer than the white cloud-shapes, were wafted into the saunterer's mind, and he rose from his wayside stone to seek the city. The sunshine was gradually extinguished as he came within the black coils of Spindleton. He passed a little Bethel offering itself as the fount of living waters; a small brick Zion where some were recognizing the shekinah; and at length an organ-peal allured him into a stately Gothic edifice, whose tower looked proudly down on the poor conventicles beneath. It was a fine interior; the congregation was fashionably dressed, the choir sang sweetly. The preacher was handsome, with a ruddy eupeptic look, middle-aged, gold-spectacled, a model of respectability. His sermon was a rebuke of those who are "wise above what is written," among whom he included agitators trying to interfere with the institutions of the country. It was nothing to those fanatics, about to meet in Spindleton, that patriarchs held slaves, or that Paul returned the fugitive to his master; fancying themselves wiser than Abraham or Paul, they were really dangerous infidels undermining all authority. This part of the sermon evidently gave much satisfaction.

There were only three or four in the congregation who looked like work people. As all were going off our workman observed an elderly man in coarse dress, whose face, or its momentary expression, interested him. He followed him a little way, then came to his side and accosted him.

"Fine weather, sir."

"Yes, stranger, weather's good enough."

"Saw you in church; what did you think of the sermon?"

"Well, sermon's good enough fur a sermon, fur's thet goes, but he'd oughter had a cotton-bale fur his pulpit."

"A cotton-bale!"

"Jess so. That's wut it all meant. He was preachin' to fine-dressed bales in the pews, and you and me was the spools. Every body 'bout here's either bale or spool."

"I've heard that cotton is king."

"Then ye've heard wrong; Cotton is Godamighty."

"You're in a cynical mood to-day."

"A wut?"

"You're in a comical mood to-day."

"Strikes me that wasn't jess wut ye said afore. Must 'a' been pickin' up fine words som'ers. Workin' in the mills?"

"Just come. Mean to try for work to-morrow."

"Well, they'll card ye inter fine shirtin's, an' yer big words too. This be my way. Good-day to ye."

The younger workman walked slowly away with a dubious look, as if not satisfied with the conversation. After moving some thirty paces he turned, and saw the old man gazing after him. He stopped and returned the gaze stolidly, upon which the other beckoned, and the two met half way.

"Young man, I should like to know jess why ye spoke to me jess now."

"I thought I'd like to make an acquaintance, for I don't know a soul in Spindleton,—no offense meant."

"No, there's no offense. P'r'aps ye'll obleege me with yer name."

'Brooks,—Peter Brooks."

The elder workman's eyes probed the younger very keenly for the few more minutes of cross-examination, but in the end his voice grew more friendly.

"Well, Mr. Brooks, ez ye're minded to know something about the Spindleton fellers, maybe ye kin come 'round to-night to the Out-an'-Outers. No end o' gab, an' 'taint allers wuth much, but ye'll find how the wind sets. 'Bout seven."

"Where? and may I give your name at the door?"

"Room back o' Baxter's Bar. 'Taint exactly private, seats free, but only workmen allowed. Ef it's wanted, my name's Jethuel Minor. Pretty well known, but not a pop'lar character. Good-day agin."

Peter walked through several dingy streets to the tenement which for thirty-six hours had been his abode. It was the boarding-house of seven or eight workmen without families, who were already lounging about the dining-room waiting for their meal. This consisted of cold pork and beans, which the men swallowed rapidly, as if eager to be at something else. After the repast the new-comer was approached, with some shyness, by a fellow-boarder.

"Take a hand at high-low-jack?"

"Don't mind."

The game was played in an upper room, and for cent stakes. Peter soon lost some dimes. His stoicism under steady bad luck raised him in the esteem of the others, and when at length he rose to go, several hands were offered which he did not appear to see.

Out into the street again went Brooks, intending to

make a tour of the poorer quarters. But he soon wearied of this. The sad sameness of every thing and every body; the endless rows of small houses broken at intervals with squalid barracks of the ragged regiments of toil; the group of loafers at the street-corner which, after he had passed, turned up at the next, as if all had slipped around to waylay him again with vacant or sullen stares; all this produced in his soul a hard depression, like that written on the whole face of Spindleton as it toiled through its taskless Sabbath. He paused to read the advertisement of a "Spiritual Seance" to be held that evening. It announced that Mrs. Ellerton, the celebrated Trance Speaker, would "deliver an inspirational poem on a subject selected by the audience;" that "Dr. Abel Dovedale would hold a seance;" and that "Raphail Summerland would voice the spirit-breathings at the harmonium." As he turned away from this, a threadbare colporteur placed in his hand a tract against "Lying Spirits." Peter Brooks then returned to his lodging-house, took some sips of a dismal decoction called coffee, and consoled himself in his room with a smoke.

Brooks was glanced at sharply that evening as he passed through Baxter's bar-room to a half open door, beyond which he found the assemblage of Out-and-Outers. He took his seat in the lower part of the room, with an air of familiarity which was presently put to confusion; for when a boy asked him what he would take, he replied "nothing." He was informed that the room was paid for by every body taking something. He then asked for "grog,"—a generic anachronism which raised a laugh around him, amid which a man said " Bring the stranger an eye-opener." Then Brooks laughed, but nobody else did ; he found it was no joke ; nor was it a joke to sip the "eye-opener" when it was brought. The new-comer longed to be invisible, and made himself as small as possible.

There were about eighty persons present, counting by heads, but, counting by heads' contents, only two —Jethuel Minor, and the seventy-nine-necked Out-and-Outerism opposing him. Jethuel must have been speaking before Brooks arrived, for when presently a small man, with flat ashen face arose, the whispers went round—" Miller," " Englisher," " Now Jethuel 'll catch it ! " Mr. Miller, from whom so much was expected, began in a high key and screamed invectives till his voice gave way. The capitalist was the devouring dragon against which his rage was directed. He lived in a palace, dined on roast turkey hevery day, drank wine like a lord, never siled his kid gloves with work, wile we slaves for 'im and 'ardly get the crumbs from 'is table. Very likely his lordship 'as 'is favrits — a sarcastic bow to Jethuel — who 'ave a good word to say for 'im. [Laughter.] Wen a feller 'as a bit o' the turkey 'e can afford to say grace. For these hand all other musseys the Lord make us thankful ! [Loud laughter.] But there's a thousand 'ungry mouths in Spindleton for hevery one that gets enough to say grace over. Capital's grindin' the face of the widdy and horphan ! Capital's a-robbin' 'ard-'anded labor of 'elth and 'appiness. [Applause, after which, while the orator took a sip of something, Jethuel said, "Tell us wut ye're agoin' to do about it, Danby Miller."]

"What am I agoin' to do? Mr. Minor wants to know what I am agoin' to do. I'll soon tell him what I'm agoin' to do. [Another sip from the glass, continuous throat-clearing, and other dilatory items suggesting that the Englishman's prescription was not quite ready.] Capital's got to disgorge. It's got to give us shorter howers an' more wages. ["S'pose it won't," said Jethuel.] S'pose it won't! Then s'pose we won't work. ["Will that bring yer turkey ye're so fond of?"] Well, it'll make the grass grow in the streets o' Spindleton. If capitalists 'aven't got 'earts they've got 'ides, and we can take it out of their 'ides."

Some applause followed this retort and the speaker was quick enough to perceive that he had better stop there. He was the most glib of the majority's tongues, but a more impressive utterance was given to the bitterness deep in the workmen's souls by the faltering and sullen wrath of others who followed. These men were unable to save anything from their wages; there was no spark before them which hope might keep alive with dreams of its one day flaming above their desert and leading them out of bondage. The *raison d'être* of Out-and-Outerism was hopelessness; its only relief was a war-cry as hopeless as its pain.

"Wall, stranger, what's your idee?"

Brooks affected unconsciousness that this question was addressed to himself. It came from a fellow whom he promptly brevetted "bully," and whose eyes had several times stared at him with sullen spite. This fellow now whispered to some near him, and they all clamored for the "stranger" to pronounce under which king he had enlisted.

"I have nothing to say."

It may seem an innocent remark, but as Brooks uttered it the room became sultry with suspicion. It was not the voice of a workingman. A thrush may pass for a wren so long as it is silent. Peter Brooks' short speech had not only betrayed him, it had revealed a lot of things about him that he never dreamed of.

"Nothin' to say!"

"But keeps up a devil of a thinkin'?"

"Mum's the word!"

"How much d'ye git for the job?"

Such were the sarcastic cries that hurtled through the room. Brooks sat silent, but there was an amused look on his face at which the crowd waxed wroth.

"Who brought the spy?" cried the seventy-nine throated Out-and-Outer.

"Don't be fools," said Jethuel, rising; "I met that man for the first time to-day, by accident, an' seein' he was a workman an' a stranger, asked him to come 'round. What's he done that you should all o' sudden take to worryin' him?"

"Oh, he's your friend, is he?"

"Thought so."

"Damn all such ——"

"One moment, gentlemen!"

As Brooks said this, rising to his full height, there was a hush.

"I am a stranger in your town; I have been here two days; I hope to get work in a mill to-morrow. That is as much as I choose to say about myself just now. If any body chooses to think any thing more about my affairs he's welcome—provided he keeps a civil tongue. I came here to learn something about the people I'm going to live among. I've learned enough for one night, and now I'm going to bed."

"No, you ain't," cried the bully, stalking to the door, "things ain't settled yet."

"Settle them to suit yourselves, but allow me to pass."

"No, you don't!"

In another instant the bully was spinning among the benches and Brooks quietly moving through Baxter's bar-room. As he reached the street he touched a package of documents in his breast pocket, which, had they been handled by the Out-and-Outers, might have made his teapot tempest serious.

"A spy!" said Brooks, as he lay on a bed softened only by his weariness. "Precisely!"

# CHAPTER VI.

### THE COTTON WITCH.

IT was in the days of the Cotton Witch, whose miracles seem incredible to the young generation,—how she took certain malvacean plants, with capsules of white wool, of these made men, and so decorated them that they were chosen rulers and divines. One day the Cotton Witch took a notion to unmake what she had made ; she fired a gun—and lo ! all the malvacean princes and priests disappeared. Some now say that this fantastic creation of the Cotton Witch never existed,—none who belong to it being discoverable,—but they are mistaken ; the splendid cotton people really lived, and Spindleton was their capital.

Peter Brooks sought work at the Union Mills, but there was no work to be had there ; there were more than a hundred applications on file. As he was about to leave, a gentleman, who had just been conversing with some others, accosted him.

"What is it you want, my man ?"

"Work, sir."

"Ah, we are overstocked, but I hear they want hands at the Print Works, Prescott Street."

Brooks hastened to the Print Works, and the manager there put some questions to him.

"What region are you from ?" he asked at last.

"South."

"It isn't often we have applications from that section. We may find a place for you next week. Meantime if you will call on Captain Meshach Jones, number ninety, lower door, he may be glad to see you. Tell him you are from the South, don't forget that."

Captain Meshach Jones was not found at any Mills, but in the back room of a small unfurnished house, into which Brooks was ushered by an ingeniously ugly doorkeeper. The captain was of middle age, black with broadcloth from head to foot; but for his red nose he might have been mistaken for a preacher. Our workman did not find him prepossessing—especially not his white eyes, one of which by a cross movement seemed trying to cover the over-curious stare of the other. His face—the nose excepted—was colorless, and it was a cracked voice that said to the ugly usher, "You can go, Scully."

"Well, sir, what do you want?" said the captain to Brooks.

"Work."

"Who sent you to me?"

"Manager at the Print Works near by."

"Ah—take a seat."

As Brooks looked round for a chair he glanced out of the window and saw a group of roughs in the back yard.

"Where are you from?" asked the captain in a friendly way.

"I've been working near Boston."

"Do you belong to any party in politics?"

"Does that make any difference in my getting work?"

"Well, you see—the manager at the Print Works don't know it, oh no, don't suppose he knows it—but it isn't mill-hands we are wantin' to-day. There's a political matter on hand, and I told him if he met any workmen out of work I'd like to see them. He must have known you are of the right stripe—that is—ah—he must have known you were out of work. Oh, bless you, he don't know no more'n a child!"

While Brooks was debating whether "Whig" or "Democrat" were trumps, he saw distrust gathering in Captain Meshach's cross eye, and said, "I'm a Democrat."

"A fine able-bodied fellow, too, Mr.—didn't catch the name?"

"Brooks."

"Well, you see, Mr. Brooks, times are bad for us up here, in the cotton business. The southern people are getting mad. They've been writin' from the plantations to our leading men in Spindleton that they won't stand this abolition business any longer. They say they'll make grass to grow in the streets of Spindleton. Think of that! Well, the question is, what's to be done? Now what do *you* say, Mr. Brooks?"

Brooks shook his head solemnly and dubiously.

"You're out of work. Thousands are out of work, and the abolitionists want to make Spindleton swarm with niggers to take the bread out of your mouth. And where will the work be and the bread when the South ships all the cotton to Europe—all because o' them pesky abolitionists? That's what they say.

They are publishin' all the northern firms that ain't friendly to the South, and all places where the abolitionists are allowed to hold meetin's. And, would you believe it, they've got Spindleton down! It was sent to one of our bosses in a Georgia paper, and it's in that drawer. Does seem to have been a little abolition meetin' here six months back, kind o' private like, but none o' the boys hearn of it. But the abolitionists have give out for a big meetin' Thursday night in the nigger meetin'-house. What do you think of that, Mr. Brooks? Are we a-goin' to allow that?"

"What can be done?"

"Done, Mr. Brooks! What was done at Riceport the other day, where not one of the infidel set went away with a sound skin! It's the Lord's work—it is. They're all infidels. Why, one of them lit a match and burnt the Constitution of the United States—burnt it to a cinder. A man told me he seen it done with his own eyes, and wondered it didn't bring down a judgment. Are we again to stand that kind o' atheism in Spindleton?"

"Should think not," said Brooks.

"Any family?" inquired Captain Meshach, tenderly.

"None."

"Them that obeys orders this week gets five dollars down and five one week from to-day, and more if they get into trouble, and sure of a place in the mills if they want it."

"I must think over this," said Brooks, rising.

The captain's straight eye glared at him an instant,

the cross eye searched him successfully, the thin lips spoke unctuously.

"Of course we don't expect trouble, Mr. Brooks, but we must be prepared for the worst when excitin' meetin's like this takes place. Our citizens are naterally excited and may be roused to violence. We must have men on hand to—to keep order."

"To keep order!"

"Yes, Mr. Brooks, to keep order. Hope I've not been misunderstood?"

"I think not."

"I hope not. We must do our best to keep order, and when we're warned of danger we must employ extra men. This duty has been allotted to me, and I must perform it to the best of my humble ability. I may be abused and slandered—slandered, sir—for my efforts to discharge my duty, but that duty shall be fearlessly done."

"Good morning, Captain Jones."

"Good morning. It's my official duty to admonish you not to mention any thing said in this room."

"Thank you," said Brooks, with an affectation of meekness which made Captain Meshach livid.

"This way," said the captain, opening a door into the inclosure of the roughs, "you'll find a gate at the bottom of the yard."

The rowdies gazed at Brooks as he passed, and when he had disappeared Captain Meshach went out to them.

"Boys," he said, "he's an abolition spy. If you see him about anywhere a good handlin' won't do any harm; but be careful; he's strong and likely to be dangerous. He oughtn't to be there Thursday."

A few hours later Brooks was at the anti-slavery rooms in Boston telling the story; after which he at once returned to Spindleton.

The abolitionists held their meeting in Spindleton, and mustered all the stronger because of the information Brooks brought them; for that peculiar people delighted to flock where they were least wanted. Stephen Foster was there with his bitter arraignment of the clergy, as dumb dogs whose cowardice was guilty of all done by the wolves. His startling generalization was illustrated by the crushed hat he wore and a coat picturesquely split down the back. "This hat," he said, "was battered in by the church in Riceport, and this coat" (turning his back to the audience) "was torn by the ministers of Christ in Vermont."

"Damned infidels all of you!" shouted a voice.

"What church in Spindleton do you preach in?" cried Foster.

Splash went an egg into the speaker's face, followed by a mad yell from the crowd. The roughs rose *en masse*, showing themselves to be two-thirds of those present.

"At 'em, boys!" cried a ringleader.

Straightway the mob began climbing over the benches toward the pulpit, waving sticks and roaring. The front benches were occupied by abolitionists, chiefly women, who made gallant obstruction and were considerably bruised. The mob was determined to get at the leading abolitionists who sat in front of the pulpit. Garrison's beaming face was visible above the raging mass he vainly tried to still. The melodious voice of Phillips was drowned as a flute might be by drums. Angry yells greeted the colored orator Charles Remond. Matters began to look serious enough; the mob evidently meant mischief. Suddenly a stentorian voice near the door cried—" Let's hang that nigger, any way!"

Just then from a remote corner stepped forward a quaint little man, with large luminous eye, whom few even of the anti-slavery men recognized as Thoreau, and placed himself in front of the rush, so quietly—as if he did not see it—that the crowd was surprised into momentary stillness. "Doubtless," he said, "you all remember that fine passage in the Bhagavatgita where Krishna says to Arjuna, Thou and I have met many times." The mob was breathless. "I may now say that you and I have met in various ages of the world." Here somebody exploded in a laugh, which made the crowd laugh. The mob that laughs is lost. The ringleaders vainly tried to rally their forces. Thoreau was heard to the end of his estimate of how many births the mob and the abolitionists had gone through. A few howls and cat-calls were all that could be achieved against the subsequent speakers, and a "successful meeting in Spindleton" was reported in next week's *Liberator*.

It was from that paper that our workman, Peter Brooks, learned the particulars of the meeting. He had set his heart on being present, but alas, while these scenes were occurring, he was withheld by inglorious repose in a cell of Spindleton police-station.

## CHAPTER VII.

### FRAULEIN ROSE.

ON the day following his interview with Captain Meshach Jones, Peter Brooks had again tried to obtain employment, but in vain. In the evening he went to a Music Hall, and found a dismal performance going on. It was a company of roughs instead of the workmen whom Brooks hoped to meet there; and there were no women at all except those who appeared from time to time on the wretched little stage. These were tawdry and tiresome enough, and our workman was about to leave, when he observed a fellow staring at him impudently, and apparently speaking of him to three others drinking with him. Brooks was by this time accustomed to the rude glances that greeted a stranger at Spindleton,—result, perhaps, of instinctive hostility to a new competitor for wages,—but this fellow's look was unusually sinister.

At this moment the pianist announced that a German *cantatrice*, Fraülein Rose, would appear for the first time in the United States, and sing in the peasant costume of her country. The Fraülein was very different from the preceding singers; she was modest, pretty, fresh, and began her ballad with a clear sweet voice. But her broken English was received with derision and grotesque mimicry. The interruptions began so immediately that Brooks suspected a conspiracy; and when somebody called out "Let the girl have a chance," he applauded vigorously. Just then loud hisses broke out, and the poor girl moved from the stage weeping. Brooks could not repress a cry of "Shame!" and at that moment heard a brutal voice beside him, "Is that your girl?"

Brooks recognized the fellow who had been inspecting him so insolently, and lost his temper.

"Puppy!" he exclaimed, "speak when you're spoken to."

The fellow raised his stick, and was felled with a blow. Instantly two others leaped on Brooks, and when one of these was disabled, another rushed viciously at our workman and clutched his right arm.

"Four to one's hardly fair," called a voice from the circle that pressed around, and somebody grappled one of the assailants. The fight threatened to extend, when the saloon-keeper and pianist managed to stop it. Then policemen rushed in, and finding Brooks with two men at his feet arrested the three. They were marched to the station and there ushered into the presence of Captain Meshach Jones.

Brooks saw a sparkle in the captain's cross eye, but the straight one stared on and gave no sign. He wrote down the accusation, "causing disturbance in a saloon," with the name, age, and address given by each prisoner, and nodded toward an inner door.

"Take the prisoner Brooks into number five, and come back for the others."

As Brooks passed out he gave a steady look at one of his assailants; he thought he had seen him before that evening, and carried the fellow's photograph in his eye. About midnight he remembered that it was Scully, the captain's ugly usher.

Only on the third morning after the fray was Brooks brought before the magistrate, who asked why he had not been brought earlier. He was told that there seemed to be some mystery about this prisoner and it was suspected that he had given a false name. There had been delay for inquiries, but nothing had been discovered, and no one appeared against him.

Soon after his discharge Brooks read a report of the riot at the anti-slavery meeting the evening before, and suspected the reason why his case was postponed. He resolved, too, to postpone his case against Captain Meshach, and to leave Spindleton. Personal encounters there were becoming monotonous, and he was in danger of becoming famous. He would go and try Peacefield, whose name at least promised repose. It required but one more evening to settle his small affairs at Spindleton, and next morning he was at the depot ready for the early train.

While so waiting our workman observed a young woman dragging a wooden trunk along the platform, and hastened to her assistance. When she looked up to thank him he recognized in her the German singer who had fared so badly in the saloon. She presently sat on the box; and as Brooks paced the platform he saw tears in her eyes. He debated within himself whether he should speak to her. Her continued distress in the car, where they presently sat, almost alone, determined him. He saw that she was an honest simple-minded woman, and in trouble.

Taking a seat near her he said in German, "You are in trouble, and seem to be alone." Her eyes filled with tears again; she gazed silently out of the window for some moments, then looked into the eyes of her neighbor.

"You speak German," she said, "but you are not German?"

"I am not. I saw you Tuesday evening at the Music Hall and was angry at your outrageous treatment."

"It was all planned beforehand. Here are letters telling me I would not be allowed to sing there."

"It is infamous," said Brooks, looking over the scrawls.

"The manager wants to be rid of two other girls there; but their friends plot against every new singer. He told me."

"You must have been in need before you could go to such a place, Fraülein——"

"Rose—Mathilde Rose is my name. Yes, I have very little money and no friends. Mr. Senker—he that keeps that saloon, his father is a Hanoverian like me—could not help me with more than a dollar, but gives me a letter to one in Peacefield who may get me some work. At home, near Verden, I got up little plays at Christmas and Fastnacht; I had a pretty dress, from our carnival, and hoped to earn something at a beer-house concert. My father taught me English; he learned it in England."

Here she broke down again. Our workman could not make up his mind to leave this poor Fraülein to her fate, but was sore puzzled about the way to assist her.

"Can I help you in any way?" he presently said.

"You are kind, you can not help me. I came from Germany to find my Franz, but can not; now I must give up."

Her blush rendered it needless to inquire her relationship to Franz. The mention of that name made her feel that she had taken this casual friend into her confidence, and indeed the Fraülein was plainly glad to talk with any one whose tone was kind.

"How did Franz come to leave you?" asked Brooks.

"Do not think it was his fault; no, my Franz is true. My father did not like him; he would not let us meet. Franz came from Baden to a farm near us, but he had no relations, and he went to America. My mother was dead, my father loved me—his only child—I could not leave him; so Franz had to give me up. My poor father was drowned; out of his money near three hundred thalers came to me, and then I must be in the same fatherland with Franz. My money is gone, I can yet work for bread. If I get not work I can die, and not be sorry."

"Did you ever hear from Franz after he sailed?"

"One letter came and my father found me reading it; he snatched, he burned it. I had not yet noticed the address, but on the envelope is 'Boston.' I hoped it was a little place, and that he might get the letter I wrote there, but I never heard from him except that once after he left Bremen."

"Do you know just when he left Bremen, and the name of the ship?"

"Yes; it was April 10th, last year, on the *Silesia*.

Oh sir, is it possible to learn any thing of him by that?"

"I fear not, but we can try," said Brooks, writing down the items.

The engine screamed; Peacefield was near. Our good Samaritan found this case sufficiently embarrassing. The oil and wine required were not of the kind that money could buy.

"Where are you going in Peacefield?" he asked.

"Heman Wilder, Boarding House, 37 Merrimac St.," she read, from a letter in her hand.

"Very well," said Brooks, copying the address; "now let me advise you. I will pay a man to take you and your trunk to that house. Even if Heman Wilder can not give you employment you had better stay in his house for a time, paying board. I can lend you some money. At any rate stay there till you see me or hear from me. I hope to call this afternoon, and if you have no employment, will try to find you some."

"Who are you?" said the Fraülein, trembling; "I am frightened. You saw me in that low place at Spindleton, where good men do not go—and yet——"

"Were you not there also, Fraülein?" said Brooks, with a reassuring smile. "I believe you had honest reason to be there, and you must believe the same of me."

"Did you see the fight that night? Mr. Sadler, that's the pianist, said a man took my side and was set upon by the men who hissed me, and he knocked them down—Oh—oh lieber Gott! it was you!"

His blush under the Fraülein's clear eyes had betrayed him.

"It was you, it was you!" she said, trembling with emotion. "Are you a prince in disguise? Have you met me to-day on purpose?"

"No, I never dreamed of seeing you again. I could not get work in the Spindleton Mills and am going to try Peacefield."

There are unconscious expressions that can not be mistaken. Fraülein Rose looked into this man's face, then at his coarse dress; through the surprise in her eyes beamed perfect confidence.

"I may never know who you are," she said, in a low, reverent tone, "but you have lifted a weight under which I was sinking. I obey you. No—I don't want any money yet, I have over three dollars; but I thank you from my heart, little as that may help you."

"It helps me more than you think," he answered gently. "Now remember; remain at Heman Wilder's till you see or hear from me. On this paper is my name."

At Peacefield depot Brooks paid the driver of an humble conveyance to convey the Fraülein to her boarding-house. For himself he took from his large wooden box a fashionable overcoat and hat, with which he entered the toilet-room, returning presently with some garments which were placed in his box. At the hotel to which he drove he escaped scrutiny, —but his box! That huge chest, suitable for an emigrant, remained ostentatiously in the hotel entry, a problem for clerks and porters, until it was personally demanded by its owner—Randolph Stirling.

# CHAPTER VIII.

### PEACEFIELD PINES.

ISSUING from his hotel, merry at relief from his masquerade, Stirling passes through the main business street of Peacefield, makes inquiry of a wayfarer, saunters through an avenue of superb elms and edifices, leaves the town behind, and after a happy half hour's walk stops at the gate of the old mansion known as "Peacefield Pines." The spacious lawn, the flowers and trees, were so beautiful that he moved but slowly to the door. There he asked for Mr. Derby Leigh.

"He is in Boston, sir," said the rosy maid-servant.

"And Mrs. Leigh?"

"She has driven into town. Would you like to see Miss Hilda, sir?"

She went off with Stirling's card, and he was soon yielding himself to the enchantment of a wondrous drawing-room, wainscoted like his own home in Virginia, and hung with portraits of ancestral Leighs. One especially lovely face was beaming on him as if with friendship, when the daughter of the house entered, hat in hand.

"I am sorry my father and mother are absent," said Hilda.

"I have no very urgent affairs with either of them,

Miss Leigh, and can call again if you will tell me when Mr. Leigh will be able to see me. I am a friend, I may say, and lately a student with Judge Minott of Cambridge, who has given me a letter to your father."

"Father would be sorry to miss you; he will return by a rather late train this evening, but be home all day to-morrow. He thinks Judge Minott one of the best of men and would be glad to serve a friend of his."

"I have little to trouble your father with except a number of questions. I had indeed thought to consult him to-day about a matter that has engaged my sympathies and put me under some responsibility."

There was now one of those inevitable pauses which follow the gambit of opening acquaintance. While Hilda was expecting a remark on the picturesqueness of Peacefield, Stirling had moved a pawn that required her attention. Stirling found turned toward him a face whose type he had never before seen in the North, and but rarely in the South,—a placid, or almost languid, face, very fair, with translucent complexion, wavy brown-and-gold hair and soft brown-and-gold eyes. She was of large frame, and might have been supposed a well-advanced spinster until her voice—the only sure test—revealed the nearness of her teens. Her repose, her largeness, a way of half-closing her eyes while listening, impressed Stirling with a feeling that the Fraülein's little romance might well be confided to this grave and gracious young lady, if she offered occasion. Hilda's answer was sympathetic, but her eyes were incurious.

"You may feel sure of father's interest in whatever you consult him about. Will you not stay to luncheon? Mother will then return: she will be glad to see you, and also to hear about the Minotts."

"Willingly," answered Stirling, with a smile hardly comprehensible to Hilda, who little knew how long it had been since her guest had really lunched or dined.

"That is well," said Hilda, "and as it is early perhaps you will enjoy a stroll in our grounds."

As Hilda with her furzy russet hat, a bit of warm red ribbon about her throat, led the way through an aisle of pines to a grove of many-colored trees, and there moved on the carpet of brown and tinted leaves, Stirling recognized in her the creation of Indian Summer. The day folded its veil tenderly around her, the leaves rustled rhythmically under her tread, a serene joy overspread her face, as if her youth were maternally quieted by this afterglow of summer. Stirling too was content. The rude world he had been mingling with was here as a fable, the past was really past; even the Fraülein's face, bathed in tears, vanished out of memory under the unconscious spell of this guileless Vivien of the Peacefield wood.

They had walked a quarter of a mile, conversing but little, yet with a growing satisfaction in each other's society, when they reached a small gate beyond which was a cottage.

"If you will wait for me here," said Hilda, "I would like to call on an old colored woman, an aged servant whom we have to look after."

Hilda entered the cottage and Stirling strolled farther in the park about a hundred yards, where he stopped to pick blackberries from bushes that made a hedge at that part of the grounds. While thus listlessly engaged he perceived two men, suspicious characters he thought, crouching under bushes beyond the fence, near a road. They did not see him, and were absorbed in their silent watch for something or somebody in the direction of the cottage. Stirling felt that they meant mischief, but was puzzled what to do, for they were beside an apparently public road. He resolved to return to the cottage where he had left Miss Leigh and report what he had seen. When he knocked, Hilda herself appeared, pale, trembling, her eyes flashing.

"Come in, pray," she said hurriedly, then locked the door behind them.

Stirling saw before him a handsome young mulatto, and three women of the same race, one aged, all much frightened. The man was a fugitive slave. That he saw at a glance, and he knew why these men were crouching under the hedge. He had seen such men dragging just such a trembling runaway through the streets of Warrenton, followed by a train of gaping boys. He did not need, and hardly heeded, Hilda's information, being already deep in the difficulties of the case.

"This man," she said, "has escaped from his master in Maryland; he was tracked to Boston, and ran from there last night, traveled all night on foot, and reached here at daybreak."

"He has been tracked here," said Stirling; "I have just seen two men watching this house."

Hilda sank into a chair with horror, but recovered herself when the women began to cry.

"Hush!" she commanded; "no noise at all! Now

what can we do? This man is under my protection and must be saved."

"There is danger," said Stirling, to whom she had appealed; "the law respects no protection short of Canada. For that country he must race with his pursuers. Do any of you know any man in this region who has ever helped a runaway?"

The fugitive drew from his breast a bit of paper on which Stirling read: "John Moor, Marble Works, Cemetery, Peacefield." The man said this address had been given him in Boston. The women knew something of Moor; his place was two miles distant. Stirling pondered for a time.

"Miss Leigh," said he at length, "can a swift conveyance be got without being brought too close?"

"The stable is half way to the house, and the dog-cart is there, with a boy."

"You," said Stirling to the smaller of the women, "walk quietly to the stable—don't appear to hurry—and have the dog-cart and driver in readiness. And you," addressing the larger but younger sister, "are you willing to give this boy your clothes and wear his for a short time?"

The poor creature was aghast, and the mother raised her hands in alarm.

"I'm willing to dress in the man's clothes," said Hilda. It was now Stirling's turn to be aghast. The possibility of this sublime maiden being carried off by negro hunters—visions of parental consternation—rose before him. How like his sister Gisela she now looked, her languor gone, her repose that of the smooth cataract : fancy Gisela in the clutch of a slave-driver!

"No," said Stirling, "that would not do at all. We must have the dark complexion. The men must be deceived and follow this woman, supposing her to be their man. She must run ; they will overtake her ; she must not say a word but hide her face with her hands and appear to cry. I will walk with this man to the stable, then come back. This woman in his clothes will wait till she sees me coming ; then let her leave the door and hurry towards the town. I will not lose sight of her, and will come up in time to save her from any worry. She must not say a word."

"This fugitive must use my gown at any rate," said Hilda, "for the men who are watching saw us both coming and should see us both leaving. Maria, come in here with me and we will arrange things."

Hilda's dress was presently thrust through the door ; the mulatto put it on and walked with Stirling to the stable where a negro stable-boy was waiting with the dog-cart. The fugitive being sped on his way to Moor's Marble Works, with money in his pocket, Stirling hastened back. As he came in sight of the cottage he saw the woman in man's clothes leave the door and run along a small road into the woods. He hurried on, but presently saw with dismay that the men had a covered buggy and swift horse for their pursuit. Stricken with fear, he leaped a fence, ran across a field to the wood, and there plunged along the road, but he could see neither the woman nor her captors. Running a hundred rods farther, he mounted a small hill, and then saw, half a mile beyond, one of the men opening a gate for the other to drive through. Cursing his stupidity in not reflecting that the men would never try to carry a fugitive without a vehicle, Stirling was bewildered. Fortunately a grocer's wagon came along the road on its way to town. Stirling hailed it.

"Young man," he said to the driver, "if you want to earn a dollar or two, take me up and drive into Peacefield like lightning."

"Get in!"

Stirling was out of breath for a few moments, but presently told the youth that some fellows were carrying off a woman and must be caught. A whistle of amazement and a tremendous lash on his horse were the driver's comment on this strange story. No word passed till the gate opening on the high-road was reached.

"Where am I to take you in Peacefield?" asked the driver.

"Let me think a little."

The few moments' silence that followed was broken by the young driver's pride in his horse.

"That one cut was enough, sir,—don't she dash splendid? She knows sutthin's up."

"Drive to the police-station."

Stirling's instinct told true: as they came in sight of the police-station he saw the buggy in front of it.

"Here is your money. You had better wait outside a little time to see if I need you again; but don't answer any questions—mark, my friend, you've done good service, now do me that."

In a few moments Stirling was in the office confronting a constable, and summoning what calmness he could.

"Did some men bring a nigger here just now?" he asked.

"Well, we don't generally answer questions here till we know who's asking them. Have you any business with me?"

"Yes; two men ran off with my nigger in that buggy out there."

"How am I to know that?"

"There's my card."

The constable read—"Mr. Randolph Stirling. The Palms, Warrenton, Va."

"Of course," said Stirling, "if my nigger chooses to leave me when I'm traveling north I can't help it, but I'm not going to have him abducted by force."

"Wait a moment, Mr. Stirling, we must see about this. Two men did leave a nigger here and they've gone off to find the Marshal. They said this wasn't their man, but he had got theirs off, and we must keep him till they brought the Marshal."

"Well—only let me see that nigger and you'll hear all about it."

"I'm ready to do whatever's lawful, Mr. Stirling, but we must wait till the Marshal comes. The negro is quite comfortable in the other room, all by himself. You needn't be afraid, provided he wants to go with you. He hasn't spoken a word yet."

Stirling fretted a good deal about poor Maria, knowing how terrified she must be. He dismissed the driver who brought him, and ordered a carriage to await him at the door. Just then the two slave-hunters returned with the Marshal. They preceded Stirling a little into the station and he hurried after them. He saw them at the end of a corridor where the constable was unlocking a door. He swiftly followed them into the dark room, in a corner of which crouched—Hilda.

Overwhelmed with amazement and fear, Stirling was about to cry out, when he saw Hilda touch her lips; he was also calmed by the slightly mischievous glance she cast at him. Hilda made up well as a young man, but her color had been put on hastily—a mixture, one would say, of coffee and soot. She was aware that this was her weak point, and had crouched in the darkest corner, where she drew her hat over her face as well as she could.

"Come now," cried one of the Marylanders, "get up here, you damned——"

"Stop a moment," said Stirling, placing himself in front of Hilda—" is this your boy?"

"No, but he's got on our boy's clothes, I do believe, and he's come a trick on us."

"Show the Marshal your documents. Let's see if you've got a warrant to catch any nigger at all," said Stirling, wondering what Hilda would think of his swagger and vulgar dialect.

"Jim Bounce's got the papers; he took 'em off to get the warrant while Bob and me watched the house where the boy went. While we was watching the feller made off and we follered——"

"But it isn't the fellow," said the Marshal; "I gave Mr. Bounce his warrant an hour ago, and that's not the fugitive described in the papers. Come, gentlemen, we are ready to try and return your slave if you get hold of him, but you'll find that hard enough without trying to carry off somebody in his place."

"This gentleman," said the constable, pointing to Stirling, "claims the negro as his property, and gave me this card."

"Peacefield seems overrun with masters and slaves to-day," said the Marshal, examining Stirling's card.

"My God, I do wish Jim Bounce was here!" exclaimed one of the slave-hunters piteously. "It was his man; I never seen him till I see him go into that house. This feller looked like him behind."

"Probably," remarked Stirling, "Mr. Bounce has gone back to the house with his warrant and by this time has got his own nigger. As for my boy there, I sent him out to that house to wait while I transacted some business with Mr. Derby Leigh; if he found a runaway nigger there, flying from a cruel master, he might have swapped clothes to draw off these men. Niggers will be niggers. If these men haven't been so sharp as the darkies it's their lookout. But I don't believe they're right. I didn't notice the boy's clothes this morning, but they look about right."

"Can't we wait here till Jim Bounce comes?" whined the slave-hunter pathetically.

"These gentlemen," said Stirling, bowing politely to the Marshal and the constable, "may be able to accommodate you, but I have already lost more time than I can well spare. If my boy Sam there wishes to leave me and claim his freedom he has now a chance; I admit that, Mr. Marshal, for I brought him north at my own risk; but if, as I hope, he has found me a good master, and wishes to stick by me, and see his old mammy and daddy again, I trust the Marshal will protect us from further annoyance and allow us to go in peace."

The Marshal, impressed by Stirling's little speech —it was in his best Dane Hall manner—bowed assent.

"Well, Sam, my boy," said Stirling, "what do you mean to do?"

Hilda, shunning the gaze of the sharp-eyed Marylanders, leaped forward and knelt before Stirling, grasping his hand. The Marshal was touched by such affection.

"Constable, let this gentleman and his servant out without interruption!"

"Darnation seize Jim Bounce!" cried a despairing voice behind them as Stirling and Hilda hurried away —she holding her sleeve to her eyes as if crying, and so hiding her clumsy complexion from too much light.

But the attendant constable was a connoisseur in human figures, and when they reached their carriage Stirling saw on that functionary's face a knowing smile as he searchingly regarded Hilda's form. Hilda was pushed roughly into the carriage, but the constable was not to be deceived; he distinctly winked at Stirling.

"Young men will be young men," he whispered.

An instantaneous debate passed in Stirling's mind whether he should knock the constable down or give him five dollars.

"Young men know whom they can trust," he whispered, slipping something into the official's hand.

"Tell the driver to go up that high road as fast as possible, and he'll be well paid."

They were none too quick in getting off. The rumor had reached Peacefield negro-quarter that a fugitive slave was being carried off, and a score or two of furious men rushed to the police-station just as the carriage dashed off. But not without a black face being seen in it. The mob at once pursued, crying "kidnappers"; the negro driver heard the cry, and when stones crashed against his coach held back his horses. Stirling thrust his head out and called to the driver, "Don't be afraid; we are leaving the kidnappers behind and saving this boy. Drive fast, straight to Peacefield Pines."

At that moment a stone struck Stirling's head, and he sank back into the coach. "It is nothing," he said, and became insensible. The driver, who knew nothing of the blow, dashed on; he had no fear that any kidnapper would wish to be taken to Derby Leigh's house. The mob was left far behind. To Hilda, holding the apparently lifeless man in her arms, the horses moved as snails.

The Leigh household was in terrible commotion. On her return home several hours before, Mrs. Leigh found the colored woman from the cottage weeping with terror. She was met with the wild story that her daughter, dressed in man's clothes, had gone off with a strange gentleman. She had to be stern with the bewildered woman before she received any intelligible account; she drove to the telegraph office to call her husband back by first train, then to the office of her brother, Dr. Endicott. The physician, with what meager information she could give, started off in her carriage, and she returned home in his brougham. She found and read Judge Minott's letter of introduction, then went to the front gate and watched till she saw a coach rapidly approaching. She felt that it was coming there and swung open the gate. She required all her courage after a glance into the carriage. To see her daughter, her lovely, luxuriant Hilda, now sooty, blood-stained, clasping a man's head, so shook her nerves that she could hardly follow the coach.

"Bring the men," said Hilda to the servants gathered at the door. "Coachman, this gentleman was struck by a stone—we shall need your help. Maria, stand by the horses' heads and keep them still. Emma, some brandy."

She remained seated, with Stirling in her weary arms, until the gardener, coachman, and stable-boy were ready to lift him into the house, where he gave signs of returning consciousness.

Dr. Endicott had driven to the negro-quarter, where he was told that a fugitive slave had been taken to Moor's Marble Works: he drove there and learned that the mulatto was far on his way. He then drove to his sister's house for further inquiry, and arrived in good time to attend to Stirling. He found the wounded man conscious, but weak from excitement and loss of blood. He could not say yet whether the wound was dangerous, but bound it up carefully. He then turned his attention to Hilda. She had almost become her tranquil self again. Only a big bruise on each arm told that ruffian hands had been upon her.

Dr. Endicott's conservatism suffered by sight of these bruises, and when later he returned from a drive into Peacefield he reported, with illicit satisfaction, that the mob, distanced by Stirling's coach, had got hold of the negro-hunters, who had to be locked up for safety.

Mr. Derby Leigh was met at the depot by Dr. Endicott. His apprehensions being relieved about his family, he at once entered Stirling's room; he inquired where his trunk was, and whether there were any thing he wished to have attended to. Stirling mentioned his hotel, and then said he would like to have Miss Rose, at Heman Wilder's boarding-house in Peacefield, informed that the man who traveled with her from Spindleton was prevented by an accident from calling, but he would surely come to her and fulfill his promise, if he lived. Stirling's voice became very feeble, and Mr. Leigh had to lean over him to catch the last words.

## CHAPTER IX.

#### A MORROW OF MYSTERIES.

MR. DERBY LEIGH that evening undertook the visits to the hotel and to Heman Wilder's boarding-house, and returned with a batch of what he least liked—mysteries. One mystery was a huge wooden box of clothing, brought from the hotel after much hesitation in accepting the evidence that it must be Stirling's. Another mystery was the impression left by his interview with Miss Rose. He had found himself conversing with a servant, and when he gave her Stirling's message she was greatly agitated. "Oh, sir," she exclaimed with tears, "I hope he is not much hurt—is he, sir, is he? He is so good and kind! Ah, I would help him!" Mr. Leigh was in a hurry to leave, but left his address that she might call and ask about her friend the next day. This Miss Rose, he could not but see, was pretty and otherwise attractive; there was also a certain dignity about her, servant as she was, which prevented his questioning her about her relations with Stirling. When he reached home, this simple gentleman, who never had a secret in his life, was perplexed almost to irritation. His wife and daughter were alone, and fixed on him eyes so fraught with questions that utterance of any particular one would have been misleading.

"Well, Constance," he said, "I have seen little more

than the nose of the person upstairs, but if Hilda there didn't guarantee him I might have doubts of his identity."

"Father!"

"Why the man's only trunk is a big and rough box —an emigrant's box—and the only person he has any communication for is a servant girl in a Dutch boarding-house. Is that a man for Minott to introduce into my family?"

"Yes, father," said Hilda, encircling his neck with an arm that ached as she did so—"that is Judge Minott's friend; it's well you haven't really seen him yet, for I should lose faith in your eyes. I have known him a whole year in one day, and a truer gentleman never crossed your threshold."

Mr. Leigh never appealed from a verdict sealed with a kiss, but on this occasion was bold enough to remark that it was curious.

"Hilda," said Mrs. Leigh, "I don't yet know just what your knight has done, or whether you owe him fealty of Maiden rescued from Dragon, but I *would* like to know whether the German servant is also a rescued maiden."

"Not the least doubt of it," said Hilda. "Did she say when she would come, father?"

"No; but your uncle said when you must go to bed, unless we want two invalids in the house— namely, at nine, and that you must not rise till he has seen you. These are my parental orders. No, not another word, only my kiss. Good-night, my darling."

Derby Leigh's voice did not often quiver; the terrible thought that this heart on which his life rested had been near to danger and harm, was almost too much for him. Hilda suddenly clasped him in her arms and caressed him as if he were a child. Mrs. Constance took the occasion to have out the cry she had been reserving for her pillow.

A servant? Then, reflected Hilda on her way up stairs, she will probably come early,—soon after the people have had their breakfast. She found Emma, her maid, waiting in her room, and somewhat hysterical. She soothed her, and then enjoined that if any body should call after the wounded gentleman, that person must not leave without the name being first brought to herself. This injunction was carefully repeated and Emma promised obedience.

Next morning Hilda returned to a troubled consciousness. The pallid blood-stained face of the man struck down at her side shaped itself before her waking senses. Her uncle had good prevision in forbidding her to rise the next morning; her back was stiff and both arms ached. At cost of a twinge she rang her bell, which was answered by Emma.

"When uncle Endicott comes—"

"He came last night, miss, to take care of the gentleman."

"Well, you may go; but don't forget about the Ger—Don't forget that I want to see any one who comes to ask after the gentleman."

Soon after Dr. Endicott visited Hilda, and gave her permission to rise when her limbs gave theirs.

"Now, uncle, dear uncle"—the half-closed eyes were leveled at him—"tell me the exact condition of

Mr. Stirling. I'm not one to worry. How bad is it?"

"Well, child, the blow was about as deep as it could be without fracture. He has not had a good night, and worse may follow. But he is sound and strong, otherwise, and if erysipelas be escaped the wound will heal fast."

"Give me a kiss, uncle, and come again when I send for you. And now, remember, I am an invalid, and must not be crossed in any thing; will you please give that order to every body about the house?"

"Hilda, are you turning humbug after all?"

"Uncle, from this time I am a nervous and agitated invalid, and if I happen to have a whim it must be respected."

Dr. Endicott went off laughing, and as he was presently driving through the gate he met the Fraülein, who asked if that were Mr. Leigh's house. He gave her a scrutinizing glance with his answer, and drove on. Emma, who answered the Fraülein's ring, had too much unsatisfied curiosity to bear in mind her mistress' instructions.

"The gentleman is hurt bad," she said; "did you see it all? how did it happen?"

"No," said the Fraülein, "I do not know about it. He was friendly with me. Can I see him?"

Emma stared at her and smiled at her accent and manner.

"Who is that?" called Mrs. Leigh, just passing through the hall.

"A young person asking about the gentleman up stairs, ma'am."

"Ah," said Mrs. Leigh, a faintest frown gathering on her brow as she approached the door. "Emma, you may go; I will see this person."

"Pray, madame, will you tell me how the man is, and what has happened to him?"

"He was struck by a stone and much injured."

"Ach, lieber Gott!" exclaimed the Fraülein, her eyes brimming.

"Is he a—a relation of yours?"

"No, madam."

"A friend."

"Yes, madam, my one, my true friend. Can I see him?"

"Not now, he is too ill."

The Fraülein bid Mrs. Leigh "adieu," and turned slowly away from the door.

Casually entering Hilda's room, after dismissal from the front door, Emma found that young lady restless.

"Has no one been here yet to inquire for Mr. Stirling?—How can I trust you, Emma?"

She saw the guilt in Emma's face. The maid flew down stairs, and, the Fraülein having gone, ran wildly after her on the high road. She was easily overtaken, for she had sat down on a wayside rock to weep. She was led back to Hilda, who said: "Thank you, Emma," in a forgiving tone, and added, "You need not come again till I ring."

"Take a seat," said Hilda to the Fraülein, rather coldly. "I am not allowed to get out of bed just now."

"Are you ill, miss?"

"No, but they're afraid I will be. You can speak to me in German, Fraülein; I will tell you if I don't understand any thing."

The German looked at the lovely American on her luxurious couch with wonder, while Hilda's eyes closed for a moment, as if fearing they might reveal her anxiety, which stirred a little by sight of the attractive object of Stirling's solicitude. This was no commonplace servant.

"You called to ask after Mr. Stirling," said Hilda, the eyes slightly opening.

"After him that is hurt—ah! I could not sleep for thinking of him in pain. I came as soon as I could. Ah, miss, is it dangerous? The last hope of my life will die—Oh,—"—the last words ended in tears.

"We all hope it is not so bad as that," said Hilda, vainly trying to get kindliness into her voice by reflecting that allowance must be made for foreigners.

"Is he a relation of yours?" asked Hilda.

"No, Miss."

"A friend?"

"My only friend."

"You know him intimately."

"How? I know him, I feel him to be a true and loving and godlike heart, however he may look on the outside. One can not judge by appearances."

Hilda was so bewildered by this remark that her scheme for this interview was disarranged. The outside? She looked into Fraülein's eyes for light on the dark saying, but none was caught from their sky-blue simplicity.

"He has been very good to you, then"?

"Ah, indeed was he! He found me without home or friends; he raised my heart out of trouble; once more I found hope."

"Where did you first meet him?"

"In a railway station. He helped me with my box and afterwards we have traveled together. Then he spoke to me, oh, so sweetly!"

The languid white face on the pillow was suffused with a blush; the long eyelashes came down this time to repress something—was it a flash or a tear? It was some moments before Hilda ventured to speak.

"He wished us to send you word that he would come to you and fulfill his promise to you if he lived."

"Ah, that is like him! I can see him, I can hear him as he said it. It is wonderful. What was there in poor me that he should load me with favors?"

Hilda considered the Fraülein's question. There could be no doubt that she was pretty, ingenuous—though perhaps slightly sentimental—and fairly educated; why might not the warm-blooded southerner, mastering the scholar, be fascinated by this servant girl? But, alas for the suggestiveness of those words about the meeting in the depot, "he helped me with my box and afterwards we have traveled together!" If, as Hilda now feared, there had been wrong, it must be some treason, and this girl was its victim. She had been too cold to the poor child.

"Is he your man, miss?" asked the Fraülein.

"My man!"

"Has he got work here?"

"Work? What can you mean? Keep to your

German, Fraülein, I understand it better than your English."

"I mean is my friend a servant on this place? He could not get work in the mills at Spindleton and was trying to find some here."

Hilda was thoroughly mystified. While she reflected there rose in her vision that emigrant box carried to Stirling's room; she remembered her father's passing doubt about his identity. Her hero of the morning was tottering on his pedestal. For the first time in her life she seemed to be getting a glimpse into the dark depths of man's perfidy. This was indeed the gentleman whom Judge Minott had introduced in glowing terms—Hilda had read the letter—but in some way he had deceived this poor German girl; who must now be undeceived, however painful the task.

"My friend," said Hilda, "come closer to me. No—leave that hard chair, here is one beside me. There! Now, take my hand; I have been cold to you but am not so now. You have had troubles."

"Ah, I have had troubles; I have long been alone and never expected to have a friend again, when your workman took my side—he fought for me, he helped me with his money, he promised to—to—"

"To do what?" asked Hilda eagerly, the Fraülein having ended her sentence with a blush and with tears.

Hilda drew a little sigh of relief. She could hardly have explained why; she was even more puzzled than ever about the relation between this young woman and Stirling, but the revelation that he had fought for her in some emergency set the Virginian somewhat straighter on his pedestal.

"We shall be good friends, shall we not?" said she, pressing the Fraülein's hand. "Tell me now all about yourself and this man. He is not our workman; we have never seen him before yesterday; he is here only because he is wounded."

"So!" exclaimed Fraülein Rose with amazement; "then you do not know?"

At that moment Mr. Derby Leigh entered the room. He did not know that the Fraülein was with Hilda, but bowed politely to her.

"You darling papa," said Hilda, as he kissed her, "for once in your life you've come too soon."

"Then I'll go at once, but I had a secret to tell you."

"Darling papa, why didn't you come sooner?"

"Can this young lady spare you a moment?"

"Fraülein, will you step outside a moment?"

The girl having gone Mr. Leigh informed Hilda that, it having become necessary to open Mr. Stirling's box, a workman's suit was found, which he had explained by saying that, in traveling to observe the working classes, he had used that disguise.

"How droll!" said Hilda.

"What sort of girl is this?"

"A good girl. She was about to tell me her story, I believe, when you came in. Do call her now, and tell mamma I think still she will prove to be one of our knight's rescued maidens."

A few moments after, Hilda was listening to the Fraülein's romance.

"And this promise to you, which he said he would fulfill if he lived?"

"Ah, that: he took down the name of my Franz's ship, and the time he sailed, and said he would try to find him; he promised too to try and find me some work. Ah, is he not kind?"

"He is indeed," said Hilda, turning away to laugh at the comedy she had been acting with the simple Fraülein. At last she turned her eyes, which merriment had moistened, on the wondering and abashed girl, and took her hand again.

"Forgive me, Fraülein, I am laughing at myself. I had formed some ridiculous fancies about you and this gentleman down stairs. For he is not a workingman as you suppose, but was only dressed in that way for a kind of—of masquerade."

"Lieber Gott!"

"Don't think he meant harm. He meant good—to just such people as you; and yesterday he was wounded while saving a poor slave. Don't you remember your Märchen of princes going about in disguise?"

"Indeed, I asked him if so he was."

"You have made me happier, Fraülein; will you not come again to-morrow?"

"Indeed I will, miss," answered the pleased and blushing girl.

"And do not tell any one the story you have told me; and do not talk of your friend here except to me, and do not ask about him when you come again. I will tell you that."

At this moment Dr. Endicott knocked and was admitted. He bowed politely to Fraülein Rose, whom his niece introduced, then turned to his blithe patient.

"You seem to be a rather lively case of nervous and agitated invalid, Hilda. Well, is there any thing I can do, I'm just going home."

"Nothing, uncle—but yes, there is. I wish you would take this friend of mine to her home in Peacefield in your carriage."

"With pleasure."

"Oh no," exclaimed the Fraülein, "I will gladly walk."

"My niece must be obeyed in every thing—for this one day; so I beg your company, miss," said the doctor, opening the door.

Soon after Dr. Endicott had driven off with the Fraülein, to the astonishment of all, and of Emma in particular, Hilda surprised her parents by rushing upon them, as they were walking on the lawn, and declaring herself exceptionally well.

"But you look anxious, both of you," she said; "what is it?"

"Well, Hilda, your father and I are considering what we can do for Mr. Stirling. He may require nursing. We might bring Maria from the cottage, but I fear Lucy could not take care of her mother, by herself."

"Mamma," said Hilda merrily, "do Rescued Maidens give up their wounded Knights in that way? That German girl, about whom we have been mystified, is Mr. Stirling's acquaintance of two hours; he defended her from insult, helped her in trouble, promised to try and find her work, and to try and find some trace of her lover. The poor child has followed some despairing youth all the way from Germany without knowing where he is—a veritable bride asking for her beloved!"

"Well, that is odd," exclaimed Mr. Leigh.

"Hilda, for once I believe you're romancing," said her mother.

"Not a bit, mamma. Now she and I are your rescued maidens: she must remain here; Emma is to be married next week and this Fraülein is the very person I want. The gardener may watch with Mr. Stirling at night, but if woman's help is needed Fraülein and I—"

"Hilda, do be serious!"

"Child, you've taken laughing-gas!"

There were other parental exclamations, to which Hilda listened with the sweet submissiveness of one sure to have her way.

The next day Fraülein Rose, as she was preparing to walk to the Leighs' house, found their carriage at Heman Wilder's door. In obedience to a letter that came with it she prepared her trunk, was driven to the mansion, and installed in a pleasant room there. She moved through it all with a sort of dazed happiness.

"My mother," she said to Hilda, "would sometimes call me her Dornröschen, and she must right be. I am favored by fairies and tooken out from the briers."

Stirling thus seemed in a fair way to become, for a second time, an interesting object of maidenly care; but, unfortunately for the pathos of such situation, Dr. Endicott interfered the very next day.

"I know it's cruel news, my dear Hilda," he said

sadly, "but nothing can save this youth from—getting well almost immediately."

"Uncle!"

"Why, what young fellow wouldn't keep his broken head to be a hero nursed by tender damozel?"

"Incorrigible bachelor!"

"But it can not be helped, the poor fellow is already well enough to go home with me; for it is I that must tend his wound."

And so the wounded knight came down in casque of white bandages, and was driven off by the officious physician.

# CHAPTER X.

### FROM THE SHAMBLE TO LEROYLAND.

ABOUT the time when his friend reached Peacefield, Wentworth for the first time touched the " sacred soil" of Virginia. The first house he entered there was not, however, especially sacred; it was the human shamble of Messrs. Gephart & Co., in a town not far from the District of Columbia. The Bostonian had stored up all his cynicism for this visit, and presented a *blasé* front to the slavedealer's keen eyes.

" Is it cash ? " asked Gephart.

" Yes."

" You only want a man ? We've a nice lot to-morrow, man and wife."

" I can't wait. I'm not sure about wanting more than the man."

" Well, I'll show you what we've got."

Wentworth followed the dealer through several groups, and at length fixed his eye on a handsome defiant face, one of five in a room through which Gephart was hurrying.

" Stop a moment," said Wentworth, " let's look at these."

" These are for far south."

" You mean they are sold ? "

"Not yet, but they must be sold on condition of going down south."

"Why?"

"One thing and another. That yeller gal's got to go because some youngster's taken a fancy to her. The Missis won't 'low her nigher'n Louisiana. Rest got into trouble, mostly thieving, and let off on condition of being sent to the plantations."

"What of this young man?"

"Wust o' the set. Kep' the whole neighborhood in terror with his devilry, and at last burned down a barn jes for a fourth o' July bonfire. Would 'a' been hung if his master hadn't promised to sell him to the plantations. You're not after cotton hands, sir?"

"Is that man married?"

"Wesley, are you married?"

"Yes, sir," answered the barn-burner, curtly.

"Where's your wife?"

"Don' know. Ain't seen her this two year."

After one or two other lots had been inspected Wentworth and Gephart returned to the counting-room.

"Seen any thing you like, sir?"

"I suppose that fellow who burned the barn can't be trusted?"

"Well, you see, that don't matter on the plantation; not much chance for mischief there."

"Cheap lot that, of course?"

"Nat'rally; bad character, forced sale, strict conditions; any body making oath to take him to a cotton state can get him for five hundred."

"I'll take him."

"I didn't understand you was going that way. What state, sir?"

"South Carolina."

"When do you start?"

"Day after to-morrow."

"Where's he to be delivered?"

"Can I take him now?"

"There's papers to be made out."

"I'm at Willard's in Washington."

"Can't send him there; he must go from here straight south."

"I shall be on the Acquia boat day after to-morrow."

"If you don't mind adding five dollars he shall be at the Acquia Landing when you get there."

"All right. Papers must be sent to Willard's to-morrow morning, showing clean title; the money shall be exchanged for the man next day at Acquia, with signed oath to take him to South Carolina, and through tickets shown to that state."

"Tied," said Gephart.

"Oh, you needn't tie him."

"Perhaps our talk up here isn't plain to Carolina gentlemen; it's our bargain that's tied, sir."

"Ah yes, of course," said Wentworth, blushing at his slowness. "I thought you might think it necessary to tie such a dangerous character. Can I see the rascal alone a moment?"

"Certainly. Jes walk in the yard; I'll send him."

Wentworth strolled into the yard, which was inclosed with high walls, and waited beneath a tree at the farthest corner until he was approached by Wesley Hampton. Intelligence and insolence mingled in the handsome face, whose complexion was that sometimes called " saddle-colored." He confronted Wentworth with a reckless look that speedily vanished.

" My man," said Wentworth, with a gentleness that made the negro start and tremble,—" I have bought you, and you know the conditions; you must be taken South."

" Yes, sir."

" Well, now, listen to what I am about to say, do not forget a word of it, and do not show any excitement. You will travel with me day after to-morrow, and I may not have a chance to talk with you privately till we get to Richmond. But however I may treat you at Acquia, or on the way, from the time you belong to me you are a free man. Don't speak of it, don't look it, let nobody suspect it ; be perfectly quiet and act like an obedient servant. I am your friend, and you shall be free, but I shall want your help too. Now remember, be careful ! "

" O master ! O Lord ! " gasped the negro.

" Keep quiet—look sullen—don't let those negroes know a whisper of what I say. Be dumb except when alone with me. Mark you, man, a blunder may cost your liberty. Don't thank me. Now's your chance to show your sense ; look as stupid as you can and as sorry and sullen as you can. Now we'll go in."

" Just a moment, sir," said the man, turning his eyes to the northern horizon, and wiping with his sleeves the drops of sweat that started out on his forehead.

" By the way," said Wentworth," " you said you had a wife; where is she ? "

" Gone where I've been trying to follow her—to

Georgia. She belonged to Mr. Bullen and when he died two years ago all the niggers was sold. She was sold to Georgia. Niggers from here mostly go there, sir. That place couldn't be worse than where I was, and I wanted to go there too. Easiest way to go there was to kill somebody—they don't hang only free niggers—but I hadn't it in me to more than fire a house."

"Well, Wesley, we shall visit that region, and if you know where she is—"

"—I know exactly—"

"We may be able to help each other a good deal. But we must be good actors. Now down with your face, and go in!"

A week later Wentworth and his smartly-dressed servant sailed from Charleston to seek a coast island famous for its variety of cotton, a considerable order for which had been intrusted to him, through the influence of a friend, by a New England firm. He would thus not be without excuse for his presence on plantations, should any be required. The little steamer that plied as far as Leroy Island had place also for his horse and buggy, purchased in Charleston. It was under a beautiful dawn that the two men landed and immediately set forth for the planter's residence. The roads were heavy, but Wentworth was beguiled by the rich vegetation, the forest aisles and arches, the vast ferns, the birds of brilliant plumage. Gradually, however, the sparseness of human life and the silence became oppressive, and then Wentworth forgot both the beauty and the solitude in listening to the story of Wesley Hampton's life. This man, who had been surreptitiously given some education by a pious old mistress, did not fail to recall the kindly hearts that had sometimes mitigated the rigors of servitude, and confessed that he would not care for liberty if he had a kind owner and felt secure against being parted from his wife.

At length Wesley drove up to the door of Leroy House. The long veranda of the white mansion, adorned with lemon-trees and oleanders, the flower-beds on the lawn attesting tender care, had already in a way introduced the mistress of the house before she appeared. Mrs. Leroy met Wentworth affably and said she had sent his card to her husband, who would soon return. She smiled pleasantly while he was apologizing for his intrusion and regretting that Mr. Leroy should be disturbed. Meanwhile fruit and wine were brought; and while he was enjoying this refreshment the planter arrived.

"I am glad to see you, sir, and hope you will feel yourself at home."

The man who with these words grasped Wentworth's hand was about forty years of age, but with a more youthful look in his dark eyes and rosy cheeks. When Wentworth apologized and declared he had no business of sufficient importance to call the planter from his affairs, Leroy interrupted him merrily.

"You are welcome without any business at all. Any gentleman who comes all the way out of the world to visit our little nook needn't apologize. There are the children now, peeping at you as an interesting novelty—Sumter, Eva, come in!"

The boy scampered off, but a little dame of some

nine summers entered, nestled about her father, and beamed welcome on the stranger. Wentworth found every thing assumed for him. As he had not been asked whether he would have food, he was not allowed to say whether he would remain: he was simply shown to his room, and told that dinner was at half past two. When he presently descended he was received with friendly interest by two pretty young ladies—somewhere between seventeen and twenty years of age—and " all this time," he reflected, " not one of them knows who I am, why I am here, or that I am not a rogue."

After dinner Wentworth was asked whether he would drive out, or walk, or sleep in a hammock, or play graces, or do nothing at all. He selected the walk and was guided by Mr. Leroy, his wife, and the two elder daughters—Fanny and Bertha—through a glade with archways of flowering trees to a rivulet flowing amid palmettos. The air was warm, the young ladies wore light white raiment and wide straw hats, and the Bostonian was charmed away from his misgivings about his right to all this cordiality. Supper was ready soon after their return. Wentworth was warmed into a new kind of happiness by this unexpected hospitality; he talked like an old friend of the family, told his best stories, and resolved that he would never withhold any fact about himself from such confiding people. Now and then, however, he became grave and reflected whether a perfectly frank word on his part might not turn these bright faces pale, and transform his trustful host into an enemy. A little time afterward, when Mr. Leroy and

Wentworth were smoking together on the veranda, the first step toward a confession was taken.

"Mr. Leroy, I have heard of southern hospitality, but yours is more than I could dream of any one extending to a stranger."

"I know a gentleman when I meet him, Mr. Wentworth, and while he is under my roof all that I have is his."

"But you have not inquired who I am or why I am here?"

"Well, you have come a long way to see me; the first thing after a journey is rest, and the making of acquaintance; when the time comes for any business you may have with us, I shall be at your service. It happens to be my inclination—and I may be a sharper fellow than you think—to let you say as much or as little about yourself as you like till I have occasion to ask more."

"I am grateful to you and your family for this confidence and kindness. Now I wish to say this much about myself. I am from Boston. The dearest friend I have is a Virginian; we have been for some years classmates at college; he and his friends have given me letters of introduction to gentlemen in various parts of the South; I am traveling that I may learn more of this region, the people, and especially more of the system of slavery. In coming to this plantation I did not count on being a guest in any private house: my buggy is loaded with provisions, and even a tent. I meant to buy a lot of cotton for a New England firm, ask to be shown over the estate, learn as much as planter or overseer chose to tell me about the hands and their work, pay my way, and travel on elsewhere."

"A very fair purpose, Mr. Wentworth! As for the cotton, you will have to deal with our warehouses in Charleston. For the rest, I fear you'll find little to repay your journey, but you have the freedom of my estate and of the cabins. You are welcome to all the information we can give you. I don't expect you to fall in love with our institutions, but the more facts you gentlemen of the North have about us the better. We didn't make the world, and take it as we find it. On this plantation, where my father and my grandfather dwelt before me, there are some seven hundred men and women, white and black, all hard at work making their living—and making it as they must. We are all alike servants of a necessity. There is not an idle one among us,—not even one of my daughters in there."

"I have said my best friend is a Virginian; now I may say the most generous treatment I ever received is from a Carolinian. It is worth many journeys only to have this conversation with you."

"Handsomely said, sir: it would surely be better for the country if northern and southern gentlemen could exchange ideas instead of affronts."

The notes of a guitar flitted out on the soft evening air. The two elder sisters sang together a Spanish song, which blended with murmurs of the trees, and the light of an evening star that almost cast shadows. And this was a cotton-plantation! Wentworth glanced in at the window on the tableau of fair and happy faces, and remembered the words of the man whose body and soul he had bought—"If I could only feel secure against being parted from my wife!" Fancy an auction-block set beside that happy group, and a cold-blooded stranger putting up that lovely lady, those daughters, to the highest bidder! 'Here, gentlemen, is a first-rate lot. Stir yourself, girl, and show the gentlemen how you can play the guitar!' Wentworth shuddered at the thought, and it flitted away among the bats.

When the gentlemen rejoined the ladies there was more music, which was suspended during a visit from the Baptist preacher. A good phlegmatic sort of man, apparently, was this Mr. Haswell, who had the chief care of souls on the plantation. He now came to make some usual reports. Old Nancy was dead at last. They say Old Joe was seen near the house last night— that superstition continues. "Aunt Nancy died this afternoon; she sent her love to you all—especially Miss Fanny, with thanks for the preserves, and hopes she will give her heart to the Lord." (The sisters droop their heads: Fanny drops a tear as she says "poor Aunt Nancy.") Blind Peter was rather better, and Dr. Burrows believes he will last the winter; "the old man talked a good deal about you, Miss Bertha—your visit cheered him up. Old Adelaide hopes you'll come again; she's had a blessed vision, since you sang her that hymn, which she mustn't tell to any body but you." The minister continued these reports for some time, little knowing how deeply they interested the stranger present.

"How many are to be baptized Sunday, Mr. Haswell?" asked Leroy.

"Yours and Scott's together, there'll be thirty gathered in. Scott's Virginia man, Charles, who killed your hand Humphrey, has been converted and will be baptized Sunday. There's great rejoicing over him. Jane's to be baptized at the same time. I think they'll be married before long."

"Won't you spend the night, Mr. Haswell?" said Mrs. Leroy, as the preacher took up his hat.

"No, thank you. I must call on Petty a moment to-night, and start for Scott's early. Is there any thing you've got to suggest about next Sunday's sermon, Mr. Leroy?"

"I believe not. Old Nancy, as you know, was a faithful servant. Fanny, is there any thing you wish said?"

"Only this—she was always glad to hear the new hymn Cousin Lucy sent me, 'Nearer, my God, to Thee.' Mr. Haswell knows it."

"I've heard you and Miss Bertha sing it, but I don't remember all the words. Could you send them to me?"

"I'll send them to-morrow."

"Daughters, why not sing them on Sunday?" said Leroy.

"That indeed would be a help," said the preacher.

The young ladies having consented, the preacher left, and soon after the family retired. Wentworth lay awake with his thoughts for some time, then sank to sleep, and to a dream of moving over a blue sea with Stirling.

## CHAPTER XI.

### A CAROLINIAN PROSPERO AND HIS ISLANDERS.

EARLY the next morning, while Wentworth lay contemplating his pretty room,—its snow-white drapings, its brass-mounted mahogany furniture, dark with age—his man Wesley brought his boots and a whisk for his clothes.

"Good-morning, Wesley; have you had a good rest?"

"Perfect, sir, thank you, and hope the same of you, master."

"Yes, I slept well. I suppose your new acquaintances have a good deal to say about this place and the family?"

"Yes, sir; Mr. Leroy and his family are famous among colored people a hundred miles round as the best people in the country to their servants. Every hand wants Mr. Leroy for a master."

"Did they ask you about yourself and me?"

"They were curious, sir, but I remember what you told me; I only let them know I came from a hard master to a good one."

"They all like the Leroys, then?"

"The only fault they find in them is that they ain't saved."

"Aren't saved!"

"Mr. Leroy don't go to meetin', sir, 'less it's a

funeral, and won't join any church. Every month the 'piscopal parson comes round and preaches in the neighborhood; the family go to hear him; but most colored folks don't look on that as any religion at all. The parson stays here when he's in the neighborhood, and plays cards with them, and they all dance. That's why they say the family ain't saved. No fault found with them but that."

"Well, Wesley, they are 'saved' enough for me if they treat their servants well."

"You are right there, sir. Even the overseers here are good—'cept one."

Breakfast — an overwhelming breakfast — was through by eight. There was rejoicing at the arrival of St. George, eldest of the Leroy offspring and nearing his majority, who had been sent on a responsible expedition to a remote part of Georgia to superintend the transfer of some negroes consigned by a law-suit to the Leroy estate. The youth was good-looking, sun-tanned, full of animal spirits, and proud of having acquitted himself successfully in this important trust. Wentworth read in St. George's eye a suspicion that he was after one of his sisters. When he was introduced as "a gentleman from Boston," that theory dissolved into the supposition that the guest was a Yankee manufacturer come for bargains. St. George was transparent as a rivulet, and happily his babble was rather melodious.

"You must not consider it necessary to rise so early, Mr. Wentworth," said Mrs. Leroy. "We have to be early people, but you can always get some breakfast later."

"Thank you for the indulgence, but I have been lately used to college hours and desire to make the most of my time. I find my northern notions about you southerners at fault; you are supposed to rise late, spend your time in hammocks, or sipping juleps and sherbets, while watching negroes at work; but I find you stirring with the early birds. I fear Boston aristocracy is at this moment in déshabille."

Wentworth's frankness made an agreeable impression; the ladies turned on St. George glances that said plainly—you see he is a manly fellow, comes out with what he thinks: we like him, and so must you.

After breakfast a bell was sounded through the house and grounds by a small negro lad, who magnified his office; some thirty servants, Wesley among them, filed into the room and occupied seats along the wall. Leroy read a psalm from the family Bible; the sisters sang a hymn in which St. George joined, but not the negroes,—one or two of the women, however, swaying to and fro with the music, their eyes closed. Then all kneeled, and the planter, with reverential voice, read a prayer.

Horses for Leroy and his guest were ready at the door, and they were soon on their way to the fields devoted to upland cotton. From a hill-top Wentworth presently looked for the first time on the white wonder of plains whose plants, bending and rising under the wind, made a creamy sea, in which there were forms that looked in the distance like sportive bathers. The scene was strangely beautiful. The bolls were all expanded; there was no effect of snow on the landscape, for a tint as if left by a golden dawn toned the expanse to a character of its own. When an intervening quarter of a mile was passed, Wentworth listened for some voices from that soft foam, but heard none; the sportive bathers had turned to silent negroes picking bolls and bearing them in baskets. They were picturesque,—the men in shining straw hats and white or blue shirts, the women in white gowns, and some with gay bandana head-dresses. Beneath this sky, amid these fields, they were æsthetically in the right place; their dark faces and natural movements were harmonious with the animation of the scene. But their silence was oppressive. Only one voice Wentworth heard as he presently walked along the rows,—an old woman's voice crooning a funeral hymn, with long spaces of silence. This was the solitary note that reached him from the scene that appeared so gay in the distance.

An overseer moved about vigilantly, but bore no whip or visible weapon. Long before Darwin was heard of, natural selection on southern plantations had evolved the rebellious out of existence, and preserved the submissive. One man, unarmed, could command these hundreds. But he could not make them laugh or sing.

After the rest of the morning had been passed in examining the steam-gins, Leroy proposed that they should return home; at which his guest's regret was evident.

"I hope, Mr. Wentworth, you are not under necessity of hurrying your observations; it takes a little time to show even what little we have in this monotonous region."

"It is not monotonous,—I am much interested,—but I must soon start on my further travels."

"If you must go I must speed the parting guest; but I should do so with uncommon regret. I think you would make a mistake in rushing through what you have come so far to see."

"I am very grateful to you and Mrs. Leroy—"

"Are you?" interrupted Leroy laughing, "Then show it. Mrs, Leroy and the girls are planning a little something-or-other which your leaving would upset."

"But—"

"Ah, confess, there's no necessity in the case, only politeness. You do not wish to press on our hospitality. But consider the other side: may I not desire to know New England as much as you the South? Is it fair to see our ways, then run off before I have begun to explore yours? No, sir—you will find me shrewd as a Yankee, and not be released so easily."

"You southerners are a race of lawyers. I accept your hospitality and stay till Monday."

"Sufficient unto Monday is the evil thereof. For the present I must reflect that I am under promise to give my Lily a ride home, and to be in good time for dinner. Mammy—that's cook—has a haunch of venison in hand, and if it has to wait she becomes a whole negro insurrection in herself."

In such merry mood Leroy galloped with his guest to a cabin in a grove—the school-house as he explained where the children of several families were taught by Miss Stringfield, the parson's sister; she was originally employed by the Leroys for their own children alone, and lived with them, though absent the last night. There was no lack of voice among these little laborers; the cabin was humming like a hive; but it grew still with excitement when the two gentlemen entered. Miss Stringfield, a tall handsome lady of some two and twenty years, received them graciously. The children sang one English glee for them: after which Leroy asked for a recitation, declaring that the teacher was accomplished in that way, and particularly successful in training orators.

"Oh, Mr. Leroy," said the blushing mistress, "you always make a swan out of your goose."

"But I never make goose out of swan, Lotty. Come, bring us out an orator—which shall she, or he, be?"

"Sumter would have a right to be jealous if I didn't choose him, for he spoke 'Marion's Men' well on Wednesday."

"Let's have it, sonny."

The boy came forward—cynosure of eyes glistening with his reflected glory—and took his stand on the neatly-decorated platform. He was nervous at first; when he came to "The British soldier trembles," the Briton's agitation got into Sumter's voice; but he soon righted himself and went on bravely to the end, receiving due applause.

"A noble poem," said Leroy.

"And nobly recited, here in Marion's land—by one bearing his gallant comrade's name too," said Wentworth.

"I wonder how it is the South does not produce poets to sing her own deeds?" said Leroy.

"Perhaps such are growing in this room," said Wentworth.

"We may have the Marions, but hardly the Bryants," said Miss Stringfield.

"May I take Lily?" said Leroy.

"Certainly—Lily get your hat."

"It will be your turn next time, Eva," said Leroy to another little one, who looked rather grave.

"If you can carry Miss Lily, surely I can take Miss Eva," said Wentworth.

Blankets were laid behind each saddle, the children sat like Amazons; and when Wentworth, who had never known much home life, felt the little arm clinging to him, another was added to the silken threads which the sunny South was beginning to weave about him. The horses were gentle pacers, the day was charming, and they took a circuitous route in order to give the children a longer ride.

A drive in the afternoon with Mrs. Leroy to visit some of her pensioners; listening to their dreams and lore and patois; a lesson on his return in the play of graces; a tale told the children; made time pass swiftly for the guest. In the evening, while the three gentlemen were smoking on the veranda, bursts of merriment from within broke on their ears.

"Lotty Stringfield," explained St. George; "I suppose she's telling them a yarn about her visit to the Barnwells last night. There never was such a woman for yarns. I do believe if Lotty had only seen a watling fence there she'd have the girls crying or laughing about it. She's a one-er, is Lotty. Just look, sir!"

Wentworth glanced in at the window that opened on the veranda, and saw Miss Stringfield, buttressed by Eva and Lily, the rest massed in semi-circle around her. It was a pretty picture; the teacher in that frame of young faces, all in the mellow candlelight, was of unique beauty. St. George threw away his freshly-lighted cigar and went to join them.

"Between you and me," said Leroy with a laugh, "I sometimes think that boy of mine is half in love with the parson's sister."

"Judging by her looks his taste were not bad."

"But she's two years older."

"That does seem a little too much."

"Too much! I should say so."

"Still, if that's the only thing against her, he might do worse."

"I must say, that's the only thing. She has not much money, but she has what money can't buy, good sense and heart. She is educated; she comes of good family—the Stringfields of Virginia. But surely only infatuation would make a youth marry a woman older than himself."

"In some of the happiest marriages I have known the disparity of years was on the lady's side. It might not do for all, perhaps not for St. George, but there are men who might be all the better for a sort of maternal as well as wifely influence."

"An ingenious paradox!" said Leroy laughing. "I fear it would hardly be safe in this region, where girls mature so early."

"Perhaps Virginians may not resemble Carolinians in that."

"Possibly. Miss Stringfield's mother was a Baltimore beauty, and she was educated there."

"That is the city called Beautiful, so far as its women are concerned."

Next day Leroy took his guest to a remote part of the plantation where his best Sea Island cotton was produced. The border of this tract was swampy, and at one place so disagreeable was the toil that it was reserved for evil-doers—"Not a hell," Leroy said, "but a sort of purgatory." Rice and a few other things were produced there for use on the estate. It was on the edge of a savannah hedged with jungle, in which grew enormous fungi and other rank growths.

"A negro's eyes are remarkable," said Leroy; "one of his eyes is a magnifier, the other a multiplier. One snake becomes a thousand vipers, and presently an army of dragons. Slimy imps lurk about here, and ghosts—especially about a certain old graveyard half-adopted by the swamp. Thus the poor fellows make their own purgatory."

"What are their chief offenses?"

"Lying of course is habitual with every slave; it is his natural defensive shell under which he draws up like a tortoise. Drunkenness is their chloroform for all troubles. Then they are very jealous. A pretty girl on a plantation is as dangerous a creature as Helen of Troy. The rivals become panthers when they fight."

"And the punishments?"

"The discipline is developed out of the conditions

of each plantation. The punishments are subsidiary to the one great end—the best average crop. An overseer indulging persona lvengeance is discharged ; it would tell on the crop. A hand disabled for one day means two hundred and fifty pounds of cotton disabled. The regulation is—hurt sometimes but never harm. There are disagreeable kinds of work for the refractory."

"But in the case of crimes?"

"The law is merciful to a homicide worth a thousand dollars. Imprisonment is more costly to master than slave. Why sentence him to hard labor when he has it already? Slaves can not be punished like free men. Courts compound their felonies. There are negroes in all these states who would have been hung long ago had they been free. Fortunately the negro is rarely a daring criminal, for he is the man least restrained by law."

"In the cabins which they visited Wentworth recognized many indications of the good will with which Leroy was regarded by his subjects. He already realized that he was on the estate of an exceptional man. The slave system could not be studied in all its actualities on this plantation : here were the lights, but he must seek elsewhere for the shades.

But the thought of leaving the Leroys saddened Wentworth. In this sunny land confidence between him and them had been a quick growth. There was already friendship between him and Leroy. This island to which he had drifted was so environed with beauty of strange and alluring kind, so full of antique charm, that old romances—as if Ponce, and Prester

John—were made real. Or had he not found the Isle of Prospero and Miranda, and—

"Caliban," bluntly asked his northern conscience. "Oh yes—out with it! Caliban is Prospero Leroy's long-heeled, thick-lipped slave, for whom you were just now pleading at Cambridge. How brutal beside the planter's pretty masque!"

Whereto his Minott-Stirling conscience answered, that he had engaged his abolition-conscience to remain for a time in judicial suspense. There is always something provincial about a man's conscience —even a Boston conscience. What would his friends there say if they heard he had bought a slave and was the guest of a planter? They would say much that wouldn't be true—as you, Mr. Wentworth, may have been saying much that isn't true about such men as Leroy!

Thoughts like these were vaguely haunting Wentworth as he lay on the grass while Leroy was conversing with the overseer. He had heard from Wesley Hampton that one overseer was an object of negro dislike. The retributive overseer, probably this man—Corbin by name—might have horn and hoof in the slave's eye; but to Wentworth his wooden perfunctory look and manner, however disagreeable, were only a human-like part of the swamp and its conditions. The unruly might keep away from him and them if they chose. The man wouldn't be so bad, he thought, if one were sure that he had offset in corresponding forces, vigilant to allure the negro to the right and happy way as he was to enforce consequences of the reverse.

Just then came dashing up on horseback the three young ladies and St. George. Their healthy faces and clear eyes appeared to Wentworth as if summoned by his thought. What civilizing capacities lay in those maidens! What if they were watching over the rude minds around them as jealously as yon machine-like overseer watches that the average yield of his slimy savannah shall be secured!

They all rode home together—St. George and Miss Stringfield indulging in a race, the victory being gallantly surrendered to the lady, but the prize passing to him in her heightened beauty.

"Ah, poor Saint," said she, "the next time we'll try who can come in last—then you'll be sure to win."

"No, Lotty, the next time I'll ride Black Bess, and you'll be nowhere. I gave you Bob, and took Samson —who's five hundred years if he's a day—and that's the thanks I get. But laugh on!"

When the house was reached Miss Stringfield leaped from her horse without waiting for assistance; but the excited animal gave a start, her foot missed the block, and St. George sprang forward barely in time to save her from falling under the horse's feet. She limped as she entered the house, but was laughing at the alarm of the youth on whose arm she leaned.

"She's broken her leg," he called out, pale with fear.

"Nonsense," said Charlotte, lightly.

"Probably a sprain," said Mrs. Leroy, anxiously.

Charlotte was laid on the sofa and surrounded by the entire family. Mrs. Leroy discovered that the arnica was gone, and was about to send for some, when Wentworth appeared with a leather box, from which he drew a bottle of the needed lotion. The children glanced curiously at this box, and it presently divided attention with Charlotte; out of it he drew scissors, needles, spools, corkscrew, knife, lenses, nut-cracker, twine, and a dozen other useful things; causing much merriment, especially to Charlotte, who forgot her foot.

"It's only a slight punishment for laughing at Saint," she said meekly.

"No, Lotty, but for not waiting for me to help you down. I hope you'll wait for me hereafter. The race is not always to the swift."

"Nor always to the slow," said Bertha.

"Bertha," said Charlotte, "I'll send you into a corner if you say another word. Saint was never slow in his life; if he hadn't sprung like lightning I would have been trampled. Thank you, Saint, I'll wait for your hand next time."

Charlotte kept her flow of spirits during the evening, the usual circle gathering around her sofa. St. George was ambitious to carry her to her room in his arms, but she declared that an elephant required two men, and limped upstairs between him and Wentworth.

## CHAPTER XII.

### BESIDE THE JORDAN.

"I'M puzzled to think what to do with you to-day," said Leroy to his guest during the Sunday breakfast.

"Mere existence is enough on such a day," said Wentworth.

"Yes, St. Martin shares his cloak with us also, a son of Huguenots may say. The Indian Summer is not aboriginal."

"The 'Great Spirit' smiles alike on Yankee and southerner."

"On Sunday our plantation becomes a bit of ancient Judea. Indeed it is largely that all the time: one place is called Canaan, the meeting-house is Bethel, the creek near it Jordan."

"Ah, Jordan—did I not hear there were to be immersions to-day? I have never seen such baptism."

"The very thing!"

They rode off soon after breakfast, the Jordan being four miles distant. As they approached the meeting-house, a huge wooden building, Leroy said he would have been glad to make it prettier, but the negroes have a pious objection to beauty in churches. Already a long white-robed procession was moving toward the water, accompanied by a large crowd in its finest raiment. The long cotton robes of the candidates for baptism, reaching to the feet, formed a graceful and even classical drapery. When the stream was reached the negroes sang, with much enthusiasm, "On Jordan's stormy banks I stand." Mr. Haswell, the preacher, also arrayed in white, read the narrative of the baptism of Jesus, then uttered a prayer containing personal allusions, amid ejaculations of increasing fervor among the negroes. He then went slowly into the water until it nearly reached his waist, and the candidates came to him, one by one. The minister called out each name after the words "I baptize thee," and placing one hand on the back, the other on the breast, threw him or her backward till the form disappeared, and lifted them again. Meanwhile hymns were sung by the assembly on the bank. Each person baptized was received by friends on emerging, and enveloped in a cloak. There were greetings, embraces, and ejaculations of joy. The waxing emotion in the crowd became ecstasy when one handsome youth entered the water. This, Leroy whispered, was the notorious fellow who killed one of his (Leroy's) men for flirting with his sweetheart. There were shouts when he came up from the water, and a renewed outburst when he was succeeded by a comely quadroon, who proved to be the sweetheart for whom he had slain his rival. Wentworth found the scene picturesque and impressive; he could never forget the radiance on the faces of those who came from the water: to those uplifted eyes the poised hawk might seem a dove, and every noise on the air tell of their beloved.

In the meeting-house, an hour later, Wentworth was an object of keen observation. Did the negroes perceive that he was not a southerner? Perhaps his intent interest in all that occurred betrayed his alienage. There were nearly a thousand negroes present and their united voices were glorious. Before the preacher appeared the assembly began a wild chant, quick and loud, of four lines:

> His feet like polished brass,
> His legs like marble pillars!
> His head is white as any lamb's wool,
> And his voice like many waters!

When the multitude had got as far as "many" the leader had already begun again with "His feet." It was all unison, and it had a peculiar impressiveness for Wentworth; perhaps it was the first time he had heard singing strictly meant to be heard in heaven, and without intention to please any earthly ear.

Mr. Haswell's sermon was one of the many that by their poverty make cultured listeners grateful for the Bible. The good man's resources were small, partly, no doubt, because not needed, his humble hearers requiring nothing less than apocalyptic utterance in every sentence. These burning biblical sentences were as orient gems set in the Haswellian lead. Happily the humble preacher's lead did not try to glory in the presence of his chain of quotations which linked these dusky islanders with far lands and ages, bore them through wildernesses to promised lands, and raised them to the New Jerusalem. Strains of eastern poetry set to music of heavenly harps became audible as angel-voices to people whose souls had already reached their resurrection, the earth-life being sepulchred in slavery. Songs sung in many an ancient night, plaintive cries and hopes born of ancient bondage, living through thousands of years, had found their way to bondmen of the present and gave them wings to rise above a world become their grave. How many tempest-tossed souls would exchange wealth and power for the burdens of these lowly ones, to know their absolute faith, and visions that impoverish palaces shining on these unquestioning eyes! It was no mere anthropological immortality that had been revealed to these babes. As the preacher invested Aunt Nancy with imagery of Patmos the assembly saw her as a spirit beautiful beyond fairest queens, singing amid the palms. The dance of ancient Egyptians around their dead, celebrating their entrance to paradise, had simply passed from feet to face and voice in these believers whose funeral cry was—Glory!

At the end of the sermon Fanny and Bertha stood in front of the congregation and sang the hymn Aunt Nancy was said to have loved—" Nearer, my God, to Thee!" It is probable the old woman loved the singer rather than the song. The negroes listened silently; they were evidently grateful to the young ladies, but this hymn was not for them. It is the hymn of an age that dreams it is dreaming.

"What pleased me also in the sermon," said Wentworth, when they were talking it over on their way home, "was his use of hopeful prophecies and abstinence from 'the terrors.' He never summoned Satan once,"

"It would be idle," said Leroy; "the darkies think they are about square with Satan, hell being for Dives. There is a preacher at Ebenezer who has thinned his congregation with 'the terrors.' The negroes, I sometimes think, believe the devil is chained up; and at any rate he has a wholesome fear of Jordan water, which renders them invulnerable to his fiery darts."

"I shall never forget the impression of this day," said Wentworth. "Now that my visit draws to a close my gratitude is struck speechless."

"You will go then,—when we have not half exchanged ideas and experiences; Massachusetts and South Carolina being left as far apart as ever?"

Wentworth was genuinely embarrassed. Leroy must be saved from his generosity, and in some way be made to feel how profoundly it was appreciated.

"I will stay one day more," he said.

"Good! Now, will you let me know if there is anything more you wish to see or know about our negroes?"

"Yes—their amusements. We hear of their banjos, dances, songs."

"I am sorry to say you can not see that kind of thing nearer than the northern theaters. It is the burnt-cork negro alone who now fiddles and dances. I can show you any number of prayer-meetings, but there hasn't been a negro dance in this region for many years. I can barely remember seeing one 'breakdown' when I was a boy."

"How do you account for the change?"

"The cause, as I think, is profound. There used

to be insurrections, and more attempts of that kind than were reported. It was the dancing negro who was the insurrectionist. He still lived in this world; he had some worldly hopes left. By inevitable necessity he was 'weeded out' of the plantation,—roses would be weeds if they grew amid cotton. There was required a hand that would adjourn his dance to the next world, hang up his banjo to be resumed as a heavenly harp. What frolicsome spirits remained, after the worldly and rebellious were improved out of the earth, were driven into camp-meeting convulsions. The preacher who instills the belief that pleasure is hateful to God, and present affliction the measure of future bliss, is the real overseer. He has reduced flogging to a minimum; but this peace sometimes strikes me as something like that of a cemetery. I tried one Christmas to get up a dance for the negroes, but failed."

On reaching home they were met with the sad report that Charlotte's foot was worse; the doctor had shaken his head, and she was in bed, troubled by his doubt of her ability to attend school. The rest were in gloom because a pic-nic had been planned, and Charlotte had agreed to give half holiday. A pic-nic without Charlotte was inconceivable.

"It is indeed unfortunate," said Leroy, "for Wentworth can stay only one day more."

"Only one day more!" cried three ladies at once.

"I'm sorry he has tired of us so soon."

"I assure you, Mrs. Leroy — "

"But our place *is very* dull."

"Oh, Miss Leroy—"

"Mr. Wentworth feels he has been here six months since Thursday."

"You too, Miss Bertha!"

"Give it him, girls," said Leroy, with mock aside, adding, "Wentworth, I am shocked by the satire of these ladies, but what authority has a husband or father in these degenerate days?"

"My dear kind friends, I have coolly quartered myself on you, man and beast. I have no home in which you can come and quarter yourselves. Do you mean me to settle down to law practice here?"

"Do!" cried Bertha; "and we'll try the case whether you shall go or stay."

"What's the excitement?" asked St. George, just entering.

"Why, Mr. Wentworth says he must go,—he's going Tuesday."

"Of course he's going," said St. George, "do you think he's got nothing better to do than stick here with you girls? No, he's going; he's going with me for two days' shooting in Turkey Forest. I've made all the arrangements."

"Oh, that's it," said Fanny; "then all we can do is to sit by Lotty and mingle our sighs till you both come back."

In the course of the evening Wentworth conversed with his man Wesley, whom he found enjoying his stay and trying to make himself useful. At night he lay awake revolving the situation in which he found himself, but without finding it grow clearer. Then he sank to sleep with a pleasing memory of the planter's daughters, in their simple white dresses, singing to the slaves.

## CHAPTER XIII.

### ONE DAY MORE.

WENTWORTH was half awakened by chatter of birds, so near his window that he could see their tiny forms traced in shadows on his curtain, with the boughs on which they sat. Sorrowfully he looked out on the fading dawn of his "one day more" in this beautiful abode, where he had found friendship. But need it be one day only? At least he might accept St. George's invitation for a shooting excursion. It was plain that the young man would be grateful for his company.

"Poor Charlotte is worrying dreadfully," said Mrs. Leroy at the breakfast-table.

"Is her foot worse?" asked Wentworth.

"No, or not much; but it is out of the question for her to attend her school to-day, and that troubles her."

"Tell her not to mind that," said Leroy; "we'll send word that she has sprained her foot, and the children will be consoled by a holiday."

"Mamma, what does papa mean by consoled?" asked Lily, whose private question happened to be heard by all, and caused a smile.

"He says the children will be so glad of a holiday that they won't feel so bad about Charlotte's foot; but papa doesn't think how much you all love her, does he, Lily?"

"No mamma, he don't. I'm sorry, and like to have her well."

"Lily," said Leroy, "mamma has suggested a possible and even plausible, but hypothetical and by no means essential construction of my phraseology, nevertheless——"

"Don't listen to him, Lily,—he doesn't mean any thing at all this time."

"What does Charlotte wish to do?" asked Leroy.

"She hinted about the children coming to her here, but that will not do; she'd never get well that way."

"It would do if it were necessary, but it isn't."

"So I told her, but you know, Mr. Leroy, what kind of person she is, and how she hates not to fulfil all her engagements. There are also two new pupils coming to-day, Mrs. Millward's children, and Charlotte had set her heart on giving them a pleasant reception."

"Mamma," said Eva, just entering, "Miss Charlotte's crying."

This news caused Bertha to slip out, and a sympathetic silence reigned around the table, till St. George said it was "too bad to have Lotty troubled that way." Then Wentworth had an inspiration.

"Leroy," he said, his face flushing, "in response to your generous desire to have me remain I said 'one day more;' this is the day—may I enjoy it as I like?"

"With all my heart."

"Then let me attend to the school in Miss Charlotte's place."

"Oh Mr. Wentworth!" echoed round the table.

"That is just the one service I feel able to do for those who have done me many favors; it would ease my mind and perhaps the sufferer up-stairs. I can not do all she does but I will do my best."

"Where are you running to, Eva and Lily?" cried Leroy.

"I'm going to tell Miss Charlotte," said Eva.

"Wentworth, this appeared to me a small matter, but nothing is small that will give you any satisfaction. I honor a teacher, yet can't quite like to have you set to work; this fine day too; but I shall not oppose one word to your desire."

Next was heard Charlotte's own voice from the head of the stair.

"Tell him I will not hear of such a thing!"

"Gracious! she's got out of bed—run, Fanny!"

"I beg you, Miss Leroy, to tell Miss Charlotte that if I can not be of any service here at all I can not be happy, and will leave at once. Or perhaps you'd better tell her she's too late—I've gone. Come, children!"

Wentworth glided away, the children rushed after him, and Charlotte from her window saw him disappearing with them.

The "one day more" crept into others. The picnic and the shooting were indefinitely postponed. The doctor said Charlotte would be lucky if she could drive out at the end of the week, and Wentworth said no more about leaving. Every morning he walked with the children to school; in the afternoons enjoyed any pastime proposed; in the evenings smoked and chatted and found happiness in his growing intimacy with these new friends. Just how he fared with his pupils will perhaps never be made known with historical exactness; but it is known that in several homes simultaneous reports were made by delighted children which brought simultaneous notes begging the Leroys to come and see them, and "bring the gentleman who has taken Miss Stringfield's place, the last few days." Moreover we have the report of Eva and Lily, who, on returning with Wentworth the first day, were unable to pursue usual amusements, even neglected domestic duties of the baby-house, but sat clasping Charlotte's hands, their joint memory conveying to her eager ears some account of what was said and done.

"Soon as he came he shook hands all round and asked every one's name. . He talked first to Susan and Charley Millward . . they are nice, Miss Charlotte . . he said he hoped they'd like the school and all of us. . Then Andy Scott and Tim Barbour got to laughing . . yes, Eva, and Belle too, for I saw her . . and Mr. Wentworth didn't take no notice . . *any* notice, Eva. . He rose up . . just as pleasant as could be. . And he said we needn't take our books, 'cause he had something to say. . *Be*cause, Lily. . The boys stopped laughing . . and Belle too. . And all was so still. . He said you had sprained your foot and couldn't come, and he would teach till you were well. . He loved to teach. . He said so many nice things, we all listened. . My! Didn't we, Eva. . He said he wanted to ask us questions. He asked, is it right to make a noise in school . . And nobody said a word. He said perhaps that young gentleman . . that was Tim, my! wasn't Tim pale . . He will tell me is it right or wrong . . Tim says wrong . . Will someone else tell me why it is wrong. Nobody spoke . . He said we must not be afraid, he was our friend . . He said, noise isn't always bad, and laughing is good, but in school we ought to be quiet . . If any body was about to be noisy in school he ought to say to himself, if I am noisy another boy or girl might be so too, and all may be . . then there couldn't be any more school at all . . Miss Charlotte who is trying to do you good would bid you good-by and never come back . . Oh —oh . . Don't cry, Lily . . Children might be happy in school. He liked that . . and laugh too if there was any thing to laugh at . . And it wasn't making fun of anybody, and hurting their feelings . . But giggling and playing in school, is mean . . *are* mean . . He said, will any one tell me the difference between laughing and giggling. Eva, can you tell me? Oh Miss Charlotte. I was choking, but he looked so . . Eva says, we giggle sometimes and can't tell why. That's right, Eva, he said . . Just think, Miss Charlotte, I was right. He says, when people laugh and don't know why, they are giggling . . That ain't . . *isn't*, Lily . . always wrong out of school . . And what do you think he did? He just went to the blackboard and drew a lot of children . . not us, but any children . . Some had their mouths wide open laughing fit to kill . . one was poking another . . two or three hiding their faces with books . . And then a picture of the teacher . . it wasn't you . . but she was pretty . . she was holding her fingers in her ears .. 'cause o' the noise .. *be*cause Lily. And oh how we laughed! He said, you're not giggling now because you've got something to laugh at .. He wanted to show us how a school would look if all fell to laughing .. giggling .. and he was going to wipe it all out, but Andy says, please wait till Miss Charlotte sees it .. He said no, I'm glad it made you merry, but we must now go to our books .. To-morrow we'll talk again .. and he taught just like you .. and there wasn't any noise all day .. And oh Miss Charlotte, but he *is* nice!"

Again, next afternoon, swing, hoops, baby-house, were forgotten, dolls pined in neglect; this time not Eva and Lily alone but Sumter also contributed to the report, while Fanny and Bertha swelled the audience.

"Oh, Miss Charlotte, such a talk! He got the boys to talk too .. He talked about how people ought to treat each other .. Every body ought to be polite .. 'Specially to Miss Charlotte .. No, Lily .. He said teacher, though .. He asked Charley Millward how a gentleman would treat a woman .. Charley said he would be polite and do things for her, and he turned out to be right .. He asked Sumter, why. Sumter said *be*cause men was .. *were*, Lily .. stronger than women .. most always .. Mr. Wentworth said he saw St. George dash and catch Miss Charlotte and keep her from falling under the horse .. St. George was against the horse's hind legs, and the horse kicked and it's a wonder he didn't hurt him .. but St. George didn't think about himself .. Real gentlemen think of others first .. 'Specially ladies

.. He told us the story of St. George and the Dragon .. He said the Dragon meant any danger at all .. and the Princess any woman at all .. Then he talked about old people and how young people should behave to them .. they ought to offer them their seat .. and listen to what they think .. He asked Tim why .. He said because they had lived longer .. He asked Susie Millward if living longer made people know more .. She said yes .. She was right .. 'Sir' means older .. So does Senator, and what else Sumter? .. The Indian 'Sachem' means Aged Man .. Old people may be mistaken, and not know so much as young sometimes, but they ought to be respected .. The young people will grow old and then they'll want to be respected."

Every morning, as it seemed, Wentworth devoted a half hour to such conversations; the children were so eager to hear them that none was ever late. Duty to parents, to each other, to animals, were successively discussed and many a good story told. One delicate theme he thought of dealing with—duty to servants; but he had forgotten there was no school on Saturday, and it never came off. His week was out. The doctor said Charlotte could resume her duties on Monday.

After dinner Wentworth was invited to see Charlotte in her own room, where he found her looking quite well, though she remained seated in her wicker chair.

"How glad I am to see you—and your pretty room too," said Wentworth, looking around, rather artfully, for he saw that Charlotte was finding it difficult to speak.

"Thank you," she said, "we women pet our rooms. But sit down and be devoured with thanks—poor as they are—for the riches lavished on my children."

"Oh, no! How glad I am your foot is nearly well."

"And able to take me to school. You've good reason after all your work."

"Miss Stringfield, may I see your foot?"

"My foot?" exclaimed Charlotte laughing, "what on earth for?"

"Of course, if you object—"

"Well, there," said Charlotte, as a shapely foot peeped out.

"Oh, thank you, but I meant the culprit foot, the invalid foot; I want to thank it for the happiest week I ever had."

"Mr. Wentworth, you've sealed your doom, and that of my wretched foot too; now it will never get well—Oh, oh, a twinge already! You've got to go on, and on, and on, teaching those children to the last syllable of recorded time!"

"But think of the cry of the children; had you only seen their sparkling eyes when I said you would be there Monday!"

"I have seen some children's eye-sparkles too in this room. I mean to be serious. I have seen these Leroy children growing under my eyes this week, mentally and morally. I have heard about others. You have got at their hearts, and what you taught is graven on their minds with a diamond."

"This is indeed encouraging."

"But it is discouraging to think of it ceasing. Oh, why can not a beautiful thing last forever!"

"The beautiful work went on before I came and shall go on now that I leave. I found those children devoted to their teacher, the thought of what she would approve always in their minds, their studies advanced; the cabin grew poetical as it was revealed what loving art had set there at its task."

Charlotte did not venture to speak, but her cheeks were eloquent. At length she said, "When?"

"Do I leave? Monday."

"Now be confiding! You can say to me what you would not to the Leroys, and I shall not tell them: are you leaving from inclination or by demand of duties? Do trust me!"

"I will," said Wentworth, after hesitation. "The imperative duty is not to press unfairly the boundless generosity of these dear friends. I have had two weeks of happiness, but must go."

"You are making a mistake. But I will not argue it now; we are all about to drive out, and I will be obliged for your arm down stairs. Thank you. Now I will beg as a personal favor, that you will not leave Monday, but stay one day more."

"How would that help you?"

"Why," said Charlotte, limping a little, as they approached the stairs, "it will be my first venture—my foot you know—I might have to move about—there are a dozen reasons why I want you Monday."

"That is sufficient; you want me—I stay."

"What's the matter, Charlotte," cried Mrs. Leroy from below, seeing the teacher leaning on Wentworth's arm and limping; "have you hurt yourself again? You moved about briskly this morning."

"You hateful woman! You can't let a body do a bit of acting but you must come out at the wrong time and catch 'em!"

With these words Charlotte ran down stairs with a ringing laugh and stood there awaiting her escort.

"A clear case of false pretenses," he cried—"Oyez, oyez!"

"Please the court, if weak woman can only get things from tyrant man by false pretenses—"

"What mischief has she been up to?" asked Mrs. Leroy.

"Not guilty, but don't do it again," said Wentworth.

"Never! An' may the blissed saints reward yer 'onor!"

## CHAPTER XIV.

A SUNDAY PIC-NIC.

THE Rev. Phayr Stringfield did not come to the Leroys on Saturday, as they expected, being under promise to stay that night with the Scotts, but sent word that he would return with them from church. Wharton Church was ten miles distant, but it was a pleasant drive, and the monthly service there was occasion for a parish pic-nic. The ancient building was in shape of a Greek cross, without architectural pretensions, but grateful to the eye by reason of its large and solid dignity, and its situation in a venerable grove of white oak and hickory. It was a colonial edifice, more than a hundred and fifty years old certainly, built of large red bricks. Above one gable rose a square tower, with belfry. There was a tradition that when, for many years, the church was deserted, slave traders had made it their headquarters, imprisoning there the smuggled Africans till disposed of among the planters. The walls inside, lofty and spacious, had no ornament save texts in evergreen, and black wooden tablets with golden letters, on which were inscribed the Decalogue, the Lord's Prayer, and the Apostles' Creed. The massive pulpit was perched high at a central angle, and two reading-desks were passed in the ascent to it. The round-arched windows were stained only by the autumn foliage visible through them.

More than a hundred persons gathered for the morning service, generally of the wealthy class. All greeted each other as they entered, and were seated some time before the clergyman arrived. Wentworth found the airy church, so full of light, the placid faces, the red and golden leaves outside the great windows, all so restful, that he dreaded to have the sweet silence broken. But the clergyman came, the old litany was read, the hymns sung—without choir or organ—and Mr. Stringfield began his sermon. A striking figure, certainly—tall, slightly bent (though not more than thirty), long-headed, heavy-browed, with small mouth; the large nose buttressing a full brow under bushy brown hair; the gray eyes of variable shade, the pale complexion at times overspread with swift color. His voice was sympathetic, his manner was simple, and almost sleepy when he began; but there was a certain charm in the eye, which appeared as if resting on the pastoral scene he described. For the subject was the Good Shepherd. His manner became less languid as he passed from the primitive shepherd life—gradual extermination of the violent and preservation of the peaceful animals by human vigilance and fidelity—to the symbol which grew out of it. The rude picture drawn by some hunted Christian on a wall in the Catacombs of the Good Shepherd bearing a lamb in his arms, the later splendors with which art invested the humble theme, were described with fine touches, Some doctrinal details followed which Wentworth lost. The present was too interesting for the past to charm him away; Leroy Island was too full of wonders for his imagination to wander even in Palestine; before him rose visions of the white-robed slaves beside their Jordan, the Leroy sisters singing in the island Bethel, and Charlotte bearing the lambs in her arms. How unconscious they were in their gentle service! What awaited them in the future? And what would befall those sheep of poor Haswell's pasture, so dumb before their shearers?

How far the clergyman had gone in his sermon Wentworth knew not, when his reverie was broken by a movement at his side: it was a bronzed old squire feeling for his handkerchief; tears were on his hard cheek. Wentworth raised his eyes to the preacher, whose head presently appeared encircled with soft light, while his voice was pure melody. Do not imagine, he said, that the Good Shepherd gave his life for the sheep only in Palestine, or bore in his arms only the lambs of flocks long perished. On these islands and savannahs he moves to-day. Whenever hearts are faithful to their lowly trust, there is he: wherever maternal love sleeplessly watches over souls that may stray where evil passions lurk, wherever paternal prudence guards young steps that may move upward or downward, where lower tendencies are restrained by high example, sorrow soothed by sympathy, wrath turned away by the soft answer—there see the Shepherd daily giving his life for the sheep! Think not that an age of asylums and schools has outgrown the need of individual care for each several mind and heart, with its several sorrow or danger. It is the Good Shepherd whose patient care cultivates the individual thinker, the finer character, the pure love and friendship, the happy life, in our homes. Shall we not consider the poor, as well as provide poor-houses? Shall we not be good shepherds to our servants, so helpless in our hands? While worshiping the Great Shepherd on high, shall we feed his African sheep only for our own fatness? Their lot is not to be deplored; it needs only our compassionateness to be made almost enviable. No political systems can make human beings happy; under any system that must remain the work of the Good Shepherd who cares for every soul, and feeds the heart's hunger with his flesh and blood.

These thoughts, spoken with great freedom—no cautious interpolations—arrowlike, feathered with pathos, shining with sincerity, found their way to every breast, and there turned to roses. The sacrament followed, after which the congregation distributed itself in groups under the trees. Hampers were brought forth, cloths spread on the grass, so near each other that all virtually dined together; and there was plenty of mirth.

"I'm sorry for you," said Leroy, taking Wentworth's arm, "but the school-children have spread your fame and you're in for it; one party bids for you with partridge, another with sucking-pig. The parson's delighted to have a vice-lion, for he hates to eat and talk before preaching again. So meet your fate like a man!"

Wentworth was presently bowing to blushing maidens with chicken or pastry in their dainty fingers, and apologies struggling from full mouths. Men grasped his hand, matrons thanked him, for the happiness he had given their children; several asked him to fix a day to visit them; young ladies, lily-like in their pretty dresses, besieged him with dainties till he cried mercy. He was rescued by Leroy, who brought up the clergyman.

"You'll drive home with him, Stringfield," said Leroy; "for the present know this—Wentworth is my friend and I am his."

"Then I'm his friend too," said the preacher.

"And I am yours," answered Wentworth, warmly.

The clergyman hastened to his vestry; the bell sounded, and the pic-nic resolved itself to a congregation again. The subject of the sermon was "The Day of Small Things." Wentworth's attention did not wander again, and he heard counsels that helped him to recognize the days that were surprising him with rich experiences.

Wentworth had brought Bertha in his buggy, but it was arranged that he should return with the clergyman. While he waited many of the flock gathered round their pastor, and after he had started a gentle lady stood in the way to say that she must tell him how he had helped her that day. Farther on another stopped him to say, "Never before have I heard such sweet thoughts from human lips." And far in the woods they were again waylaid.

"May I speak a word?" said a young man, advancing timidly. "I am from North Carolina, a stranger in this country, where I have come to live, but have no friends; I came to church lonely and sick, but now I am well and happy."

"That makes me happy, my young friend; give me your name and place, and we will meet again."

He pressed the youth's hand, and they passed on—the preacher remaining silent for a time.

"These people," he at length said, rubbing his eyes with two fingers, "have discovered my weakness. I'm as fond of being praised as a child. I'm as tickled as can be now because they liked my sermons."

"If any one did not feel what you said to-day he must be a stock or a stone," said Wentworth, with a slight dimness about his eyes too.

"Sometimes I come here heart-sick like that young man; but these people preach to me—they don't know it, just a warm word or look—and I go away happy. What a cheap thing happiness is! But one thing brings me down when I think of it—the emptiness of that negro gallery. Only four coachmen in it this morning. The negroes will not come to either of my two churches, yet no people in the world are such church goers. They would live in meeting-houses if they hadn't to work. It isn't a question of race; they crowd to white Baptist and Methodist preachers. How do you account for that? I've tried all my bunch of keys on that problem. Do you happen to have a key about you?"

"If you had asked me last year I could have offered keys warranted to unlock all questions concerning negroes."

"And where were you last year?"

"At Harvard university."

"Ah, you found omniscience easy there? But you are a southerner? No? I knew you were not a

Carolinian, but thought you might be from the South-West."

"I was born in Boston, and such keys as I have to southern problems were manufactured there."

"Out with them! Here we are amid the brave pines, man to man: is thy heart right with my heart, son of Rechab, then your hand; our buggy shall be a chariot of truth. Now tell me, in a word, what you think of us southerners, our institutions, laws, climate, negroes, geology, botany—but forgive my frivolity! I declare to you, after I have just got over the strain of preaching what must affect people for good or ill, I'm unfit for serious society. Not a grave thought in my brain, but only a buzz of conceits."

"Well, out with them! Those ground-squirrels are in keeping with these Gothic pines."

"Leroy knew what he was about when he confided me to you. And you, a Boston man, are friend of that prince of planters! Where did you know him? He was never north in his life; he and I were at the University of Virginia together. A unique man! The old Frenchman who sowed that seed in South Carolina will never die so long as Laurens Leroy lives. I don't know what the Merriwether mixture may do for his children. His wife was Margaret Merriwether. He met her at Charlottesville. Leroy had too much heart to keep the faith of his Huguenot fathers, but I can't make him an Episcopalian either: he worships the sun—Soli Invicto, you know—which shines alike on good and evil——"

"—Southerners and Yankees—"

"Exactly. Now we're not all up to that—or down to that: which should it be, Mr.—?"

"Wentworth. I think it should be 'up,' Mr. Stringfield, when we're talking of Leroy."

"I sometimes think a little more divine wrath were better for him."

"The wrath of the Lamb, perhaps."

"Good! he has that; baseness hides from his gentleness. Ah, 'wrath of the Lamb,'—thank you for my next text; I hope you're used to having your pocket picked; my fingers are providentially contrived for that industry."

"Perhaps you are taking stolen goods."

"No matter; honor among thieves ought to oblige, but doesn't always. Now let us go back to that empty negro-gallery. That conspicuously absent colored man is my Mordecai at the gate,—only I don't want him to kneel to me, but with me."

"You spoke just now of the strain of sermons that must affect human beings for good or ill. Your sermons to-day assumed in your hearers freedom,— power to be providential to others, active or indolent, unselfish or self-indulgent. Is that applicable to people whose moral responsibilities are on the shoulders of others? Grant, as you said, that the slave's lot is not deplorable, one would say it must modify the moral conditions of his nature. Whether it be so, you can say better than I."

"No, I can not; one can't read a page too close to the eye any better than one too far. But what is slavery? The subjection of one will to another. The home and society are impossible without that. The principle is only extended when this particular subject is disabled from choosing his master."

"But that added thing may make a vast difference; as a half-ounce of bone more or less in a bird's wing may bind it to earth or bear it aloft."

"Sometimes our freedom appears to me over-rated: life is so complex, we are so ignorant, so laden with inherited tendencies,—might we not be happier if half the problems were decided for us and our paths determined?"

"However better, it would cost us the comprehension of such sermons as yours. St. Anthony warning the fishes against snares of the fowler were weak beside a Baptist pointing them to a pool secure from the net, whence they pass to become gold-fishes in a sea of glory."

"Therefore Haswell succeeds with colored folk and I don't. Have you heard Haswell?"

"Yes. His whole Bible was the book of Revelations, while yours includes the sermon on the Mount."

"Well, I have put my question and got my answer. You must be aware that our answer to northern argument exudes from these pines, that our corollaries are supplied by our feathered fauna. But you may be astonished to hear that I am eccentric enough to thank you for your thoughts, which I will ponder. You will increase my gratitude if you give me your opinion on this question: how can a parson, who can not preach to these negroes, yet benefit them?"

"Mr. Stringfield I have been talking too much, I meant to sit at your feet, and have been garrulous."

"You have said too little: you will have to say

more. I let you off now, for here's the house—but not for long. I'm a horse-leech; also the garrulousest man you ever saw—

"Well, Eva, how goes it, dear? and there's Lily of the Valley too,—mind the wheels, sweetheart. Ah, Lotty, aren't you a little pale? I get kisses, you see, comrade."

"Oh! punning to Mr. Wentworth already!"

"Let me recommend you to be a venerable parson, Mr. Wentworth; it's sometimes better than this; Fanny and Bertha are shy and only give me one-and a-half apiece—before company."

# CHAPTER XV.

### A SUCCESSFUL CONSPIRACY.

"WELL, Wentworth, how do you like our parson?"

"Like! I love him."

"Hallelujah!"

"But, my dear Leroy, why didn't you hint what I was to hear?"

"Impossible; there's no predicting Stringfield, except that he'll always be strong; he spreads himself like a green bay tree one month, but it can not be found the next—in place of it a palm, or maybe a sweet-brier. What was he to-day?"

"Several things—now I heard the Pastorale, and now the house was filled with the sweet perfume."

"That man declines calls to cities; he might be a bishop; he sticks by his two country congregations—Wharton and St. Marks, he calls them his Rachel and Leah—and when we tell him to marry, says he has two wives already."

"Which is which?"

"He says he can't tell till the morning comes. In fact, I didn't dare to talk to you about Stringfield. I love him so much that my estimate can't be trusted. I thought he'd come out for a smoke after supper, but I suppose they are making him take a rest."

The truth was, Charlotte had spirited away her brother to her own room, brazening out charges of being "too mean for any thing," had closed her door solemnly, and sentenced him to imprisonment for one hour.

"They may gnash their teeth down stairs, but here you've got to stay, brother Phayr, unless you want to see your sister explode with what she's got to say. Better take an easier chair, and here's your cigar—it will keep your mouth shut while you listen. There! Do you feel like the Grand Turk? You'd better!"

"I—I—yam, I mean I do."

"Well, yawn now, for you won't afterwards. Listen! This Mr. Wentworth is a man —"

"Thought as much."

"You need boxing. Well, you never saw such a man in your life."

"I must defend truth—I've driven ten miles with such a man. A powerful intellect, polished till it shines."

"Fifteen minutes taken from your captivity by that knowledge. A man of that kind doesn't come into a little neighborhood like this without being felt. He's been working miracles without knowing it. You needn't smile; I'm not in love."

Charlotte then told the story of Wentworth's twelve days on the island, ending with the sad words—"and he declares he must leave Tuesday."

"Well?"

"He must not!"

"And you're not in love!"

"No; I'm the exception. But I'm in love with my

school, and he has opened a new path there; he must see us fairly on it before he goes. That for one thing. Brother Phayr, in all history never but one man came to Leroy Island for a high human purpose, except you; are we to let him slip in this way?"

"Is it reasonable to expect a scholar like that to bury himself on this island?"

"What else does my brother do? Now I have extorted from Mr. Wentworth, under promise that the Leroys shall not know it (mark!), that he would rather remain longer but can not trespass on their hospitality—and they, every one, longing for him to stay!"

"That alters the case without making it more hopeful. People of fine instinct will not easily perceive the generosity of accepting much generosity; in that they are right ninety-nine times in a hundred."

"This is the hundredth. Brother Phayr, you see through the whole thing; it will certainly be better for him and us to keep him longer, and you must help."

Mr. Stringfield smoked in silence for a few moments, then broke into a laugh.

"It is so funny, Lotty, for us to be contriving how to catch a hare that wants to be caught, but enters neither snare nor gum."

"He goes to my school to-morrow; it must be his gum."

"You'll find yourself mistaken; there are schools in Boston too. That man's soul is stirred by the profoundest problems of his time. These charming talks with your children are as easy to him as for me to smoke this—where did you steal it, Lotty? If he stays it will be for severer work than that."

"I have felt that too; but thought that if my school, the girls' plans for excursions, Mr. Leroy's friendship, Margaret's—well she's downright in love with him—were all twisted together —"

"I think not; he will go with a heavy heart, but he will go, unless you can add another strand to your rope."

"That must be you! put your arms around him tight!"

"The arms must be stronger than mine."

"You have something in your mind: do you mean a love affair?"

"No, Lotty; the new strand must be black. If this man remains it will be for the sake of the negroes."

"Heavens!"

"I can't tell you all I think now. Mr. Wentworth is a new kind of man, a mind bred by an era; his presence here means more than he realizes. He is no vulgar abolitionist, but his interest in the slave has brought him here, and he has a new interest in the master."

"What a fool I was not to see that!'

"I will think it over, and do my best. And now, haven't I a right to be jealous? You haven't asked a word about poor me, and I with splendid news to tell. No! it's too late—I bury it in this solitary breast forever. Leave your Phayr and go to your What's-his-name!"

"You bushy-headed, stony-hearted brother, if you don't tell me, I die instantly at your feet."

"Stop! my feet are not at my neck—you're choking me! Well, I've got lease of Selwood."

"At last, at last!" cried Charlotte, moved to tears. "Now we shall part no more. Oh my brother, why did you not tell me before! Oh the joy of it! Do they know it down stairs?"

"No, I kept the secret for you. Scott got Ravenel over last night and he unexpectedly agreed to my terms."

In another moment Charlotte rushed out to publish the tidings,—joyful indeed, for Selwood was a cottage near by which they had been long trying to secure for Mr. Stringfield. Although the clergyman's residence in the neighborhood would involve Charlotte's withdrawal from their abode, the Leroys knew that his coming was the only security for her remaining long. She would still be their near neighbor, and her brother also. The event was thus of immense importance to them, and Leroy insisted on bumpers of champagne to the new master and mistress of Selwood.

Afterward Mr. Stringfield drew Leroy away for a stroll in the moonlight. Leroy having spoken with warmth of Wentworth, the clergyman told him about their conversation on the way from church.

"It's really too bad to have him go away; we've tried to keep him in vain," said Leroy.

"Have you had much talk with him about the condition and prospects of the negroes?"

"Not enough; he has asked questions and I have answered freely."

"Tell me some of his questions."

"He asked about their chief faults and offenses,

our methods of punishment; he asked about their amusements, and was disappointed not to find banjos and breakdowns in full blast."

"I don't wonder at his disappointment. Well, as you all want him to stay I must do my best to help you; but you must give me *carte blanche* and agree beforehand to all I engage."

"With all my heart."

Next morning, according to promise, Wentworth accompanied Charlotte to her school, prepared to give the children a farewell talk. It had been his intention, as we know, to speak of kindness to servants, but after Mr. Stringfield's words on the subject, in his sermon, he resolved to be silent on that delicate matter, and suggest to the teacher a talk from her brother with the children about it. So Wentworth selected "Fun" for his topic. While he was cross-examining the boys about their sports, Mr. Stringfield entered and took his seat with the pupils. Wentworth flushed a little but went on to make clear the distinction between horseplay and fun; chalked on the board a bully in knickerbockers teasing a sensitive child; and told them that as their sports trained their sinews and senses for the serious activities of after life, so their dispositions were largely formed in the play-ground. Charlotte and her brother were now and then appealed to and made to answer questions, and there was a rapid growth of freedom and confidence on the part of the children in their replies.

When Wentworth, in a few simple words, expressed the happiness he had enjoyed in the days passed with them, and bade them farewell, the children's eyes began to swim. Mr. Stringfield restored their smiles by holding up his hand, with "Please, sir, may I speak?" He then spoke a few words of gratitude to the teacher who had taken his sister's place, carried a vote of thanks from every little hand, and proposed a holiday, to be improved by all walking over to Selwood where, he was glad to inform them, he and his sister were coming to reside.

When two cultured intellects, representing the subtle spirits of widely different societies, are brought into affectionate contact, the result sometimes surpasses the surprises of chemistry. While this Harvard man was talking to the children about "fun," showing the large relationships of sport and amusement, spiritualizing them, certain vague feelings in the clergyman crystallized to a purpose. On the way to Selwood he managed to get Wentworth to lag with him behind the others.

"You said good things, Mr. Wentworth, of the serious advantages of amusement for children, but what of our negroes,—these grown-up children who have no amusement at all?"

"That is the saddest thing I have found in the South. When poverty and toil become conscious, that is the curse; when laughter dies, then terrors are in the way."

"I can not express how fully I agree with you. A morbid religiosity has overspread these plantations like dry-rot, blighting all beauty for these Africans. For them no flower blooms, no bird sings. Do you remember my question yesterday which you did not answer? No? I asked how you thought a clergyman they would not hear might yet benefit these colored people."

"I remember the question, but I can not answer it."

"What do you think of this?—suppose such a clergyman should make a sustained effort to recall human gladness to their hearts, to surround them with some kind of beauty, to beguile them from care by some little amusement?"

"How strange that you should say this! I thought of talking to the children to-day about kindness to servants, but some words of yours in your sermon determined me to bequeathe that to one from whom it would come with a better grace. Kindness to them would, with me, mean too much,—for instance, teaching them to read, which is illegal."

"There were centuries during which the masses could not read, and yet the Church taught them many beautiful histories and truths; it was by means of music, images, pictures, legends, symbols——"

"Plays."

"And plays, acted in the churches by priests. It occurs to me that our colored masses, forbidden to learn letters lest they should read controversies about themselves and conspire, appear much in the position of the Europeans before printing was discovered. Yet those people were reached by the Arts, had a fair culture, and their serfdom was softened."

"You amaze me. Do you really think any thing of that kind can be done in the South? Would not the same influences that banished the banjo resist all amusement?"

"Possibly; but sufficient unto the day is the puritan.

ism thereof. One needn't cross a shaky bridge till he comes to it. I believe that if these laborers could be amused with pictures, poetry, music, for a few hours a week, their lot would be better than in the banjo-and-breakdown days; and not so bad a lot on a plantation like this, where they are kindly treated, never parted from their families, and need not be more anxious about to-morrow than the lilies."

"A few days ago, after sitting in their dismal meeting-house, and hearing from Leroy that they dreaded decoration, also that they had no amusements, some such thought as yours rose in me like a dream, and flitted away. What miracles, I thought, could a little paint, a little illusion, work for these children, for whom gilt were the same as gold. Say it were a theater, introducing them into elegant society, beguiling them with some romance from their small round of cares and the inner chains. Do you mean to treat this dream seriously?"

"I mean that we should try to do a small thing, if we can't do more. Consider this island. Here is a planter with a thousand slaves, children included, for whose welfare he will do all he can. Here are so many starving souls whose bejeweled heaven with eternal concert proves their craving for the beauty unknown to them on earth. We have a company of fairly educated people with talent, taste, benevolence. There are ladies who can sing and recite, lads too; and there is one woman who is a born mimic and actress—even my sister there. Here is a demand, here a supply; they are one inch apart."

"In geology it takes a long time to add an inch to a stratum."

"But man may do in a day as much as nature in a thousand years. Perhaps you would like to free these slaves to-day: it can not be done, even if it were well. But, whatever larger thing you or I might desire, or respectively work for as ideals, might we not try to effect some smaller thing where we see eye to eye— one that might become a large thing in the end?"

"A thousand times yes!"

"Ah, possibly a large thing—even probably. Leroy has taken you over his plantation,—nay, he has taken you over Georgia, Alabama, Mississippi; should you leave to-morrow and travel the coast you will see continuous cotton-fields, cabins, negroes; then you would find you had tried to analyze an ocean to obtain elements which Jordan creek can give you just as well. But could you only be content to stay and help us with some humane experiments, and we should succeed, what is to prevent our success spreading like a fire over regions where the stubble is the same?"

"My fellow-dreamer, I swear I will not go! I will live in a cabin, I will be slave of your lamp, will do any thing to follow such an aim, even if it fail."

"Well, now let us overtake that party; they are casting evil eyes on me for keeping you to myself."

When Charlotte and the children were overtaken they were already waiting in the veranda of Selwood, not having brought the key. Fortunately Leroy came with it; but before he had unlocked the door Wentworth, glowing with enthusiasm, spoke to him.

"Leroy, I have a great favor to ask."

"It is granted."

"It is that you will make some arrangement by which I may remain longer, perhaps even till after Christmas."

"Wentworth, what is this? you ask a favor and then grant me one. Charlotte, Stringfield, come here! what spells have you cast on this man—he says he will not leave us!"

"But this is too good to be true!" cried Charlotte; "Mr. Wentworth, have you really said so."

"I have; but I must be employed somehow. I must make believe to earn my bread and butter. May I lecture to the children now and then?"

"I engage," said Leroy, "to make you admit I am in your debt before the year is out."

# CHAPTER XVI.

### TAMING A TIGER.

THE fact that the Leroys had a guest from Boston,—handsome, scholarly, apparently rich,—became well known in the island after the Sunday at Wharton. It caused some sensation in every household, but in one breast excited emotions of a painful kind. Robert Ravenel, a rejected but desperately hopeful lover of Bertha Leroy, had seen the new-comer driving her in his buggy toward Wharton Church. In connection with the fame of Wentworth's accomplishments the sight had suggested a dreaded theory, afterwards to be branded on his heart as fearful fact: this Yankee manufacturer was after one of the rich planter's daughters. But which? A funereal thump in Robert's breast gave answer. There was but one lady on earth to whom all must aspire. Such was Robert's bad case after he had seen them on their way to church—himself unperceived—and he was filled with longing to plead with Bertha once more. This desire of his had done her friends a service: it was he who had persuaded his father to let Selwood to the parson, knowing well what pleasure that would give the Leroys.

The Ravenels were a Huguenot family whose heads, for a hundred and fifty years, had kept vendetta against the church which had persecuted their ancestors. The sins of the Carolinian English Church had been steadily visited on its Episcopal successor in the fifth generation by this one branch of the Ravenels. There being no Presbyterian Church on Leroy Island, a room at Rochelle, their family seat, witnessed weekly assemblages of the household for scriptural readings, some old divine supplying the sermon. St. Jean Ravenel, presiding magistrate of his county, was not a hard man apart from his attitude toward the church of the other gentry. He lived in the fashion of his fathers, grand without gaiety, read Latin, French and English classics, and was a generous patriarch to his sons and daughters. He could not quite forgive Leroy—whose grandmother was a Ravenel—for not supporting his pet feud against the Episcopal Church, and might have frowned on Robert's suit had he known of it. These feelings had prejudiced him against the clergyman, whom he never saw, and hardened him in the matter of Selwood. Mr. Stringfield might have succeeded better, perhaps, had he approached St. Jean personally, but he had been represented by Leroy, whose appearance reminded the old gentleman of his duty to Huguenot shades. He raised difficulties about the house, and did not conceal the fact that he did not want the parson in the neighborhood.

After Selwood had remained without tenant for a year, Mr. Scott took the matter in hand again. Robert was seated with his father in the Rochelle veranda when Scott's messenger came with the note. The old gentleman read it with vexation.

"Tell your master, with my compliments, that I can not come," he said, putting the note in his pocket.

"What is it, father?" asked Robert, when the messenger had gone.

"They are worrying me again about Selwood. It is Scott now; he wants me to meet Stringfield at his house and talk it over. I have talked it over; it's settled."

A cloud came over Robert's face, but he said nothing. He began thinking of the pleasure it would give Bertha and those around her if his father were more friendly in this thing. He felt that he and his sisters were in some way isolated, and it might even be that Bertha left him without hope because of the separate traditions of their family. They never attended balls, because of their hereditary Calvinism, and never went to church because its colonial predecessor persecuted Huguenots. After long silence, Robert, rendered desperate by rumors of Wentworth's honors in the Leroy family, ventured for the first time in his life to oppose his father.

"Father, doesn't it seem rather useless to keep Selwood closed all this time?"

"If I choose it so, I can't see that it concerns you, sir!"

"Oh, of course not. I was only thinking—that is I—"

"Well, sir, let's have your valuable thoughts."

"You shall have them, father," said Robert, with a look that startled the old gentleman. "It concerns me—it concerns my sisters—that we should have the reputation of being unfriendly to our neighbors, and never mix with them, and not oblige them in a thing like this. You have my thoughts, father, valuable or not, as you please."

The particulars of the storm that followed Robert's outbreak need not be given. St. Jean was at first aghast, then accused his son of ingratitude, their voices at length becoming so loud that Eleanor, the eldest daughter, hastened to the verandah. She caught her father's arm as he stood, trembling with anger, pointing Robert away from the house.

"Go, sir, go!"

"Father, what is all this?" cried Eleanor.

"That ungrateful boy has insulted me in my own house!"

"I never dreamed of such a thing," said Robert with quivering voice, "I would get on my knees to you rather than insult you."

"You have done so, sir!" cried St. Jean, disappearing into the house.

Robert had a faithful confederate in Eleanor, a year older than himself, and told her all that had occurred, and the motives that had impelled him to speak out.

"You are in the right," said Eleanor, "but you know that obedience has been the rule of this house since it was founded; there is only one thing to be done—before dinner you must find father and ask his pardon, without justifying yourself in the least, and with a good grace."

Meanwhile, irate St. Jean had gone to his wife with an account of what had occurred, and was not satisfied with her reception of it. She wept, and would not say a word.

He next encountered Eleanor with the story, but she also was silent, and to his charge that his family were turned against him, tears were her only reply. He went off to his office, at the end of the garden, and had remained there nearly an hour when Robert knocked at the door.

"Father," he said, "I have come to ask your forgiveness. I am very sorry that I worried you. I had no business to interfere in your affairs; it was entirely wrong of me, and I beg your pardon, sir."

"Well, my son, let us say no more about it. I want to be alone now—till dinner."

There was, nevertheless, some constraint and undue silence at dinner. In the evening Eleanor was summoned to her father's office, though what the subject of their conversation was she did not mention. But next morning, as Robert was about riding off, his father called to him.

"Where are you going, Robert?"

"To Sullivan's Ford, sir," said Robert, bringing his horse close to his father; "the county nominations are arranged to-day."

"Ah, I had forgotten. If you meet Scott, tell him I shall come over this evening."

"Yes, sir."

The thing was done. Robert's heart gave a little leap as he galloped off—straight to Scott's, of course. Next morning he was informed by his father that Selwood was let to Stringfield.

"I need your forgiveness all the more," said Robert handsomely, "for nobody ever had a better father, and I hope, sir, you will never doubt my love for you."

Robert hoped to be the first to carry the good news to Leroy House. While the holiday company which we have already accompanied to Selwood were speculating about the rooms—which should be Charlotte's, which the study, and how they should be decorated—the eager lover was telling the tidings to Bertha. Although these had partly preceded him she was "dying to hear all about it," and was so sweet and affable that his hope rose high. Bertha inconsiderately ran on with what they were all so full of; it was Mr. Wentworth said this and Mr. Wentworth did that; until presently her words elicited no answer, and on looking up she saw a thunder-cloud in place of the hopeful face she had greeted. She was appalled and began to ask how all were at home.

"Home! I have no home. Every body can have a happy home but me."

"Oh, Robert, don't talk so; you have a home and dear sisters."

"I am almost twenty-four; nearly every man of my age around here is engaged, or married, and settled down to something; but I am a wanderer on the face of the earth."

"Well, Robert, why don't you settle down to do something useful."

"What for? A man works for love or money. I don't want money, and I've got nobody to love me."

"That isn't true; your sisters love you."

"You know what I mean. Oh Bertha!"

She heard footsteps in the hall and hoped somebody would enter, but they died away, and she must pass through her ordeal.

"I begin to feel," said Robert, struggling with his emotion, "as if some curse was on me. Our family somehow stands alone. Father didn't mean to let the Stringfields have that place, but I tackled him on it—the first time in my life—and was almost ordered out of the house; then he gave up. I did it because I wanted to break down the wall between us and other people."

"That was grand of you, Robert. I'm glad you told me that."

"Oh, are you glad? I have made you glad. Bertha, it was for you I did it. Wall or no wall is all one to to me but for you! Only try and love me—it's awful to go on as I've been since—since that day."

"I'm so sorry. Much as I like you, Robert, it's impossible to change the answer I gave."

"Oh, my God!"

Robert threw up his hands, as if shot. Then he slowly arose and looked out of the window, unfortunately just as the party from Selwood appeared, St. George being now with the children and Wentworth with Charlotte behind them. The last time Robert had seen the Bostonian he was with Bertha, and now on the instant he received authentic revelation that this smiling gentleman was her accepted lover.

"Bertha!" he cried, "tell me this—are you in love with somebody else?"

"What a question!"

"Answer me!" he thundered.

Anger answered anger: in an instant Bertha was on her feet, but not being a lover under jealous delusion, she could still be cool and satirical.

"Please, master, don't whip me too hard," she whined out.

"I know!" shouted the maniac. "It's that damned Yankee who drove you to church."

"Oh, I'm a runaway, am I? Set the dogs on me"

"I'll kill him!" shouted Robert, on whom the girl's sarcasm was wasted.

"And now, please master, I'll go, or you might kill me too; and I've heard enough foul language for one day."

She darted out the door. Her words, "foul language," roused him to some confused consciousness of his misbehavior, and he felt that he should see her no more. At such moments more reasonable men sometimes seek scapegoats for their sins; but Wentworth had already been selected to be that of Robert, who glared at him furiously as he passed out. Every one observed the glance except its object, who seemed *fey*, as the Scotch say.

"Gracious!" exclaimed Charlotte to her brother. "Some of Bertha's work!"

St. George hurried over to the horse-rack, where Robert was mounting, and offered his hand; but it was not taken, and with a few muttered words the agitated youth dashed off.

"Poor Bob," said Saint, when he returned to Charlotte, "he's awfully cut up. I didn't like what he said, either."

"What was it?"

"'Damned Yankee! I'll do for him!'"

"Don't repeat that, Saint."

Charlotte found Bertha upstairs in a swoon, with Fanny sprinkling water in her face. They soon got her to bed, but she became hysterical, and it was long before she was able to tell what had happened. She kept back Robert's brutal language, but confided to Charlotte and her elder sister the delusion he was under, and his threat against Wentworth.

"Why in the world didn't you undeceive him?"

"It was impossible. I can't tell you just why, Lotty. He lost his head and I couldn't keep mine."

"You'll have to write to him."

"Never! nor will I ever speak to him."

Charlotte laid her cheek to Bertha's, and then the tears began to flow. Fanny quietly left them together.

"And you can not love him?"

"I am not in love, Lotty. I believe I'm a baby in that kind of thing. It all seems a long way off. I'm so happy with you all, so wrapped up in what we're all doing, that this is like a great trouble breaking in. Ever since spring, when Robert spoke, I've been trying to forget it—but, oh, how frightened I am!"

And indeed Bertha's teeth chattered. Charlotte tried to soothe her, but she became feverish, and ran on with mingled tears and laughter.

"Oh, Lotty, if you had only seen him! I felt like a mouse before a tiger. Did you ever hear of a mouse marrying a tiger? That's me marrying Robert. His eyes grew big as saucers, without the least exaggeration. It's a mercy he didn't eat me."

Charlotte gradually gathered what had occurred, and it made her uneasy. She and the Leroys knew that Robert was no mere vaporer, and there was some consultation about his menaces. Of all this, however, the individual most concerned knew nothing, but passed the afternoon writing letters for the next day's mail—one to Stirling, another to Judge Minott; a third was addressed to "Messrs. Dolland, Manufacturers of Scientific Instruments, Boston, Mass.;" a fourth was to "Abrahams, Costumer, Cornhill, Boston."

The Selwood property included a large building for cotton storage, latterly used as a barn, and on this Wentworth fixed a more admiring eye than even upon the pretty cottage with roses climbing on its verandah. The Barn was now empty, and, although he heard Leroy already negotiating for its use, the big building presented possibilities of divine uselessness to this peculiar Yankee's eye which prevailed with its new owner. The Barn at once became the scene of mysterious labors. St. George was full of resources in handiwork, and Wesley Hampton had been given some training as a mechanic. Some planter of the past had happily made preparations for the crop our Utopian sowers hoped to harvest there, by leaving plank enough for a stage.

One day toward the close of the week, work at the Barn being now well advanced, Bertha walked over there. It so happened that Robert had just been to Selwood to direct some repair, and was riding past the Barn when Bertha knocked at the door. She saw him and he saw her,—he must also have seen Wentworth admit her into that long-unused building, and carefully close the door. St. George was more disturbed even than herself when she whispered what had occurred; he went out but Robert was nowhere to be seen. Wentworth was puzzled by their agitation, and when Bertha had gone managed to get from St. George the whole story of Robert's jealousy and threats.

"Poor fellow," said Wentworth, "he saw the 'damned Yankee' admitting his sweet-heart into a lonely Barn. I wonder he didn't shoot me!"

"Tell truth, I wonder he didn't; he's equal to it."

"What sort of a fellow is he, Saint?"

"Not a bad fellow; he's got a heart; but he doesn't do any thing but go to political meetings and rave about Southern Rights."

"Has Bertha any thing particular against him?"

"Think not. Bertha's young, every body pets her at home, and she never cared for beaux."

"Does this Mr. Ravenel contemplate any profession?"

"Think not. They've lots of money. He wanted to be an artist but his father put his foot down on that."

"Can he paint?"

"He used to beat every thing at drawing; he made a funny picture of every boy at school, and one day old Carter at the Landing paid him ten dollars for painting a sign for his tavern. I don't know if he paints now, but somebody told me he made a pretty picture of his sister Eleanor sitting in the verandah."

"Where do the Ravenels live?"

"Rochelle—about five miles on the high road. It's a good road for you to keep away from just now. In fact, though I hate to say it, there's danger in Bob, and you must take my pistol along when you come to-morrow. He's a red-hot southerner, he's jealous, he isn't safe."

"Thank you for the warning. I'll think it all over. But I must at once decline the pistol."

Wentworth did think over the situation very carefully. The result was that, in the course of the next morning, while the work was going on briskly in the Barn, he slipped out, mounted a horse which Wesley brought up on the moment, and rode swiftly toward Rochelle. Three miles on the way he met the formidable man himself, whom he could not recognize. Robert's horse was steaming; he snorted when reined up, and pawed the ground, as if sensible of his master's fury.

"Mr. Wentworth, I believe," said Robert with a dark look.

"Yes; and you?"

"Ravenel is my name. You are the man I want to meet."

"At your service, Mr. Ravenel."

"One of us must die."

"I hope not just yet."

"I demand satisfaction,—you know for what."

"You shall have satisfaction."

"When you please, where you please, how you please; I stake my life against yours."

"I would suggest as the time six months hence; because ——"

"Because you are a coward and can sneak off to your damned Yankee land."

"That's not the only reason. I have two or three others for not wishing to be hasty."

"Well, let's hear them," said Robert, lashing his boot.

"First, I wish to give you fair play. You are nervous. You are under the delusion that there is some kind of love affair between Miss Bertha and me. That is a mistake. I don't wonder you fancy so, for she is a lovely young lady, but there isn't the ghost of a chance that we shall ever be more than good friends. You are under the wilder delusion that she and I had a clandestine meeting in Selwood Barn, and do not know that St. George and others were inside."

Robert saw truth in the face before him; his eyes fell, his head sank, a pallor of shame overspread his face.

"These delusions so agitate you that you couldn't shoot steady. I should have the advantage. If you happen to have a pistol will you lend it me a moment?"

Robert drew out a pocket-pistol and handed it helplessly. There was a sharp report and a sparrow lay dead some paces distant.

"I'm glad that isn't you," said Wentworth, returning the pistol; "even a Yankee coward is not always cowardly enough to shoot an enemy whose hand is trembling. No, sir, we must meet when you're cooler."

"You've got me down," gasped Robert.

"There's another reason why our duel should be postponed," said Wentworth, without seeming to hear

Robert's words; "your help is needed in an important matter, and I was just coming to beg for it."

"My help!"

"Yours. But since you have challenged me and I have accepted, the Leroys will have to send some other messenger. Good morning!"

"Stop, for God's sake! You have got me down and I deserve to be trampled on. Good God, what a jackass I've been making of myself. Just wait a minute."

Robert wiped the sweat from his brow; it was some moments before he could speak.

"There's one thing I ought to say, Mr. Wentworth. You find me with a pistol and think I meant to— to—"

"Shoot me."

"I do not often carry one, and it was not for you; more likely that bullet would have gone into my own heart."

"Then, indeed, we are well met."

"I have made a fool of myself about you, and I ask your pardon. If you knew how miserable I am you might not think so hard of me."

"I can guess something: I am not your enemy; I would like to be your friend were that possible to a Yankee."

"There's my hand, sir. You're the first northern man I ever met, and I could bite my tongue out for having insulted you."

"Now that we are friends," said Wentworth, after shaking hands, "I will say what I was coming for. I hear you know how to paint."

"Daub."

"Well, daub. Now, it's a secret at present, but we are getting up some theatricals in that same Barn—"

"Oh Lord!"

"And we have every thing except scenery. We don't need much—the inside of a room, and a kind of hall, to begin with."

"I can't paint worth looking at."

"I feel sure you can paint what we require. There's plenty of canvas. Fanny and Bertha will sew it for you, and I'm certain you will accommodate the ladies."

"You are the gentleman I wanted to kill."

"Oh no, it wasn't you but your ghost; I saw it was your ghost I was meeting; *you* never meant me any harm."

"It's brave to say so, but I can't forgive myself, and—and—I'm ashamed to ever meet her again."

"Oh, you'll soon make that up."

"You don't know half. I've treated her like a brute. I've insulted her and cursed her, and accused her of heinous crimes, and acted like a run-mad jackass—"

"Come, now, I don't believe you. You're drawing it too strong—and then jackasses don't run mad. The donkey is a picturesque animal; and if you've been a little foolish, why come and be pictorial in the Barn."

"There's nothing I'd not try to do for you to atone for my behavior; but the favor's the other way—the prospect of making myself useful is the best any one can set before me."

"Good! And now we're mounted, what say you to riding to the Barn for a look at things."

The visit was made, the dimensions taken for the scenery, and Robert promised to come next day with his pigments. In parting with Wentworth he said, "If you live a hundred years you'll never know what you've done for me this day."

# CHAPTER XVII.

### ART AND ARTIFICE.

A BUSY month followed. Never since the Revolution had Leroy Island known so much activity among its white inhabitants as attended the sojourn of its first northern visitor. By the last week in November much had been accomplished: the Stringfields were housed at Selwood, the Barn was full of benches, the performers were versed in their parts. On a day, two mysterious boxes had been brought from the Landing for Wentworth, curiosity concerning which threatened some of the Leroy household with fever until their contents could partly be inferred from the First Programme. This, as submitted to the assembled family council, was as follows:

LEROY ISLAND ENTERTAINMENT.

Part Song—" Home, Sweet Home,"
Misses Fannie and Bertha Leroy.
Recitation—" Marion's Men,"   . . .   Master Sumter Leroy.
Flute Solo—Scotch Strathspey,   . . .   Mr. St. George Leroy.
Song—" The Four-Leaved Shamrock,"   Miss Bertha Leroy.
Guitar Song—" The Blue Juniatta,"   .   Miss Leroy.
Magic Lantern—The Prodigal Son,
Mr. W. Wentworth, exhibitor.
Recitation—" Crime and Remorse," Rev. Phayr Stringfield, Miss Stringfield, Mrs. Leroy, Mr. Wentworth.

"Crime and Remorse?" said Charlotte; "is that better than 'Scenes from Macbeth'?"

"Leroy and I think we had better not hint any thing theatrical," said Wentworth; "gentle Shakespeare will forgive us for not mentioning him; his rose will smell as sweet by another name."

The vigil of the first rehearsal was one of excitement. Sumter sank to sleep with Marion's Men marching on his lips; Mrs. Leroy had to warn her daughters that they were making sweet home sour with their midnight singing; and Charlotte, who was passing the night there, heard a voice warning "Lotty Macbeth" that, if she didn't stop her sleep-walking and her damns, said voice would be too sleepy to play the flute next night.

St. George had been astounded when, on the day after he had warned Wentworth against Robert, the latter entered the Barn. Saint sprang forward with alarm, and could hardly stammer an apology for his brusqueness when he saw Wentworth greeting his enemy. When Wentworth presently whispered explanations Saint said "you're a magician." Robert, with Eleanor's assistance, had prepared a large canvas, and now set to work, only begging Wentworth not to let him have to face *her*, nor let any body else know he was working at the Barn. Robert worked daily until he had painted a brilliant palatial interior. Only when Wentworth begged it as a favor did he consent to be present at the first rehearsal.

None of the Leroy children had ever seen a theater, and no Parisian stage ever gave habitué half the delight which filled these Arcadians when the curtain at the Barn was drawn and the lamp-lit scenery revealed.

"Oh-h-h! Isn't it just perfectly beautiful!" was the first chorus heard in Selwood Barn.

"Who could have painted it!" cried Bertha.

"It came from the north in one of Those Boxes," said Charlotte.

"No! Guess again!" said Wentworth.

"I know, I know!" cried Bertha; "Mr. Wentworth painted it."

"Isn't that girl smart? Why didn't we think of it before?" said Charlotte.

"Because it isn't so. I only wish I could paint like that."

"Artist! Artist!" cried Charlotte; "every body call artist!"

Poor Robert had crept to a dark corner near the door, and heard the call with terror. He was relieved by hearing Wentworth say that the artist would be known in good time, but they must now prepare for rehearsal. But under pretext of looking at Bertha's music he whispered to her the secret.

"The artist is Robert Ravenel; he and I are good friends and he has been working with us for two weeks. He's in the far corner on the left of the door, and afraid to meet you."

"I can't sing at once," said Bertha; "let Sumter come on first."

Sumter had hardly got through when a little scream was heard near the door.

"Oh, oh! There's somebody down here—there's a man here!"

It was Bertha's voice. Robert had seen her wandering his way, absorbed in her music, and crouched, with his back turned to escape recognition. His blood curdled at her cry.

"Why!" she said innocently, when all had rushed up, "if it isn't Mr. Ravenel!"

Robert came forward, looking sheepish, and Bertha clapped her hands.

"I know! This time I *do* know; the artist is Robert Ravenel!"

"Right!" shouted Wentworth and Saint together.

Robert could not escape his ovation. Leroy and Stringfield shook his hand with warmth, the latter expressing the hope of seeing him at Selwood. When last of all came Bertha,—the rest now returning toward the stage,—the culprit shrank back.

"It's beautiful, Robert, and we owe you so much for it!"

"Oh, Miss Bertha," he said in a scarce audible tone, "don't speak to me! I've committed the unpardonable sin."

"I won't hear of that."

"You don't know half. I wasn't only a brute to you, but to him—he'd never tell you, but I tried to murder him—yes, on the highway—and he the gentlest gentleman that ever lived. No, it's no use, I've committed the unpardonable sin, I'm not fit for you to speak to—I'm not fit to be here, but he begged me to come."

"Let bygones be bygones, Robert; you must come and listen, we want you to criticise—do come!"

"Where's Bertha?" cried several voices.

"Here I am! Where are your eyes, shouting at a body when she's studying her music close by you?"

In a few moments the sisters were singing their duet, and Robert was drawn by fascination to a bench behind Wentworth, to whom he whispered when the duet was over.

"Is she not an angel! She even came and spoke to me after all my crimes. I'm in hell and it's too good for me. I'm going now to hide my head somewhere, but to my dying day I'll not forget what you've done. Should we never meet again—"

"Will you please shift that scene a little forward," cried Wentworth, as if he had not heard the whispers behind him. "Wait a moment, Saint, Mr. Ravenel will put the scene where it will be brighter."

Robert was soon on the stage, and when the really needless change was made Wentworth thanked him and said: "Please don't go, for I need your help with my Magic Lantern."

The rehearsal having passed off to general satisfaction they all walked home, Bertha managing to get some private conversation with Wentworth on the way.

"Mr. Wentworth, did you and Robert have any hostile meeting? He said he tried to murder you."

"Nonsense. The fellow exaggerates everything against himself. Why, he told me he insulted you, abused you, accused you of heinous crimes!"

"He must have dreamed most of that, but he *was* terrible,—and his language wasn't proper."

"What! Did he use improper language to a lady!"

"Oh, not exactly toward me—but—"

"About me; still, I'm shocked that, before a lady, he could use coarse—"

"Oh dear me,—it wasn't exactly that either ; I don't like to repeat it."

"Language you can't repeat ! I give him up."

"Mr. Wentworth, hold your ear down," said Bertha, and she whispered—"He said *damn !*"

"Dreadful ! but I think I'll take him back again. He was in great pain, and that sometimes calls up expressions people have heard—in church."

"But how did you soften him ? I do believe you could enter the lions' den, like Daniel."

"I wouldn't be afraid if the lions were in love with pretty lionesses, and knew I was a friend of the lionesses : they'd all turn to lambs."

"That's like Æsop's fables," said Bertha, turning crimson.

"Now tell me something about these Ravenels."

Bertha gave some account of the family, and Wentworth asked if it was likely that any of them would assist in future entertainments. Fanny was summoned to advise on this point. They were not certain. If old Mr. Ravenel shouldn't take up a prejudice against the scheme Eleanor might sing a song. The younger sister Netty was bright and pretty but they knew little of her. There was a general consultation on the same subject that evening. The sympathy of the Ravenels with their projects was regarded by Leroy as so important, especially that of the magistrate, that Wentworth resolved to visit Rochelle the next day.

St. Jean and Robert were absent when Wentworth arrived at Rochelle ; but that the visitor did not regret, for he desired a preliminary interview with Eleanor. This lady met him with a warmth which suggested knowledge of his relations with her brother—her "rash brother,"—and her tears started when Wentworth said he might be rash but had as true a heart as ever beat. Eleanor was half won to the Barn movement before he came: at the end of an hour there was formed a conspiracy of three women—Madame Ravenel, Eleanor, and Netty—and two men (Robert being taken for granted) to secure the old Huguenot's favor for the entertainments. In case of their success Eleanor would not refuse her ballads, and Netty would "participate in a recitation"—euphemism agreed on for "acting"—in any small part. In view of the important end to be attained Wentworth accepted an invitation to remain to dinner, for which St. Jean and his son duly returned.

Whatever might be the faults of St. Jean Ravenel, inhospitality was not among them. To him his guest was of all men the superior. Wentworth was made at ease in his presence, and the dinner passed off pleasantly enough. The Martin-summer, as it was called at Rochelle, continued, and the gentlemen smoked in the verandah—St. Jean his silver-mounted corn-cob pipe. The Bostonian was fairly fascinated by the elder Ravenel, having never before seen so picturesque a personage. His silvery hair with its queue, his ruffles, and snow-white cravat flowing through a large sapphire ring, his ancient watch-seals falling beneath the waistcoat, and blue dress-coat with plain brass buttons, were all in harmony with the gracious dignity of the man. Wentworth thought that if he were getting up theatricals in Boston he could wish nothing better than have such a figure simply appear on the stage. When his fellow-conspirators had left him alone with St. Jean, Wentworth found that he had been too much interested in this unique old gentleman to consider properly any plan for besieging him. He opened rather feebly.

"I can hardly imagine a pleasanter place than you have here," he said, and then, with compunction for the commonplace, added,"—it's a place for communion with poets."

"Yes, we have some leisure for reading, but I find good books rare. My family have less difficulty; they are just now making an ado about a Mr. Kingsley, but I've not looked into him yet. I stick to my Moliere, my Milton, and Shakespeare; they are likely to last my remnant of days."

"In the company of such giants I don't wonder modern writers seem pigmies. I myself was brought up on Milton, and to this day he appears to me almost incomparable."

"For thirty years no week has passed without my reading something from Milton. And, by the way, if you are interested in such things I have an old edition of Milton that belonged to my grandfather; his pencilings are in it."

"I should much like to see it."

"It is at my office; will you go with me?"

Passing through a garden, and an avenue of aspens for some two hundred yards, they entered a white frame office with neatly-turned pillars in front. The walls were well stocked with books, the table loaded with business papers. The Milton was at once laid before Wentworth.

"A Hollis!" he cried, "there's his owl! But this is rare."

"And pray who or what is Hollis?" asked St. Jean.

"An admirable Englishman who lived a hundred years ago and brought out a superb edition of Milton: this copy is from his own library."

"How could you tell? That name is indeed inside, but it never conveyed any meaning to me."

"Every book in his library was bound in red, with an owl on it; if he thought the book not wise the owl was reversed. Any Hollis book brings a solid price, but a Hollis Milton is worth its weight in gold."

"This is very interesting. Where can I find more about this Mr. Hollis?"

"I own a copy of his Memoirs, and it shall be in your hands next week. If you will pardon my egotism, I passed my college life in a building named after him, 'Hollis Hall,' for he was a great benefactor of Harvard university."

The old gentleman was grateful for the promise but deprecated the trouble it might involve. Wentworth assured him it would be a pleasure, and began to turn over the pages, meanwhile summoning his wits to follow up his lucky hit; for Leroy feared that St. Jean's disfavor might even prove fatal to the innovation at the Barn. He concluded at last to try and utilize Milton.

"I never read these majestic poems," said Wentworth, "without thinking what a grand thing it would be if passages from them could be recited before masses of men."

"In the way he himself has described," said St Jean with some eagerness,—" do you remember that passage?"

"Can you find it readily?"

"Easily,—here it is, in the Plea against Prelaty."

"It would delight me to hear you read it."

"Certainly:—' But because the spirit of man can not demean itself lively in this body without some recreating intermission of labor and serious things, it were happy for the commonwealth if our magistrates, as in those famous governments of old, would take into their care, not only the deciding of our contentious law-cases and brawls, but the managing of our public sports and festival pastimes; that they might be, not such as men authorized a while since, the provocations of drunkenness and lust, but such as may inure and harden our bodies by martial exercises to all warlike skill and performance: and may civilize, adorn, and make discreet our minds by the learned and affable meeting of frequent academies, and the procurement of wise and artful recitations, sweetened with eloquent and graceful enticements to the love and practice of justice, temperance, and fortitude, instructing and bettering the nation at all opportunities, that the call of wisdon and virtue may be heard everywhere, as Solomon saith: "She crieth without, she lifteth up her voice in the streets, in the top of high places, in the chief concourse, and in the openings of the gates." Whether this may not be, not only in pulpits, but after another persuasive method, at set and solemn paneguries, in theaters, porches, or what other way may win most upon the people to receive at once both recreation and instruction, let them in authority consult."

"That is great!" cried Wentworth, "where else can be found such writing, such sublime truth."

"My grandfather has added on the margin: 'Behold a lighthouse among lanterns! These words should be written in gold over the head of every magistrate.'"

"The marginal note should be printed in gold over that owl."

"He was indeed a fine old magistrate, albeit bookworm,—my son bears his name, Robert Julian Ravenel."

"Mr. Ravenel, you were led to that passage by a happy inspiration, for it opens up a subject I am anxious to consult you about. Being in the neighborhood, and connected for a time with a school, I am trying to get up something of the kind described by Milton, something that will unite instruction with recreation—in a small way indeed, but we must not despise the day of small things."

"I am glad to hear it. Many a time, when sots have been brought before me from brawls at cockfights and dog-fights, our county amusements, I have reflected what a blessing would be some elevating recreation in this region."

"This gives me hope that you will sympathize with my efforts."

"I can give you no aid, I am old, and can barely jog on my daily round to the end."

"To have your good will in my effort to do something in the spirit of that glorious passage you have read, were help and encouragement enough."

"That you have with all my heart. And though I am too old for more, perhaps my young people may be able to render service in a thing like that."

When Wentworth returned to the verandah with the venerable St. Jean, the conspirators saw success on his beaming countenance.

"Now you must take your nap, father," said Eleanor, "Mr. Wentworth will excuse you."

"No, child,—I don't need it at all."

"But you must, father."

"Pray do, sir," said Wentworth, "or I should never dare to come again, as I meant to ask permission to do."

"You troublesome girl," said the old man rising. "My children read in their Bible 'Parents obey your children.' I hope you will remain for the night, Mr. Wentworth."

"Another time I shall be glad to do so, but must deny myself now. Good by for the present, sir."

"Good-by, and let us see you again!"

Wentworth's success caused less surprise to the other conspirators than he expected. Eleanor remarked that though her father might have a few prejudices he knew a good deal of human nature, and could tell when a man was animated by the right spirit.

"But," said Wentworth bowing, "magistrate though he is, I fear he can not always recognize guilt. I never felt guiltier than when I found myself out there practising stratagems on a large heart whose gates were all open."

" Perhaps you knew the sesame to open them."

" No, he found even that himself—it was Milton."

" Whom he holds next to his Bible," said Madame Ravenel.

Before Wentworth left the second programme was already arranged and the parts Eleanor and Netty were to take. He was met by the Leroys with upbraidings for his absence from dinner, but these were silenced by the happy story he had to tell of his visit to Rochelle.

# CHAPTER XVIII.

### MIRACLE-PLAYERS TO SAMBO.

IT had been arranged that the negroes should come to the entertainments by relays, as the Barn could hold only three hundred and fifty. Mr. Haswell, who from the first had been consulted, announced the arrangements from his pulpit; and the evening, anticipated with many speculations, came at last—a never-to-be-forgotten Saturday! Punctually at eight the curtain was drawn by an invisible hand, revealing the interior of a palace, which elicited an exclamation of delight from one voice with several hundred throats. Then Leroy made a little speech.

"My colored friends, we have come to amuse and interest you. All of us have work enough to do, and it won't harm us to have a little play now and then. We all have troubles, and it will do us good to forget them. We haven't asked white folks because we wanted all the room for you. Next time we shall have the younger colored people, and white folks must wait for the third table."

"Thanky, sir," said a voice.

"Hold your tongue!" cried other voices, to the last.

"No," said Leroy, "you needn't hold your tongues. When any song or recitation is going on it is better to wait till it is through before saying what you think or feel; but don't feel tongue-tied here, nor afraid of anybody. My daughters will now sing "Home, Sweet Home."

When Fanny and Bertha appeared in their simple white dresses there were lively exclamations—"Ain't dey pooty!" "Dey's angels, dey is!" They sang tenderly, and now and then a plaintive note from some listener mingled with the refrain. Sumter did famously, eliciting cries of "Ain't he smart!" "Dat chile'll be a preacher, sartin!"

Bertha's shamrock spells, preceded by Leroy's explanation of the Irish superstition, were sweetly woven, and her applause was "Bless her heart!" "She'd make every body happy if she could!" The music was indeed all successful, and the interval that followed was filled with a general buzz of delight more musical to some ears present than the concert. There was deep stillness when the lights were put out. All the performers except Wentworth and his assistants—Stringfield and Robert—slipped out among the spectators, oblivious of caste in their eagerness to see the magic pictures. When a great circle of light on the sheet revealed them standing along the wall the negroes sprang up to offer them seats.

"Sit still!" cried Leroy; "we are the servants now, and wish to stand."

"That ain't proper, marsa."

"Yes, it is, Ben. If you wish to please us keep your seats and watch the pictures of the Prodigal Son which our friend and yours, Mr. Wentworth, has taken much pains to obtain for us."

The pictures were pretty and caused emotional

delight. Stringfield's melodious voice was heard from behind the scene reciting each part of the parable as it was illustrated, an occasional "Bless the Lord," or other word responding out of the darkness in front. The Prodigal was seen parting from his parents, feasting with luxurious and dissolute companions, ragged and haggard among the swine, journeying homeward,—the father falling on his son's neck, the Feast of the Fatted Calf. Then Stringfield's voice filled the room—"This my son was dead but is alive again; he was lost but is found."

"Glory to God!" cried a voice from the front.

"Glory! glory!" answered a hundred.

"Show us that agin, please marsa!"

Wentworth went over the series again, and then there was a scene of wild excitement, amid which an old negro cried, "Let us pray!" In a moment all kneeled, and out of the darkness came a prayer no longer to be contained—a prayer to Jesus who "came to seek and to save de loss," that he would "bless Marse Leroy and his family, and de gemman who has showed us pore cullud people dese picters—bless dat Marse Wentfur in 'tickler—and bless Miss Fanny and Berthy and Marse Saint and Sumter—and de Lord 'specially bless missis for teachin' her chillen to 'member de pore and needy—sweet Jesus don't forget 'em [Amen!]—no, Lord, 'member 'em when dou comest in dy kingdom [hallelujah, come Lord!]—put dy arms right roun' all dar necks an say, 'Well done good and faithful servants, ye was kind to dem pore niggers, and I'm agwine to be kind to you.'"

"Amen!" The last words of the prayer were lost

in the shout, and a female voice began singing, "Canaan, Sweet Canaan," the Barn being presently filled with a great surge of sound.

Mr. Stringfield now briefly told the story of Macbeth, which was the next thing in order. The costumes sent by Abrahams would hardly have satisfied an antiquarian, but fortunately no Dryasdust was present. Wentworth as Macbeth wore semi-military dress, and Lady Macbeth (Charlotte) was an imposing figure in her black robe, hoopless, long-trained, low at the neck, on her head a dazzling coronet. When the curtain rose she was seen in the gorgeous palace listening at the door while Macbeth was committing the murder within. When he rushed out exclaiming "I have done the deed," there was a visible sensation in the crowd; and, as the guilty pair were exchanging their horrors, little Lily began to cry, Fanny soothing her with assurance that they were "only making 'tence." Wentworth made an impression with the words—

> "Methought I heard a voice cry, 'Sleep no more!
> Macbeth does murder sleep,' the innocent sleep,
> Sleep that knits up the ravelled sleeve of care,
> The death of each day's life, slow labor's bath,
> Balm of hurt minds—"

"That's so!" cried a woman.

"B'lieve you, honey," said another.

When Lady Macbeth said—"'Tis the eye of childhood that fears a painted devil," a voice cried "You jes wait till he get hold of you!" Charlotte's red hands, after she had smeared the grooms, caused murmurs of horror, and the knocking at the door that followed thrilled the assembly into awe-struck silence. On this the curtain fell. When it rose, the doctor (Stringfield) and waiting gentlewoman (Mrs. Leroy) held their colloquy, and presently Lady Macbeth appeared in white gown, bearing a candle in her hand, her face whitened to ghastliness. The sharp crash of the fallen candlestick made all start : a weird half-light was left on the scene. There was a minute of awful silence ; then the hand was raised to the staring eyes, slowly lowered, rubbed with the other, the words hissing out—" Here's a spot ! " When the curdling cry came—" Out damned spot ! out I say ! " the horror became incontainable.

" It's blood on her hands ! "

" What, will these hands ne'er be clean ? " continued the actress.

" Cussin' won't clean 'em."

" She need de Jordan, she do."

" Pore creeter, an' in her nightgown too ! "

The doctor's final words " Good God forgive us all" elicited many " amens " ; and after the wailing female voices were heard without, and the queen's death was announced, an old man cried " Thar sin hath foun' 'em out ! "

The curtain fell, the entertainment was over, but the crowd seemed loth to go ; Leroy presently found that the " keening " of the women at the death of Lady Macbeth had shaken the nerves of some ; they " hoped they was all right back thar," but so anxiously that it was deemed prudent that the actors should show themselves, smiling, hand in hand. There was no applause—no negro among them had ever been to an entertainment before, or knew the custom of audiences—but as they filed out and passed to their cabins their voices could be heard in eager discussion of what they had seen.

This thrice-given entertainment was so successful that its promoters were much encouraged. The white audience was enthusiastic, and it was soon made known that several families included one or more individuals able to assist in future entertainments. Leroy Island burgeoned with unsuspected talent. On the second occasion Eleanor Ravenel sang "Lord Ullin's Daughter," Sumter recited "Hail, Holy Light" from Paradise Lost, the Leroy sisters sang the duet "I know a bank where the wild thyme blows," and there was a beautiful magic lantern series from "The Pilgrim's Progress." In the trial-scene from the "Merchant of Venice," Charlotte made a perfect Portia and Netty Ravenel a piquant Nerissa. Wentworth took the part of Shylock and Leroy that of Antonio. The negroes were so excited by the Jew's refusal of thrice his money in his eagerness for the pound of flesh that their protests became noisy, and the Venetian judge (Stringfield) found it necessary to promise that it would come right in the end.

"What we wants to know, sah, is what fur he do it. Whyn't he take de cash an' whut he want de man's meat fur?"

"Well, my friend," said Stringfield, "Shylock's been badly used for a long time, especially by this same man, who used to spit upon him till he wanted his money, and even then said he'd do it again. Shylock is also the chief man of the Jews, and all his tribe had been so despised and persecuted that he wants to avenge his race. Bad as his thirst for revenge is, there's some feeling of justice in it."

"Thanky, sah, an beg pardon for interferin', but it's hard to bar in mind dat it's all in fun."

Portia's plea for mercy moved all hearts, and Shylock's obduracy after it caused some hearer to murmur—"Dat Jew'd crucify de Lord." But when the tables were turned on Shylock, his property taken, his life threatened, and he moved to the door amid jeers, some sympathy gathered to his side.

"Pore ole man!"

"Dey's harder'n he was."

"But dey's gwine to baptize him, dat's somethin'."

From the day of the first success Stringfield had formed a scheme which would have been too daring in a more sophisticated neighborhood—nothing less than to usher in Christmas with tableaux of the Nativity. Wentworth was charmed with the clergyman's audacity. It was determined that this entertainment should begin on Christmas-eve with lantern-pictures, Wentworth having among his slides Abraham entertaining the Angels, Ruth and Boaz, the Queen of Sheba visiting Solomon, Job in his tribulation, Job in his triumph, and the Star of Bethlehem with Shepherds. All these were to be given in the above order, and the tableaux vivants follow so as to bring that of the Nativity at midnight.

Robert Ravenel never worked so hard in his life as on the scenery. St. George hunted for ten miles round for a donkey and at last brought back the picturesque little animal which, in that region, was a show in himself. Stringfield, an accomplished chorist himself, drilled a choir of boys and maidens to sing hymns appropriate to the tableaux. Much work was required, but enthusiasm and enterprise prevailed over all difficulties. The young people of the neighborhood never before saw so much of each other as during these preparations, and the Barn was associated forever with the merriest Christmas known in Leroy Island.

On the eventful evening the Barn was crowded to its utmost capacity. Stringfield's voice, now familiar to the audience, accompanied the lantern-pictures with descriptive words and texts. Then in front of the stage moved a chorus of twelve genii, Eleanor Ravenel leading the female, Stringfield the male choristers. They were dressed in different colors, but the robes of all reached to the feet from infant waists, and all had large sleeves which, when their arms were raised, bore a purposed resemblance to wings. Each head was bound with a golden fillet, the hair falling loose beneath it. It was like a rainbow become animate when they formed a curve before the curtain ; their voices rang out their rapture and their arms were waved with energy as they sang the glad tidings. While the lantern-picture of the Star and Shepherds was yet lingering in the vision of the spectators the genii sang " While shepherds watched their flocks by night ; " at its conclusion they parted to either side and the curtain rose on Mary kneeling before the Angel. Fanny had the Madonna face, and was lovely as, clothed in bridal white, she knelt beside a tall lily, her eyes down-dropt but shoulders erect, her hands crossed on her breast. A quaint and lyrical beauty, enhanced by floating light hair, made Netty Ravenel a picturesque angel; she bore in her hand a palm-leaf. A breathless stillness prevailed, as if each feared by any sound to startle away the vision. As it faded the genii sang, "Hark the glad sound! the Saviour comes." The second tableau (Salutation of Elizabeth) was preceded by the hymn—

> Love divine all love excelling,
> Joy of heaven to earth come down.

The embrace of Mary and Elizabeth (Mrs. Leroy and Fanny) could not be seen but as that of mother and daughter—through mist of tears. Leroy was Zecharias.

The hymn that preceded the tableau of the Nativity and Adoration was "Hark the herald angels sing!" This scene was a wonder. In the stable-interior the heads of oxen seen above their stall were painted, with straw and realistic rack. Joseph (Wentworth), his legs bare and bronzed, stood behind the ass, his look reverently bent on Mary; she (Fanny) was seated with the child,—a doll of Lily's, almost as large as herself, whose face was concealed. The curtain being lowered for a moment, the genii sang "O come all ye faithful," at the end of which the same tableau was shown with addition of the Three Kings. The great planter as Gaspar kneeling between two fine-looking negroes, one (Wesley) light, the other (Uncle Zeb) very black —Melchior and Balthazar—all in rich barbaric costumes, was a supernatural sight for the spectators. The choristers sang "Brightest and best of the sons of the morning," in which a duet by Masters Andy Scott and Charley Millward gained them fame and cemented their friendship. This tableau was called for again and again, poor Joseph not having time even to disturb a flea settled on his calf, "characteristically," as Stringfield said when he saw him rub the spot, "shedding his blood for the slave." The furzy donkey was effective in the tableau of the Flight. In the closing tableau (Jesus in the Temple) St. George was Simeon. Mary had provided herself with two white pigeons which she held fluttering about her with blue ribands, and the favorite hymn "Come Holy Spirit, heavenly dove," was sung.

The effect of these tableaux is indescribable, hardly imaginable. These negroes had never seen an artistic creation in their lives; their untrained sense was as little able to see the beauty in nature as their mind to read geologic records in the alluvium they dug. The Biblical poetry had been vulgarized to them. The sun had sent new rays since the Barn was opened. The Ixion-wheel of toil stood still for one evening in the seven, and its victims were compensated with glimpses of a transfigured world.

Leroy gave his Christmas bounties from the stage, each dollar being multiplied miraculously by the circumstances. They received it from Gaspar—he had not laid aside his costume—who had knelt beside black Melchior and Balthazar before their common Lord. After this these joyful people, for whom the Star had now for the first time risen and the angels sung of good-will to men, formed a procession; headed by Uncle Zeb, with his crown on, they marched away singing—

"I'm a pilgrim, and I'm a stranger,
I can tarry, I can tarry but a night!"

Wentworth, Stringfield, and Leroy, last to leave the darkened Barn, stood to listen as the chant became fainter; after it was lost an occasional " glory " or " hallelujah " was wafted back through the mild air.

" In all the theaters of the world," said Wentworth, " no company has witnessed scenes so beautiful and elevating as those which these humble people have seen this night."

" There are splendors which can be revealed only to babes," said Stringfield, pausing to listen again— the procession having taken some turn from which the refrain was faintly heard once more—" I can tarry, I can tarry but a night."

" But a night," said Stringfield, turning toward the east where the morning-star stood above the horizon; " but it will never be a starless night in Leroyland, my miraculous Yankee ! "

## CHAPTER XIX.

#### SHADOWS BENEATH THE DAWN.

WHEN Laurens Leroy descended from his room on Christmas morning he found Jacob Corbin, overseer, waiting for him, with an ugly look on his face.

"I have nine niggers set down for Christmas work," said Corbin, "five of them for nightwork: stealing, drunkenness, insolence. Butler brought me your order that every nigger at my place must be at Selwood Barn to-night."

"Well, Corbin, this is the day of peace and good will you know; and we have something at the Barn which I believe will improve them; so I'll be glad if you'll overlook their offenses this time."

"Mr. Leroy, it will never do. I warned them all two weeks ago what they would get Christmas if they didn't behave; yesterday I picked out these nine. I can't shilly-shally with niggers—you see for yourself, sir."

"Don't get warm, Corbin. Under ordinary circumstances I shouldn't interfere, for very likely they'd all get drunk to-night. But just now we have a gentleman here who has taken a deal of trouble and expense to get up some elevating exhibitions for the negroes;

to-night we will repeat one of peculiar and religious importance, and I should be sorry to have any one miss it."

" I haven't been to the shows myself, sir, and it's not for me to say any thing against them, though I can't say the effect on the niggers seems to me good. But that's none of my business. My business is to keep the hands at my place in order, and make them do their duty to you; and I can't do that if my word isn't stood to."

" But my word also has been given, and I must stand by it; so pray tell them you'll forgive them this time, and bid them come with the others to the Barn."

The overseer disappeared, and the Leroys hurried off to Wharton Church. There Mr. Stringfield was surprised by a marvelous Christmas-gift—a crowded negro-gallery!

Some little time after his interview with Corbin, Leroy found that though the offending negroes had been permitted to go to the Barn, they had been subsequently flogged. In reply to his inquiry the overseer explained that since his awards had been overruled the negroes generally had been insolent, and it had been necessary to re-establish his authority by showing that though the sentenced negroes had been required on Christmas-night by their owner, for their moral improvement, it was not meant that they should escape punishment altogether."

" But I did request that they should be forgiven."

" Niggers can't be forgiven on a plantation, Mr. Leroy—not without overthrowing authority. The impudent rascals have been laughing at me ever since that day. I can't stand it, and it's not for your interest I should."

" Well, Corbin, I shall take no further notice of this particular case, though I don't like it. We've been going on a certain system for a long time, but I'm not sure it's the best. Since Mr. Wentworth has been here and we've been giving the hands a little entertainment, there have been numerous expressions of their kind feeling for me and my family. If you would take some interest in these things perhaps you might find a better spirit prevailing toward yourself. At any rate let there be no further floggings without extreme necessity. You must be prepared to find me more careful in such matters; I've got some new notions."

"I hope they are good ones, sir," said Corbin with effort at a smile, which turned out sardonic.

" I hope so," said Leroy pleasantly, as he mounted and rode off.

" That gentleman!" muttered Corbin, "always 'that gentleman.'"

At this interview there had been a third party invisibly present—the slave. The negroes did not like Corbin; they knew there had been an issue joined between him and *his* master in which he had been given a taste of the cup he made bitter for them. They assumed that Corbin was in disgrace and treated him with a contempt which he could only meet with the lash. Demoralization prevailed in his domain; the number sent to the whipping-post was so large that the other overseers reported to Leroy that a reign of terror was imminent. Corbin's authority could now be recovered only by a large measure of severity from Leroy himself; for this the planter was in no mood, and the discharge of Corbin became a necessity.

The humiliation of the retributive overseer was regarded by the negroes not merely as their victory but as a token of their owner's good-will. Indeed the other overseers impressed that view, and asked the negroes, when inclined to be lazy, whether they felt no gratitude to such a master. The effect was so great that "Corbin's Tract" ceased to be regarded as a purgatorial place, Leroy having declared that in future hands drafted for disagreeable service should be rewarded by some extra allowance of food or time for rest. There was no urgency about appointing a new overseer. Uncle Zeb,—or Balthazar as he was beginning to be called,—superintended work there, and no deficiency was threatened in the supplies from that part of the estate.

On the other hand the *morale* of the discharged overseer did not improve, but the reverse; he became sullen and bitter, nor could he be appeased by the pension allowed him until he could find another place. In Wentworth he saw the cause of his troubles. Until "that gentleman" (that Yankee, interpolated Corbin), came, all had gone on well. What was he poking his nose about here for, any way? Corbin had been shocked by the rumors about the Barn, especially that the planter had appeared kneeling between two negroes. He was convinced that this Yankee had gained a dangerous influence over Leroy. And now, in his enforced idleness, Corbin became the prey of that special satan that finds mischief for active minds with unoccupied hours.

Every thing conveyed from the Landing had to pass under Corbin's notice, while he was overseer, and in this way he had observed, and copied in his note-book, names on two boxes addressed to W. Wentworth. He now referred to these names—" Dolland, Scientific Instruments, Winter Street, Boston;" "Abrahams, Costumier, Cornhill, Boston." The only other name he knew in Boston was that of a certain cotton broker, and gradually the purpose grew in him to write to this man. He stated that an individual from the North had come to their plantation under suspicious circumstances, gave all the names in his possession, and begged that secrecy might be observed in making inquiries.

There was another personage on Leroy Island who was dissatisfied with proceedings at the Barn,—namely, the Rev. Ezra Harding. He was a preacher difficult of classification. The great comet of 1843 came so near the earth that its tail turned the heads of some pious people, and struck many of the impious with terror; this being especially the case among southern negroes, who passed much of that time in prayer-meetings. While the panic was at its height on Leroy Island, this preacher Harding, generally described as a " Millerite," passed through the Sea Islands prophesying the immediate end of the world—which the famous William Miller had fixed for that same year. Harding had an immense following of negroes, and, when the comet and the year had passed without catastrophe, enough of his adherents still stuck to him to form a considerable congregation. Leroy had given them the use of a deserted meeting-house called Ebenezer, originally built for the Methodists, not far from Wharton Church. He was a fiery but not unattractive preacher, yet was steadily distanced by Mr. Haswell, the negroes having a pronounced preference for immersion, which Harding denounced. Ebenezer however was far away from Bethel, and was without rivalry from Wharton Church, which had never been attended by negroes.

But suddenly there was a change. The performances at the Barn had made Mr. Stringfield favorably known among the negroes, and when they had filled his hitherto empty gallery on Christmas he spoke to their condition so pertinently and with such passionate eloquence that the accession was maintained. Sunday after Sunday when he came the gallery was crowded. But the fly that got out of Mr. Stringfield's ointment got into that of Mr. Harding. The crowded gallery at Wharton Church meant thin benches at Ebenezer. The chief white patron and nearest neighbor of Harding was Corbin, who now had ample time to discuss with him affairs at the Barn. The preacher's soul was filled with pious horrors intensified by vacancies in his chapel. He had read or heard that the theater was main door to the Pit, and it broke on his mind like another comet that such a door had been opened on Leroy Island. Against this device of Belial he began to rage in his pulpit, denouncing a certain " pretended preacher of the Gospel " as a wolf in sheep's clothing devouring the lambs. The zealous man learned from Corbin that a Yankee " living on the Leroys " was at the bottom of these frightful immoralities, and he resolved to seek out that blind guide and rebuke him to his face.

The weekly entertainments at the Barn had not interfered with Wentworth's services to the school. Since Stringfield had settled at Selwood it had become the custom of the two scholars to accompany the children, and such of the young people in the neigborhood as could go with them, on long walks, during which they sometimes paused for conversation or instruction. One Saturday the talk fell on popular superstitions. A lad mentioned that "Old Joe" was said to have been seen near the Barn. Leroy explained that "Old Joe" was a phantom surviving from a negro of that name who lived in the island sixty years before. He was a negro of extraordinary intelligence, and occult powers were ascribed to him by colored people. He had disappeared—probably escaped to another country—but the negroes believed he had learned how to make himself invisible, and was lurking in the neighborhood. He had been a sort of preacher, and famous for speaking at funerals, so he was now supposed to appear when a death was near. If living, Old Joe would be a hundred and thirty years old. The company talked of the banshee and the baying dog, monitors of death descended from Cerberus at the gate of Hades; of the correspondence of "Old Joe" with undying Barbarossa and the Wandering Jew; and between Wentworth and Stringfield many a fallacy was buried that day in the grave of its explanation.

This discussion of superstition and fanaticism was

ended by a salient example. Out of the wood rushed the Rev. Ezra Harding red with wrath. He first confronted Wentworth, charging him with leading people to "damnation," and, when Leroy interposed, turned his vials on the planter. The worst of these, however, was reserved for Stringfield. Leroy tried to calm the man, but his oil was fuel to the flame. The preacher's language became so outrageous that, for the sake of the frightened children, Leroy brought it to a full stop.

"Mr. Harding, stop just here! Say another word and you never preach another sermon on my plantation!"

The fanatic turned instantly from red to white, and was as if struck dumb.

"Your mind," said Leroy, "has been filled by somebody with lies and nonsense. The best way to get rid of your delusion is to come to the Barn and see what you are ignorantly denouncing."

"God forbid!"

"Otherwise you may be led to say from your pulpit to my servants what you have said here. But understand clearly that, while you are free to preach your doctrines there, Ebenezer chapel belongs to me, and if you say a word there against any one now before you it will be in your last sermon."

Harding trembled but answered not a word; presently he hurried off into the woods again, where he had left his horse. He rode swiftly to the house of Corbin, whom he found reading a note just received from J. Summerberry, the Boston cotton-broker to whom he had written. "I have instituted inquiries," wrote the broker, "concerning the man Wentworth, to whom Abrahams sent goods (supposed to be disguises), and find he is a dangerous abolitionist. He once tried to kill a Virginia gentleman named Sturline, and no doubt is up to mischief on your plantation. Confidential."

The preacher was for carrying this document at once to Leroy, but Corbin would not consent. "They are all so possessed with the scoundrel, they wouldn't believe a word against him. It would only bring us into more trouble. We must wait for our opportunity. You'd better be cautious about your preaching too ; the niggers will repeat what you say and Leroy will always do what he says." Corbin then informed Harding that he had obtained a position on a rice plantation near Savannah, and must carry a certificate of honesty and competency from his previous employer ; this was another reason for his not wishing a row just then. But he desired the preacher to keep his eyes and ears open and let him know every thing that should happen. He hinted that it might be better if he would accept Leroy's proposal and go to the Barn, and " act friendly ; " but Harding was too irreconcilable for that. Besides, Baptist Haswell had countenanced the affair—a plain proof of its wickedness. He consented, however, to express to Leroy some apology for his vehemence in the woods, and even to Wentworth, on Corbin's suggestion that he might "learn something" in such interviews, and render more secure his tenure at Ebenezer.

## CHAPTER XX.

### GOING FARTHER AND FARING WORSE.

AT length a real shadow fell on Leroy Island: Wentworth announced that he must go. This time, instead of pleadings and manœuvres, silent sorrow met his announcement; for all felt that the end had inevitably come. He had remained till the first breath of summer surprised him; he knew that the time was at hand when planters must take their families to the seaside. The Leroys would have had him go with them, stay with them always; he knew that as well as the mournful company he was about to leave. It could not be: he had his life to live, and it could not be on that island.

When the time of departure came Wentworth distributed among these loved friends all he had brought, —his lantern to Robert Ravenel, and to St. Jean the Hollis Memoirs lent him; to St. George and his elder sisters the costumes; to the children books ordered from Boston for the purpose; and suitable souvenirs for Mr. and Mrs. Leroy. It seemed to them all like bequests made before death. He in turn was loaded with presents. On the occasion of his last appearance in a performance at the Barn he was surprised by a present from the negroes, who had put together their cents and got Leroy to obtain from Charleston a finely-bound Family Bible. On it was printed: "Walter Wentworth, from the servants on Leroy Island, in remembrance of what he has done for them." The venerable Balthazar, who presented this, broke down with emotion; and Wentworth could only falter out his reply, at last clasping the volume, kissing it, and shedding tears with those around him. One morning Wentworth did not appear: a brief and touching note was found in his room, promising that he would return some day.

"That is the way such invisible figures as 'Old Joe' are formed," said Stringfield, when the school-walk next occurred. "Those that love and follow them, and they themselves, can not endure a parting; they disappear, leaving the soothing promise of return, though they never return. Some will think they see the dear face again hovering near in twilight or moonlight, especially in time of trouble, when they long for him. Our beloved Wentworth has gone. He will do his duty in the great world, and make it better, as he has made us and our island better. Let him linger among us, not as a phantom but a reality—in our hearts, leading us to imitate his strangely beautiful life, and to continue the pathetically noble work he has begun among us."

Wentworth and his man Wesley had driven away with the horse and buggy which brought them. In the note found in his room he said these would be left at the Landing, as he wished to present them to Stringfield and his sister. On the road he was met by the Rev. Ezra Harding. The preacher had apologized to Leroy, and two days before had learned from him that it was probable Wentworth would leave by the next boat. Wentworth, unconscious that he was waylaid, felt touched by the kindliness now manifested by his gainsayer, and freely told him where he was going. The preacher had been reduced by Corbin to the level of a spy: he expressed apologies to Wentworth for what he had said against him; but took care to meet the letter-carrier following, and send on the same boat with Wentworth a letter, with penciled postscript, to Jacob Corbin, Hayne's Mills, near Savannah.

Although Corbin's place on Leroy Island had been a purgatory for negroes, for himself it was a paradise compared with Hayne's rice swamp. In the Yankee's absence his sins were visited on the negroes, but Corbin did not forget Wentworth. He had not long to wait for his revenge. Soon after his arrival at Savannah our Bostonian got into serious trouble, to which Corbin was able to add a contribution. A Savannah paper brought to Hayne's Mills this startling paragraph:—" Abolitionists at work in Georgia.—An individual, ascertained to be a Boston lawyer named Wentworth, was yesterday charged before Justice Shelton with complicity in abducting or stealing a negro woman belonging to John Braxton, Esq., of Thorpe Hill. The case was adjourned for inquiries and will be heard on Thursday. The magistrate expressed regret that a person of gentlemanly appearance should be brought before him on such a charge."

Corbin easily obtained leave of absence and hastened to Savannah, where he placed his letter from the Boston cotton-broker at the disposal of the prosecution.

Soon afterwards he had the pleasure of seeing Wentworth brought to the court-house through a mob clamoring for the privilege of tarring and feathering "the damned Yankee." Corbin's pent wrath broke loose.

"I know all about that man," he shouted; "he's been at his work among the niggers in Carolina."

At these words the mob gave a yell and a dash, dragging Wentworth from the hands of the two frightened constables as they were ascending the court-house steps. When Corbin saw his victim in the grasp of half-a-dozen powerful hands the blood flew to his head; he aimed a vicious blow at the Yankee's face, on his own private account. The blow left its mark, however, on the cheek-bone of the judge, who at that moment leaped from the door and stood in front of the prisoner.

"Cowards!" cried the judge. "Mighty brave southerners you are, a hundred men to one! Officers, conduct that man into the court-house, and if any one of these rowdies interferes, shoot him."

"Judge Lynch," like the cur that he is, recoiled before the eyes of Judge Shelton, and Corbin was the said cur's tail, for his fist had left on the judge's face an ugly bruise. But no sooner had the officers entered, and the court-house filled to its utmost capacity, than another mob came storming along the streets, and an angry clamor surrounded the building while the trial was going on. Corbin, uneasy about the judge—who, however, had apparently not noticed him—was going off; but the commonwealth's attorney met him, and insisted on his return to support the information he had previously given. This popular attorney, unaware of the preceding scene, bowed politely to the mob who cheered him as he passed into the court-house.

The attorney stated to the court that the prisoner had stopped at a tavern called "Price's" on the big road near Thorpe Hill, the previous Friday; he brought with him a young negro man, who left Price's the same evening and did not return till next morning; when the two went off together. It would be proved that they were seen that Saturday morning talking in the field with the woman in question. The same evening the prisoner visited Mr. Braxton and offered to purchase the woman, but was told she was not for sale. On Sunday, prisoner attended the negro meeting—a significant fact. That night the negro man left Price's and can not be found. The woman also disappeared that night and can not be found. Diligent search has been made, but no trace of either discovered. When the prisoner was arrested fifty-nine dollars were found on him, and cards showing him to be one Walter Wentworth, counselor at Boston. Whatever doubt might have been felt about the case had been largely cleared away by evidence proving that the prisoner is well known in the North as a dangerous abolitionist who once made an attempt on a southern gentleman's life.

While Mr. Braxton was giving his evidence a messenger came from Oglethorpe Hotel to say that a man named Wentworth had stopped there a single day of the previous week, and had left his trunk, also a package containing documents and money, sealed and deposited in the hotel safe. An officer was at once sent, with keys found on the prisoner, to search the trunk and bring the sealed package into court.

Wentworth conducted his own case, and asked Mr. Braxton if he had explained why he wished to buy the woman.

"You said she had been the wife of your servant."

"What was your reply."

"That I knew nothing of that, and believed she was now in the family way."

Corbin having given venomous evidence, Wentworth told his plain story. "The Summerberry letter can only refer to a ridiculous 'affair of honor,' a miserable misunderstanding that brought me, while at college, a challenge from a class-mate; a meeting never occurred, and that Virginian, spelled "Sturline" by Mr. Summerberry, is the best friend I have in the world—namely Randolph Stirling."

"Son of Judge Stirling of Virginia?" asked the justice.

"The same. It is through that friend, whose life I am said to have attempted, that I am in the South now. After a winter in South Carolina, I came to visit Savannah, in pursuance of my wish to know more about the South. I went to Thorpe Hill because my man wished to see his wife, from whom he was separated by her sale in Virginia some years ago. The man reported to me a painful story about his wife, into the details of which I will not go unless required, and from sympathy with his distress I tried to purchase the woman. I suppose it was in despair, after my failure, that the man ran off with his wife. By that Mr. Braxton and I have lost our servants. I do not see why I may not as plausibly accuse him of abducting my man as he accuse me of abducting his woman. If your Honor finds it necessary to commit me on account of the Summerberry letter, I can only regret that the credit of the court and of myself should suffer by an imposition—which, however, can easily be exposed. Otherwise, and assuming that it is no crime for a Bostonian to visit Savannah, I submit to your Honor that there is no case for committal."

"And I submit, your Honor," cried the prosecuting attorney, leaping to his feet, "that this information from Boston, not written to bear on this case but providentially fallen into our hands, reveals the remarkable coincidence that simultaneously with the appearance among us of a 'dangerous abolitionist' is the disappearance of a valuable slave. I observe that the prisoner has not ventured to repudiate his abolitionism. For the rest his ingenuity does credit to the Boston bar, but it doesn't explain the facts. Could these two negroes have vanished so swiftly and completely had there been no prearrangement? Who supplied the money? How could plans be laid in a country neighborhood without connivance of this very peculiar slaveholding abolitionist? I submit, sir, that the *prima facie* appearances require committal for trial—when we may know something more about this man."

"I confess," said the magistrate, "that it appears to me important to await the package from the hotel. Meantime, Mr. Macnulty, if you have more to say on the facts before us you can go on."

The opportunity for a stump speech was tempting. Macnulty was just describing the subtle serpent of abolitionism stealing into the southern paradise, when the officer from the hotel entered. He reported that nothing of public interest was found in the prisoner's trunk. The sealed package was handed to Justice Shelton, and a letter for the prisoner which had just arrived. The magistrate examined the contents of the package carefully.

"God bless me," he presently exclaimed, "here's a letter to me!" The crowded court-room grew still while the justice silently read this letter,—pausing now and then at some yell from the increasing mob outside. At length he spoke, with some agitation.

"This package contains letters of introduction to eminent southern gentlemen, and one to myself from one of the first planters in South Carolina—which I read aloud. 'Dear Shelton,—The gentleman this introduces, Mr. Walter Wentworth, is a friend unspeakably dear to us all. He has passed some months with us by sheer compulsion; we would not let him go, and submit at last only on promise of his return. It would require a volume to tell you all he has done for us on this estate,—for our school, our negroes, our households. He goes for a few days to Savannah, which never had a more cultured and worthy visitor, as you will certainly realize when you know him.' A few words follow on matters not relating to the prisoner. There is another letter here to a gentleman in Savannah. Mr. Wentworth, will you inform me why you did not deliver these letters, or refer to them when first arraigned before me?"

"I meant to deliver them on my return from Thorpe Hill. I did not mention them when arrested because

I could not run the risk of involving the name of any citizen with my own while under a charge likely to excite the community."

"The prisoner is at liberty to open the newly-arrived letter himself," said the justice.

"This also," said Wentworth, after a glance, "is from Leroy, who gave me the letter to your Honor. I prefer you should open and read it."

It was a cordial letter, and one passage caused a sensation in the court-room. "I hear," wrote Leroy, "that my late intractable overseer, Jacob Corbin, has preceded you to Savannah, having found employment in that neighborhood. I hope you will not fall in his way, for, from what I hear, I suspect he bears you a grudge, and would not be sorry to do you a mischief. I have not put any body in his place, and indeed doubt I shall need any overseer at Corbin's Tract except foreman Balthazar—you remember Uncle Zeb, —for my hands there never worked so well. This I owe to your sojourn with us. Come back, dear friend —come back!"

"After this evidence of character, and of *animus* on the part of the witness Corbin," said the attorney, "the case against the pris—against Mr. Wentworth— breaks down. I withdraw from it, with your Honor's permission."

"There is an inclosed letter," said the justice.

"Pray open and read that also," said Wentworth.

"It is signed Richard Stirling——"

"Father of the southerner whose life I am said to have attempted."

"My dear sir," the letter began, "I have learned

your address in South Carolina, after some difficulty, and write to entreat that you will visit us as soon as possible——"

"Enough," said the justice; "there is no need, Mr. Wentworth, to read more of your correspondence. This charge is dismissed. Stop, Mr. Corbin, you have made an impression on me, outside this court and in it. Sheriff, bring that witness before me to-morrow. I am glad you have withdrawn, Mr. Macnulty, but I can not think it would be even-handed justice merely to discharge this gentleman, and turn him over to the perils of popular excitement. It can not be too widely known that a man has a right to his principles about slavery, or any thing else, if he does not injure others or break the law. If this gentleman holds anti-slavery views, it is the more to his credit that he has passed months on a plantation and left it followed by the friendship of the planter. That is just the northern man whom the South should honor, and I deeply regret that Mr. Wentworth should not have presented these letters last week; while honoring a man who preferred going to gaol rather than risk placing others in an unpopular position. Such magnanimity is not so common as to pass without my gratitude, at least. I will thank you, Mr. Macnulty, to announce to the crowd outside that the accused gentleman is proved entirely innocent. And I will be glad, Mr. Wentworth, if you will presently enter my carriage and drive with me home, and remain my guest during your stay in Savannah. The court is adjourned."

The mob, enlightened by Macnulty, cheered the magistrate and his guest when they appeared. Before they drove off Mr. Braxton came up and expressed his regret at the mistake, and said that if Wentworth would visit Thorpe Hill he should be welcomed as a guest. The apology was politely accepted, and they drove on.

"I dare not thank the judge," said Wentworth, "but may say that you were mistaken in no particular. The negro man had received from me a hundred dollars which I thought he might want for his wife. She had been compelled by an overseer to yield to his lust. My man prudently concealed from me his plans. I remember now that he got from me the address of a lawyer in Washington with whom I had left a provision for his freedom."

"It is wonderful what coincidences meet us in this world," said Mr. Shelton. "Those Stirlings are not unknown to me. A dissipated brother of mine, now dead, married a beautiful lady, also a Shelton, who had to separate from him. They were then living on a property of hers in northern Virginia. The decree of divorce was pronounced by Judge Stirling. My sister-in-law's troubles brought on illness, during which the Stirlings kept her in their house. By their aid her property was satisfactorily sold. She was a fine artist and traveled abroad. Then she settled somewhere in New York with some community in which she is now a kind of queen. Young Randolph Stirling once visited her there, and reported that she was happy, but had strange enthusiasms. Among other things she wants to abolish marriage. Poor Maria, I don't wonder!"

The carriage presently stopped at an old-fashioned

mansion, where Wentworth was kindly received by a refined family. But dark care had begun to follow him. In the solitude of his room he read Judge Stirling's letter.

"My dear Sir,—I have learned your address in South Carolina with some difficulty, and write to entreat that you will visit us as soon as possible, as we are in sore trouble about our dear Randolph. I know of no one so likely to be in his confidence as yourself, and trust you will help us to discover what has befallen him. Some time since one James Bounce, resident in Maryland, inclosed to a magistrate of our neighboring town, Warrenton, my son's card, bearing this address, saying he had it from the police of Peacefield, Mass., while there to recover his fugitive slave. Bounce asserts that it was subsequently ascertained that the negro was assisted in his escape from Peacefield by the owner of this card. The Warrenton magistrate is not friendly to us, and the information appeared in the local paper, the names suppressed but hinted. There being some excitement in the community, I wrote to Randolph for an explanation, but grieve to say that his reply—delayed for several weeks —was not satisfactory. I have no doubt that Randolph did only what he thought honorable, but he had evidently been mixed up in the affair in a way that would not be tolerated here. He said that under the circumstances he would not return to us at present. Heavy as were the tidings, we felt that this course was necessary. I sent him money, and asked him to meet me in Washington. A mysterious letter came from a Mr. Derby Leigh, of Peacefield, saying that my son had been ill in his house, but had left, and he would forward the letter when his address was discovered. I did not again hear from Randolph till recently. A letter came from Iowa acknowledging receipt of the money, and containing the astounding announcement of his marriage! His wife, he stated, is the daughter of a hotel-keeper, and he would have married her in any case—false gossip having connected her injuriously with himself because of a service she had rendered him—but he had found her lovely and lovable in herself, and was happy. This is appalling to us. We can not help fearing ruin of the hopes built on our dear Randolph. We know not what to do. We know not where he is. We crave your counsel under these painful circumstances.—I am, dear Sir, your obedient servant, RICHARD STIRLING."

It was to be a long time before Wentworth could learn what had really happened to his friend. He could not even imagine the name of the woman he had married. He could only hasten to Virginia and to The Palms.

## CHAPTER XXI.

### "TO THE RESCUE OF HER HONOR, MY HEART!"

STIRLING, whom we left fallen, but in pleasantest Peacefield places, speedily recovered, and thereafter enjoyed a visit at the home of the Leighs. He was happy to find the Fraülein well established there. Hilda declared she would never part with her Mathilde unless to the romantic Franz, and was never weary of listening to the Fraülein's folk-song and folk-lore. To hear her tale of the Pied Piper was better than to read it in Browning. Mr. Leigh was able to add to the southerner's knowledge of northern institutions and ideas, and being a large employer of labor, introduced him to the actual conditions of free industry. Randolph and Hilda formed their friendship rather on the brother-and-sisterly lines, but there is no saying what it might have developed into had the youth's visit been prolonged. In such favorable propinquity unsuspected spells are woven between natures too like for sudden love affairs, as were those of Hilda and Stirling, but fate easily breaks them unless they have a longer time to mature than Atropos permitted here. When Stirling received the distressing letter from his father, telling him that his connection with the Peacefield fugitive slave had been divulged at home, he easily made Hilda his confidante and was comforted by her sympathy. But when a more real calamity came upon him he felt that he must face it alone.

He was preparing to leave Peacefield for Cambridge, when the said fate spun across his path one of her small threads that turn to chains and can not be broken. Among letters forwarded to him from Cambridge was a dirty one from White River Junction in which terrible words were scrawled:

"Mr. Sturling, Colleg, Cambridg.

"Sir, It aint right for citty an colleg gentles to com in places an ruin poor girls as hav no mothers Nuela Rhodes is gon bad an ran way sence you ruined her repetation an her old father in misry an you enjoyn yorself Its mighty mean I think."

Stirling tried hard to regard this anonymous note as a hoax, but the bit of blotted foolscap had a fatal look of its own: after a sleepless night he made what excuses he could, answered the Leighs' cordial invitation with a promise to return some day, and was soon speeding along a road already haunted with tragical memories.

The proprietor of the Green Mountain House, White River Junction, was surprised and delighted at seeing a gentleman entering his door. His hotel had a sublime name, but sank under the weight of it when actually entered. Stirling registered his name with lawyer-like illegibility, entered the bar-room, called for beer, and began casual talk with the barkeeper. He inquired about hotels in the neighborhood, and gradually drew the conversation around to the people at the "Junction House." Alas, there could be no doubt about it : Nuella had disappeared. It was believed by some, doubted or denied by a few, that her flight was necessary to conceal the probable result of an intrigue with some student who had been "took sick at the hotel and staid some time."

Late at night Stirling walked through a chilling rain to the restaurant at the depot : the last day-train had passed, the porters were getting what sleep they could before the night-express required them ; only a red danger-signal cast light upon the railway track on which, full of dread, he passed to a further point, to see if there was any light in the private parlor of the darkened Junction House. There was a light; approaching closer he could just see Manuel's head, still as if carved, with the glow of firelight on his down-bent face. He entered a back door, which was not locked, moved through the corridor he knew so well, and knocked at the little room. Manuel opened the door wide that light might fall on the form before him ; he was bewildered for a few moments, but at last held out his hand and burst into tears. For an instant there came before Stirling the vision of a daughter's face beside the gray head, but that face swiftly grew corpse-like and vanished.

"My dear old friend," said Stirling, "I have come to see you ; if possible to comfort you. Tell me all !"

"She has gone," cried Manuel piteously, "my dear child has gone, I do not know where."

"Your sorrow is mine. Do try and tell me something about it ! Why has she gone ? You and Nuella once did me a great service. I am here to learn if there is any thing I can do for you. Trust me !"

"You were always thankful and kind, Mr. Stirling, and we never thought of you but as a true and upright gentleman. I will tell you all I can,—but much of it is my fears and suspicions, and mayn't be true. Before you ever came here there was a man named John Layman who had been courting her. She didn't like him much,—for one thing, he is ignorant, and Nuella is educated; but he's a well-to-do farmer and most people thought it would be a good match. I had my suspicions that his eye was on a house and farm settled on Nuella by her uncle that's dead. But I would never interfere with a girl in such things, unless she asked me. Nuella didn't seem quite decided until—"

"Until?"

"Well, you want the truth, sir. After you staid here Nuella couldn't endure Layman, and when he came to the point told him she could never be his wife. That made him very mad, as she told me. Nuella began to mope, and one day, when I found her crying, says I: 'Child, you have no mother, your brother is far away, Ruth is young, why not trust your old father?' The girl put her arms around my neck, and at last says: 'Father, I feel as if I longed for somebody who can never come, and I sometimes wish for one of those convents, only without the priests and errors where I could bury myself for awhile, doing some kind of work, and never seeing any body but you and Ruth, or people needing help.' From that time I devoted myself to the girl, and gradually she got more cheerful, till one day a terrible thing happened. Nuella had a class in the Sunday-school at West Lebanon, some of the nicest children 'round here. One day she got a note from the superintendent, saying she wasn't wanted there any more. It was awful. When I went to ask about it the superintendent sent me to the minister, Mr. Grace, and little by little I drew it out of him, for he hated to tell me, that there were evil reports about Nuella—Oh, think of it, my sweet Nuella, pure like the driven snow!"

"Horrible!"

"Several families had said their children shouldn't go to the Sunday-school while she was there. Well I tried to keep back the facts from Nuella, but somehow she found out there were stories about her. Oh, sir, she couldn't eat or sleep, Ruth was nearly as bad, and I was miserable as could be. I went to minister Grace again, and after a good deal of talk he showed me a letter, without any signature, saying he had kept it back to save my feelings, and would have despised it if there had not been reports. Here's the letter; I've kept it in my pocket-book. I never showed it to her."

Stirling at once recognized the handwriting as that of the anonymous note to himself.

"Rev'd Mr. Grace, Dr. sir, Nuella Rhodes ain't proper person to mix with respectble girls and teach sunday-school every body knows as she maks too free with gentles at junctn. House!"

"Do you know who wrote this?" asked Stirling.

"No, but have my suspicions that it was the keeper of a small hotel here, Tom Benton, who has a grudge because we get the most custom. His is the Green Mountain House. I got two or three notes from him before he came here; I can't find them, but somehow when I saw this letter, that man's face rose before me."

"Let me keep this note to-night. And now tell me about her going away."

"Well, things went worse. Nobody spoke to the girl at church, and same in the street; she took on so, I thought I'd leave the town, though the business is good. One day she asked me to let her go up to Boston to see her aunt Rhodes, widow of my brother, and her cousins. They'd always wanted her, but I didn't encourage it, because they are full of spirit-rapping and such notions. But I thought a change would be good. After she had been there some days she wrote me a letter—it's in the drawer here."

The letter was full of affection; it gave some humorous account of spiritualistic séances in her aunt's house; and then followed a passage of startling significance to Stirling, who read it silently:—" On Sunday evening we all went to a little hall to hear a lecture by a lady from New York, whose name is Maria Shelton. I didn't care much about going, but when that woman appeared it was like a star shining out. Such a voice! such deep eyes! she was like Tennyson's Princess. I was spellbound. No speaker ever reached my soul before. I found out where she was staying and went to see her alone. It has made me feel happier than I have been for a long time. I meant to come home Saturday, but shall stay over Sunday to hear her again. And now, dear father, I have a favor to ask. I want a large sum of money—

a thousand dollars—raised on the estate uncle left me, and sent to me here at once. You know I am careful about money and do not spend it except for something important. You will trust me, father, whoever does not. Trust me to the end!"

"I never saw my poor child again—Oh, my God!"

Stirling took the old man's hand, and waited in silence till he was able to resume his narrative.

"On the Monday when we expected her back this letter came—you may read it."

"BELOVED FATHER:—The money came safe. When I last wrote I meant to return and see you and Ruth once more before taking the step on which I have resolved. But I can not bear parting, and I have resolved to live no longer at White River Junction. For the present I must remain entirely apart. My aunt and cousins think I have returned home. I have made my arrangements so that it will be impossible to trace me, and I entreat you not to try. Do not advertise, if you love me, and do not feel alarmed. I shall not harm myself nor ever do any thing to cause you shame for me. I shall be where kindness will surround me. You know I speak truth. Now and then I will write. Farewell. Your loving NUELLA."

"Have you received any other letter?"

"Yes—this note."

"Dear father," said this note, which was postmarked "Boston"—"I am well, and happier than I ever hoped to be again. Love to Ruth, and to brother Alfred when you write. Your NUELLA."

"One thing more," said Stirling, turning pale, "do

you think Nuella ever heard these slanders associated with me?"

"Good God! I never heard of that," exclaimed Manuel.

Manuel considered this startling suggestion for some time in silence, and became much agitated.

"I feel pretty certain that Nuella never told me all she had heard. It's just like John Layman to be suspicious, and he was hanging round a good deal while you was here. He might have hinted something of that kind to her. Ah! No—I can't say."

"We'll try and get to the bottom of it," said Stirling, rising. "And now I must bid you good-night and leave."

"What, not stay here!"

"I were afraid of breaking in on you suddenly, and put up at the Green Mountain. I'll come in the morning. Keep a brave heart! I must sleep on these letters."

Stirling kept awake on the letters, and next morning his nerves were not so calm as they should have been for the purpose he had formed. On requesting an interview with the proprietor of the hotel, Mr. Benton, he found him eager for conversation. Stirling inquired about the town, its inhabitants, the price of land, meantime measuring his man.

"How many hotels are there in the place?"

"Three—that includes a small house across the river."

"Which is the largest?"

"The Junction is rather the biggest, but very noisy if a man wants to sleep."

"But for that, is it a respectable family hotel?"

"Well, it used to be considered respectable."

"But isn't so now?"

"Well, some say the women there ain't all they should be."

"It looks like clearing up," said Stirling, carelessly walking to the window.

"Yes, sir, but the wind's east yet."

"Will you please make out my bill?"

"Dollar and a half, sir."

"Be kind enough to write the account and receipt it. I'm particular about such things. There's pen, ink and paper."

"Let's see, what name?"

"Mr. Randolph."

Benton wrote out the account and Stirling, having handed the money, scrutinized the paper.

"And now, Mr. Benton, I have a heavier account to settle with you. Certain slanderous letters, affecting the reputation of a lady in the place, have been written by you."

"I don't know what you're driving at, stranger; I haven't slandered any body, but if you want to pick a quarrel you'll find you've waked up the wrong passenger."

"Here are two notes slandering Miss Rhodes; there is your receipt; they are in the same handwriting."

"And what if they are?"

"It will go hard with you unless you can prove what you have said. I am that lady's friend and her lawyer. There is no use in getting excited. You may be perfectly certain that the maker of that charge will either prove it or be in prison this day."

"It's all along of John Layman," gasped the pallid wretch, sinking into a chair.

"I'm not surprised to hear that, and if you'll now make a clean breast of it, perhaps it may not go so hard with you."

"I'll own up," said Benton, wiping the sweat from his forehead, "for I'm miserable enough about it. I never had any thing against the girl, but I did hate her father. Layman he came one day and told me the girl was a bad 'un, and she had gone wrong with a college man, Mr.—"

"Stirling. I'm the man."

"Good Lord!"

"Go an. Here's a glass of water."

"Well, sir, he tempted me like the devil, did Layman. He said he couldn't write, and if I would write two or three letters for him it would drive the Rhodeses out of town, and he'd help me get the Junction House. I didn't misdoubt what he said about the girl was true, for she'd been his sweetheart. My children went to her Sunday-school and I didn't think she was a proper person."

"How many such letters did you write?"

"Six or seven. I gave them to him and don't know who he sent them to."

"Does that include this, which you sent to me at Cambridge?"

"No. That was wrote after the girl went off. Fact was, I felt bad and sneaky when I heard she was gone. I thought the man who ruined her ought to know it and do something."

"That shows you have some little conscience left."

"Many a time I'd given any thing if I hadn't wrote them letters."

"Why did Layman say he wanted to injure her?"

"He said the girl wouldn't have him and he'd found out certain that the reason was she was dead in love with you and was going to have a———"

"Stop! don't speak his foul words about that innocent lady. It's all a damnable lie—a venomous snake and a greedy pig conspiring to ruin an angel. By God, it shall be paid for!"

"Oh, sir, what will be done to me? I'm a man of family."

"So is Manuel Rhodes. However, you did have some pity when the girl had fled, and if you want to make the thing as easy as it can be made you'll now help me undo part of what you have done. Sit down there and write a letter to Manuel confessing that, at the instigation of John Layman, you wrote slanderous letters about his daughter, and beg his pardon. That's your only chance."

The confession received, Stirling learned from Benton that Layman generally came in from his farm to West Lebanon post-office when the ten o'clock mail opened. He crossed the railway bridge with a lad who could point out the man. A group of people were waiting at the door of the office when Layman drove up in a buggy. Stirling waited until the stalwart farmer had hitched his horse to a paling, and met him about ten yards from the crowd.

"Is your name John Layman?"

"Yes."

"Some vile slanders on Miss Rhodes have been tracked to you, Mr. Layman, and you must now answer for them. My name is Stirling, a man you have charged with ruining an innocent woman."

"I never said any thing about you at all."

"You lie! You were too cowardly to put it into the vile letters concocted between you and Benton, but you have named me."

"I deny it; and if there ain't any thing between you and her you'd better mind your own business."

"That is what I am now doing."

"I didn't write any letters."

"Then you are ready to face Benton and swear you never asked him to write any letters about Miss Rhodes, and never uttered a word against her character?"

"I may have said what I heard."

"Tell me the name of somebody from whom you heard any such thing."

"I heard several people——"

"Tell me one!"

"Don't bully me!"

"Tell me one!"

"The girl's a notorious——"

The sentence was never completed. How easily may civilized man relapse through the centuries that separate him from the faustreicht of his forefathers, and, invoking majestic Law with one breath, in the next knock a man down! Layman's large form lay prostrate; and Stirling, with a constable's hand on his shoulder, said to a wondering crowd—"Gentlemen, that reptile slandered a lady of your neighborhood; he was just repeating it and I couldn't help striking him."

Stirling begged to be taken immediately to the magistrate, and sent for Manuel. The magistrate was easily persuaded to release him on his own and Manuel's recognizances, and the two recrossed to the Junction House. Stirling advised Manuel to show the confession to the minister, Mr. Grace, and consult him about every step he should take. No anger against Benton or Layman must lead him to any mismove. Stirling then said he must leave but would return, and left an address through which he might be reached. He did not wish to buoy up Manuel with hopes that might fail, and did not tell him his immediate purpose. But he felt lighter at heart than the circumstances seemed to warrant, and both Manuel and Ruth felt their cloud lifting a little before the hopeful look in his face. He ate a hearty dinner, gave a cheery good-by to Manuel and Ruth, and was soon on his journey to a distant retreat in New York State where, four years before, he had sought out his early friend, Maria Shelton.

## CHAPTER XXII.

### BONHEUR.

IN the dusk of the following day Stirling reached a remote nook in New York State, and alighted at a "crossing" where few trains stopped. Leaving his trunk at the depot, whose sole occupants were an old man and a boy, he walked, valise in hand, to the house, a few hundred yards distant, where he had found Maria Shelton four years before. He remembered it as a sort of summer hotel which she and her friends had occupied. He now found it vacant, barred up, deserted, and returned to the depot—if a small shed and lamp-room may be so called—with misgivings. He met the man and boy going off, and learned that the people who last occupied the house had left two years before for Bonheur,—a settlement several miles away. There was no place of rest nearer, no conveyance to be obtained, and Stirling set forth in the direction pointed out.

The road was new and rough, and through lonely woods, but a friendly moon arose to light the wayfarer. He had leisure to review the situation in which he found himself. If indeed Nuella had taken refuge from evil tongues with Maria Shelton, what should he say, and how act? In the solemn darkness of the forest, picking his way on a new road, its stumps scarce revealed by the moonlight struggling through a roof of trees, he saw phantom faces appear and pass: Nuella's face now beaming with the happiness of helping him, now drooping under disgrace incurred by that service; his father's face; the faces of Gisela, Penelope, pale and anxious; and Hilda's face, which lingered till he came to a puzzling fork. "I will follow my light," he concluded, and took a road that opened against the sky. Emerging presently from the wood, he saw the village-lights in the vale beneath. A few hundred yards further he met a figure in blowse and broad hat, which grew mysterious as it approached. Stirling called across the street, into which the road had now widened.

"Will you tell me, sir, if this is Bonheur?"

"Yes."

"Do you know, miss, where Mrs. Shelton lives?"

"I will guide you to her house."

Stirling begged her not to go out of her way, but she said she was only taking a stroll in the moonlight. The young woman in trowsers, and skirt reaching to the knees, had a pleasant voice and was fair; if our traveler had not suffered so many sleepless nights he might have enjoyed a longer walk. She told him as they were passing the small white houses, all newly built, that they were a poor and happy little community; some of them refugees from a world inharmonious with their ideals; others having come for the benefits of a school kept by a fine teacher; but most of them attracted by the presence of "the grandest woman on earth,—whose house you seek. Here it is. Good-evening."

Stirling stood in the long porch, hesitating, hand on door-bell, because it was so late; but he heard voices conversing within, and rang. A gentleman came to the door and invited him to enter, but he asked to see Mrs. Shelton at the door. "Tell her, quietly please, that some one would speak to her privately. I am an old friend, but prefer you should not mention that." Maria when called out did not at once recognize him, but when she did was much delighted. She was about leading him into the room where the others were, but he paused.

"I should like to know whom I will meet."

"Only Oscar Murray, who opened the door, Naboth Warriner, our patriarch, and my adopted daughter, Rhoda Shelton."

"How long adopted?"

"Come, I must instruct you at once that close questions about people are not asked at Bonheur," she said merrily.

"I need not ask. I know who she is, and before I meet her must have a confidential talk with you. I have traveled far to find her. I am tired and hungry, but can not rest till I have consulted you."

Maria put her head in at the door from which she had come and bade them good-night, as an old friend had arrived and she must take care of him.

"Can I help you?" said a voice which Stirling knew.

"Not this time, daughter."

Maria led Stirling into her studio, brought him supper, and sat down before him with wondering eyes. Nuella had confided to this woman, who had captivated her, nearly every thing; had told her of the slanders; but the deepest secret of her heart she had not uttered. Indeed she had hardly confessed to herself the love which Randolph had left with her. That episode, which had become the whole volume of her life, might perhaps have been discovered by Maria had she referred to her own acquaintance with the Stirlings, but she had never had any occasion to do so, and now first learned that Nuella, in seeking asylum with her, bore in her breast an arrow feathered by its love. She was moved by Stirling's narrative to tears, but these had to be checked by anxious thought for the morrow.

Stirling declared that marriage was the only solution. Maria urged that marriage was a bad thing; Stirling, that if it were bad as homicide it were better than such wrong as Nuella suffered. Maria said Nuella did not suffer at Bonheur, where she was a valued teacher in their school; Stirling, that her family were in disgrace and, knowing this, Nuella could not be happy. Maria said none could be entirely happy, but Stirling declared that his own life would be blighted if he were to be forever attended by the phantoms of that old father and his daughters—ruined by the man they saved.

"But may it not add to Nuella's wrongs to marry her without really loving her?"

"Why should I not love her? I do love her. If she is not now the lovely girl she was when I knew her, it is on my account. I will not dissect my heart to discover just how much gratitude there is, how much love. Enough that I believe she can not be happy without me, and know I can not be happy without her."

"Then," said Maria, yielding, "she will have to be deceived. If she thinks you have come to save her reputation by marriage, she will never consent. I know her. Another thing I may tell you: Nuella has supernatural eyes in her heart, and if you do not really love her there will be no use in saying so."

"There seems to be no help for it—she must not know that I have come here after her. My visit must be to you—meeting her a happy accident. Can you find me board near by?"

"Not while I have a house."

"If I stay I must pay."

"Very well, and I'll send the money to pay your father for keeping me in his house two or three months. Come, Ran, I'm not needy. Go to bed and don't appear till twelve, when you've got to be astounded at meeting Nuella, just then from her school."

Maria guided her old friend to his room. As she was passing out of the door she turned: whether it was that his simple "good-night" revived recollections of happy days at The Palms, or that some feeling about his mission there moved her, a sudden emotion overcame Maria.

"O you great heart!" she cried, and clasping him in her arms kissed him again and again.

It had been long since Stirling had known such refreshing slumber as he now enjoyed. It was late in the morning when he awoke, and for a serene hour he lay tracing the fairy forests on his window; memory and imagination sauntering together through mimic landscapes of the frost.

Maria met Nuella at the door, on her return from the morning school, and led her into the breakfast-room, where a plate was laid. She explained that a dear friend had come to see her, son of a judge in whose family she once passed some time.

"He visited me several years ago when we first came into this neighborhood."

"How glad you must be? What is his name?"

"Stirling. What's the matter, child?"

"His first name?"

"Randolph."

"Oh, hide me!" cried Nuella, sinking on the floor

Just then Stirling entered and understood what had occurred. He lifted the unconscious form to a sofa, and sat chafing her hands until the pallor passed away. The return of consciousness was signaled with a deep blush, and from beneath each closed eyelid started a tear.

"Nuella," said Stirling, softly.

"It is you indeed," she said, in a low tone, looking up to his face.

"And it is you, my dear friend."

"No, not the one you knew. My name is not Nuella."

"You are my daughter, now," said Maria; "are you better?"

"I am strong enough," said Nuella, sitting up; "Mr. Stirling, I am sorry to have met you with a worry."

"Don't think that. I am the one fated to worry people."

She turned a scrutinizing glance on him, but it was

he who learned most from it : he had blundered on the fact that she had indeed heard his name connected with the slanders. After luncheon Nuella was well, and, as she had no afternoon duty at school, strategy had to begin before the strategists were quite prepared.

"I will go to my room, mother," said Nuella—"I have found a mother since I saw you, Mr. Stirling— you must have much to say to each other."

"No, don't go, Rhoda—he has nothing to say to me —that—that you may not hear."

"Three's a crowd. Why, he must have traveled ever so far to see you. Where did you come from, Mr. Stirling?"

"I left Peacefield, Massachusetts, a few days ago, but stopped on the way."

"A dreadful journey—and in the cold! You are mistaken for once, mother; I know he must have come on important business."

"He has come to spend his Christmas at Bonheur, and we must all be as merry as the pious, plunged in a gulf of dark despair and dining on turkey; which reminds me that I have directions to give; no, Nuella —I must be the Martha this time; your nerves got the shock, and you two must chat till I return."

Since Stirling and Nuella had parted she had, in a sense, lived ages, but they had not aged her physically; they had stolen some of the rich color from her cheek, and from the mouth some of its dimpled mirthfulness; but the childlike voice was left, and the brow retained its pure repose. To Stirling she appeared more beautiful than before: he looked into this face as into a serene evening sky overarching a horizon of shadows ; his soul stirred with the hope of setting there the star of love.

"It seems long, Nuella, since I was listening to your favorite poems in the little parlor. Do you remember how we roamed with 'Pippa?'"

"Unhappy days for you, but—"

"Were you about to say they were not unhappy for you? I hope so; for they were not unhappy for me, and I should be glad to think I was not merely a burden to you."

"I have had unhappy days—in my life—but those appear bright when—I saw you getting well."

"Nuella," said Stirling, in a merry tone, for he saw a shadow stealing over her face, "doesn't your conscience confess to a little deception on that night when I first saw you? As I remember you somehow made me suppose there was no train to go on by; and also surprised me into a confession."

"How can I recall such remote antiquity? And if it's true, what's a woman to do with a man twice her size to keep from some mad thing or other?"

"Just what the big man ought to do when he has to keep a woman from harm—from harming herself without knowing it."

"What, deceive her! A woman should never be deceived."

"Only men?"

"Only men."

"Deception is a female prerogative?"

"I thought every body knew that. You must learn your a-b-c."

"Be my teacher!"

"Women are like the defenseless little creatures that grow to be like twigs and leaves, so that the birds shall not notice them."

"Isn't that dangerous doctrine?"

"It is. How awful must tyranny be, when its victims must dissemble for truth's own sake!"

"Women, then, love truth?"

"Too much to let it be trodden into falsehood."

"I feel flattered that you cast yours before me, for people rarely tell the truth about truth. Every body denounces deception, but every body practices it in emergencies—some selfishly, making deception a lie, some honorably, like a patriot saving his country by stratagem."

"How profound we are becoming! Tell me where you have been, and what you have been doing."

"The way is paved for a confession: I have lately been a living deception, a walking whopper; I have been traveling about in disguise."

"Now you *are* deceiving me. No!"

While Stirling told his adventures at Spindleton, his journey with the Fraülein, the slave's escape, the drive with Hilda, his wound and recovery, she listened like a Desdemona to her hero.

"Now prepare yourself, Mr. Stirling; I have one thousand questions—"

"To be continued in our next," said Maria entering. "The table must be set for prosaic dinner, and you must do something with yourselves."

"I am to set the table," said Nuella.

"Not to-day," urged Maria.

"Leave my premises, or fear the vengeance of an angry daughter!"

"Maria," said Stirling presently, "it's going to be a hard matter to suppress the facts; I wonder if it's necessary?"

"I've been thinking over it every moment since you came. My conviction is that if you should marry her, and she then ever suspected that you came here because of her troubles, a tiny worm would be at the core of her joy, and it would decay as it ripened."

"Mother, may I speak to you?" said Nuella, at the parlor door, which she closed when Maria came out to her.

"Mother, I trust you have not told Mr. Stirling of any of my troubles."

"Not a whisper."

"And you will not tell him? I entreat you."

"I will not," said Maria, re-entering the parlor.

"She does not dream yet that you know her trouble," she said, "and has just entreated me not to tell you. Nuella is as if on the brink of a mental consumption; you must act as a physician who would save his patient by concealing what might prove fatal."

Stirling was not anxious for Nuella to get through her thousand questions; he dreaded to have their conversation turn upon her own experiences. But he was more and more charmed by her presence, and as she devoted her mornings to the school he longed for a lotus-land where it is always afternoon. This peripatetic inquirer was too deeply absorbed in the personal experience through which he was passing to make the most of his opportunity to learn more about northern institutions, but he listened with interest, in the long evenings, to discussions of the economic and social principles represented by Bonheur. Maria held a sort of *salon*, assisted by Naboth Warriner, manager of the community, Oscar Murray, a retired merchant, and Thomas Alden, the teacher, her receptions being on Wednesday and Sunday evenings. Naboth explained to him their economic system,—that time is money, an hour's labor compensating an hour's labor, this being modified in favor of disagreeable labor, and variable with corn. Five hours' professional service were equivalent to eighty pounds of corn, but the corn could be had for a less time of drudgery. The social basis of Bonheur was "individualism,"—the freedom of each to think, speak, live, without any limit, save the equal right of others, to their genius. Though few of them might have heard of Thelema, the motto of Rabelais' Utopian abbey had embodied itself in this American forest village: *Fais ce que voudras*. Whatever Stirling might think of their visions, the visionaries had to be taken seriously: they were generally thoughtful and high-minded people. Nor could there be doubt that his hours with Nuella and Maria would be found under par if measured against the superior claims of 'disagreeable occupation' in Bonheur.

# CHAPTER XXIII.

### CHRISTMAS AT BONHEUR.

NO bells rang in the Christmas day at Bonheur. There was a temple in the place, a small white parthenon, but no regular assemblages in it. It was always open, and when any one of the community had something to say there, it rested on such to send notice to every house and to build fires in the temple if needed. In this way it had been announced that Maria Shelton would speak on Christmas morning.

It was a beautiful morning, the air so still and clear that the sun was able to soften the heart of winter. Stirling and Nuella started out early enough for a stroll through the village. The streets were presently alive with temple-goers; or one might say variegated with them, for "do what thou wilt" being the only regulation in dress, the figures presented the picturesqueness of a masquerade. Even the men had some touches of color in their dress. Some of the ladies had anticipated the æsthetic era, but their skirts were generally short—of every degree between knee and ankle—the Turkish or other trowsers being worn by some, but the majority contenting themselves with stockings of various shades. There could not be the slightest suspicion of boldness among them: the Arcadian atmosphere was too potent over the secluded land for Mrs. Grundy to invade it with questions of propriety in costume. To Stirling, at any rate, they appeared as happy children on a holiday, and he was afterwards surprised to recognize in the seated assembly so many gray heads.

Behind the lecture-desk the wall was hung with pictures, placed there for the occasion by Maria, which were examined by those present before her arrival. The subjects were from Palestine and chiefly scenes in Jerusalem, some of them painted there by Maria herself. In the center was a fine copy of Filippo Lippi's "Madonna and Child in the Wood." No woman could appear worthier to stand beside the picture than Maria Shelton, who presently appeared before her audience in robe of purple velvet, and with no ornament but a white flower at her breast.

She began with a quietly humorous description of her arrival in Jerusalem; the discomfort caused by competition for making her comfortable; the guides denouncing each other as infidels, Jews, Moslems, apparently the only species of crime in their decalogue. Next she described the groping amid ruins over ancient streets sunk to ruts, leading to tombs whose inscriptions have followed into eternal silence the memories they once preserved. Maria's artist face appeared as she described the panorama of alternating antiquity and modern splendor, with the permanent figure of human degradation crouching under gilded walls of Christendom as once under palaces of the Pharaohs. Reverently and tenderly she spoke of prophets, poets, sages ; of the spiritual flower of their race, whose effort to save the poor from despair had woven a halo round his own and his mother's head. Her voice grew passionate as she pointed to the burial of that sacred city under ruins of time, under more ruinous holy wars and oppressions, till left with ditches heaped with blind guides and their followers—priestly guides, hating each other even more than the dragomans whose curses compete for your guidance to Calvary. The Holy City was then made a type of imperial Christendom, with its crumbled shrines, its moral highways buried under rubbish of superstition, its great souls succeeded by selfish guides, its Saviour dragged down to be the patron of each vulgar sectarian shop, on which one seems to read "Pope & Co.," or "Canterbury & Co.," or Calvin & Co.," "Soul-savers to H. R. H. the Prince of Peace." The old shrines broken, the old streets lost, the guides untrustworthy, Christmas tells its sweet tale of a supernatural Mother and Babe to a generation that keeps watch by night, but sees in the East no pointing star. Now must each turn to the firmament within, where shines the star of love and thought. For those who have left the conventional guides to follow that inner light the new star burns through the darkness of our time, and guides the pilgrim to a true Bethlehem. And may it not be here, she said, even in Bonheur, veritably as in the past? Behold in this old picture the paternal and maternal spirit in the universe out in the lonely Wood: the Voice in the Wilderness is there also, and the dove of peace. In these our American woods the ancient miracle is renewed for those who cease to seek it amid ruins of the past, and the parasites with which they are overgrown.

Such was the tenor of Maria's Christmas discourse; but how impossible to convey the charm of her speech, and how unimaginable the beauty of the woman transfigured in mild enthusiasm! A profound silence followed her last word, the audience sitting still as if loth to move. Then an aged woman arose and cried —"O Maria Shelton, blessed art thou for the sweet thoughts thee has spoken this day!"

"Yes!" cried Thomas Alden, "the oldest of us are her children, and we rise up and call her blessed."

By one impulse all present arose and stood for a few moments in silence. Maria moved forward as if about to speak, but there was only the faintest movement on her lips. She bowed low, then walked from the platform and disappeared through a door near it.

"Friends!" cried a voice near the entrance. It was a new and startling voice, though not loud, and every head was turned. Was this an eagle transformed to a man! Tall and lank, clothed in brown wool, gray-bearded, mouth wide and thin, nose hooked, the forehead overshadowed with thicket of iron-gray hair, the eyes steel-like in hue and glitter,—this man was one to command attention.

"Friends, I am a pilgrim to your woods, I am a seeker of the New Jerusalem, and if you will listen to me I will tell you where that holy child Jesus is, and where Herod is, and where the babes are massacred. My name is Gideon,—Captain Gideon,—and I beg madam, the lecturer, that I may be heard."

"The stranger has the same freedom to speak here

as ourselves," said Maria, who had reappeared with cloak and bonnet.

Those who hoped to hear any thing about the Babe of Bethlehem were disappointed. For any thing in this captain's address, Christmas might as well never have dawned on the world. The negro bondmen of the South were Jehovah's people; the slaveholders were taskmasters to be overthrown in a Red Sea,— they were also Cain slaying Abel, and particularly they were Midianites whose raids on Israel this Gideon had been punishing in Kansas with the sword of the Lord. Strong as was this eagle, the atmosphere of the temple was too etherial just then to sustain his wing. After a few minutes of Jehovistic wrath he fluttered down; but, from his more quiet and hesitating harangue that followed, a pathetic and sometimes thrilling story was gathered. There in the far West slavery was trying to make a fair land into its own image. On every acre of Kansas it meant to set up an auction-block for the sale of men, women and children. On the other hand a small band of the soldiers of liberty were there to die rather than the great crime should be done. The captain gave many instances of the wickedness of the Missouri Midianites, many examples of the righteousness—terribly retributive—of the Free State men; but the most impressive and touching part of his speech was that in which he described the slaves running to them, stretching out their hands for deliverance. In conclusion he made an appeal that they should all send some contribution to the Kansas committee. "For myself," he said, "my life is consecrated to the work of liberating the slave, and if I could only persuade one soul here to join me in that cause of Almighty God, I should feel that he has sent me out here with a message to that soul."

The few comments made on his address must have suggested to Captain Gideon that he was somehow missent to Bonheur. A man rose up to say that he thought the southern negroes better off than the same race in the north, and about as well off as the toiling whites ; a woman, that her sex was enslaved, and charity begins at home ; but the severest trial for the captain was a speech maintaining that the Bible was on the side of the slaveholder.

One person, however, had been deeply moved by the captain's speech,—Nuella. As the people were moving away she desired Stirling to accompany her in approaching the old man, who was walking off with bent head, and an appearance of dejection. He started at hearing his name.

" Here is a lady who wishes to speak to you," said Stirling.

" How d'ye do, madam," said the captain with a polite bow.

"I wish to ask if you have ever met a man in Kansas named Alfred Rhodes ? "

" I know him well. There isn't a better man out there than Colonel Rhodes."

" Was he well when you last saw him ? "

" Perfectly. He has a fine claim out there,—a first-rate piece of land is Rhodes's—and the ruffians would be glad to get hold of him and his place ; but they've got their match. He has one or two neighbors near his cabin with families, but isn't married himself."

"He is my—relation. I hope," said Nuella, with a candid blush, "that you will feel that many hearts are with you in your brave work, though their hands are too weak to help. I was interested in your address to-day—more than I can express. Good-by!"

In the afternoon Nuella and Stirling took a walk in the woods. Their conversation naturally turned on the addresses in the temple.

"Bonheur is an open secret," said Stirling. "Naboth may say what he will about standards of value, but the basis of the community is a great-brained woman."

"Listening to her to-day I was at times in a trance, and as if beholding angels descending on a ladder."

"For me, I remembered the saying of Socrates' young friend, that to listen to his discourse was a sufficient end of life."

"You luxurious man! Ah, Mr. Stirling——"

"Well, Miss Rhodes."

"Why Miss?"

"Why Mister?"

"I don't believe I could say simple Randolph. You'll have to give me a day or two to try it over by myself."

"After to-morrow it must be Mister no more. What were you about to say?"

"I've forgotten."

"You said it was luxurious to want to listen to Maria for the rest of life."

"The rest of life! The words have two meanings. Most of those in the village have come from tempests, clinging to fragments of their wreck, and found rest on Maria's heart; but you, starting out on a fair sea, how could you dream of rest in poor little Bonheur? You visit your southern friend, depart, and if you remember us it will be with a smile."

"I may be more of a waif than you think. What does each know of the other? Many a Bonheureuse believes she alone knows real trouble."

"It's not mere trouble that makes people leave the great world for a convent, or a place like Bonheur. The heart is born for an unbounded world, and if it turns away from it the motive is either religious, thinking to find the gate to a boundless world, or something that renders life with mankind impossible. Not even the charm of Maria could give rest to one flying from a vocation in the world."

"How long do you expect to remain in Bonheur?"

"During its life or mine."

"Then you are happy here."

"I would be happier with more to do."

There was a hopelessness in Nuella's tone, rather than in her words, that weighed on Stirling's heart; he found nothing to say, and they walked in silence till Nuella felt that she had been making their walk too gloomy.

"Mr. Stirling——"

"Oh!"

"Mr. Randolph, then!"

"Better."

"I haven't asked half my questions yet."

"You said a thousand, and have asked nine hundred and ninety-nine. I've counted,"

"Tell me more of that Lady Hilda, who put on the negro's clothes. That's a woman! Maria would do a thing like that."

"So would you."

"Do you think so? really? I have dreams of brave free action, rising above custom, ignoring sex—like Lady Godiva—to strike some stroke for justice. It would be glorious to do as your Hilda did, on the moment, so absorbed in the duty before her that questions of clothes, of what people may say, of consequences to herself, could never even occur to her!"

"It was indeed sublime to see her blackened, and in the coarse clothing of a slave. Were I an artist I would paint the picture."

"I suppose she watched over you after you were wounded. When are you to be marrried?"

"Nuella, does it always follow that when one is watched over and helped through illness by—but there, I will be merciful. No; her uncle was a doctor and took me to his own house. Afterwards I saw a good deal of Hilda, but we didn't fall in love. Perhaps she was too happy in her home; perhaps I was too—too——"

"Too what?"

"I suppose there are mysterious conditions for love as for diamonds; all the elements may be brought together in right proportions, but the gem doesn't flash out."

"You know all about it, Mr.—Randolph. You've been in love."

"I have not been, I am in love."

Just then fate put in a word. Hearing a step

behind them they turned and saw Captain Gideon approaching, bag in hand, on his way to the station.

"I hope, young lady," he said, after shaking hands with both, "that your heart is as good as your face, and that you will encourage this young man to serve the right, like Colonel Rhodes. I do not know what you are to each other. I pray God to bless you both and lead you to set about his work. Do not let earthly affections draw you from God's work. There are great wrongs to be righted. Woe to them that lead lives of ease when God is calling for helpers! Blessed are they that lose their lives for his sake! But I can not tarry. Farewell!"

Their eyes followed the captain's gaunt figure until it disappeared.

"What a strange man!" said Nuella.

"Strange indeed; he strikes me as suffering a sort of sane insanity."

"Do you know," she said, "while he was pleading about Kansas a longing to go there came over me? I felt that perhaps the service of life might be found there, if not its happiness. He must have mesmerized me; if he had come to me and said, 'Rise and go with me,' I might have followed him."

"I suppose the face of your brother—I supposed it was a brother you asked about—rose before you. But, Nuella, it pains me to hear you talk in that tone, about finding your life's service without its happiness. Is it not morbid?"

"Perhaps—partly. Yet I should like to go where I could bind up wounds, or help poor negroes flying from pursuers, and minister to brave men defending liberty. Yes!" her eyes flashed, "I should like to go with that man!"

"Nuella, go with me!"

"What did you say?"

"Go with me!"

They were the eyes of a child that turned to those of Stirling, but the eyes of a woman that started at what she read there,—then drooped toward the earth.

"You have taken me at my word suddenly," she said, trying to speak lightly; "going to Kansas is a serious business."

"Perhaps you mean going with me is a serious business. It is even so; to me infinitely more serious than going anywhere. Nuella, wherever you go, go with me! Nuella, I love you; where you go I will go; we must part no more."

Nuella stood speechless, gazing on the dead leaves,— only a faint last autumnal tint discernible on them here and there. Light snowflakes were beginning to fall; nature would weep for her, and for this love that came too late, though the tears were frozen. At length her eyes, tearless but full of pain, turned piteously to him.

"Randolph, true and good as ever, come close, for once let me clasp you to my heart—for once, *my* Randolph!"

"For once and forever."

"For once and for the last time," she said, trembling in his arms.

"No, Nuella, no!"

"Yes,—we must part. I can not be your wife,

though love for you has long been the secret of my life."

"Nuella, my love, what is this?"

"It is as I have said. It is not much I could have brought the man I love, only my devotion; but one thing I would have to bring him, and that I now can not—an untarnished name."

As Nuella said this she disengaged herself quietly from his arms and stood apart, as if the abyss were already yawning between them. The youth's whole nature flowed out to this womanly soul, standing there the martyr of love and innocence. He stretched forth his hands, but she did not come; her resolution fixed her apart, as if a statue in which the eyes alone were alive.

"Nuella, this is all some miserable mistake; what is any silly gossip to me if I have the wife I love, and know her to be pure and true?"

"It is noble to say that, it is like you, but your honor is dearer to me than your love. You must now hear all, hard as it is to tell. Malicious tongues have accused me of unchaste conduct, our family has been publicly disgraced, and we are defenseless against the slanders. The disgrace is ineffaceable, and I am hiding at Bonheur."

"You shall find honor and protection in your own home, and at my side," cried Stirling, starting forward.

"Impossible," said Nuella, waving him back.

"Now see, Nuella,—we happen to be in the same case. I also am in disgrace at home. I am unable to return there because I helped a fugitive slave. I am disgraced for something I did, you for what you never did. If nevertheless I long to make you my wife, to have you share my disgrace, why should you not let me share yours?"

"It is different. You are accused of what in my eyes is to your honor."

"And you, Nuella, is not your accusation based on something that in my eyes would be to your honor? It can not be that malice could fasten on you without some fact to pervert, and I know that fact would be something worthy of the woman I love—Nuella, you do not answer. I entreat you in pity, tell me that. There was something, and I swear, before you speak, you were slandered for what would make me proud of you."

"I am frightened. I fear your reasoning. Be merciful—never let me lower the man I love in the eyes of those to whom his name belongs. No, Randolph, never can I be your wife. The air grows bitter—this snow stings. Let us go back to Bonheur." She started, but he held her by the arm.

"Speak out like your frank self, my Nuella—be bold as your innocence. You say you have loved me; was not your secret known? did it not turn some jealous man into your enemy?"

"Let us return—the snow is thickening."

"Nuella, Nuella, I entreat an answer."

"I am not able, I can only obey my heart—it says, beware!" Now her tears began to flow, and he caught her in his arms again.

"You have been suffering, my sweet. Let the snow fall—you are in your shelter. In some way your love has brought on your troubles; then I have the right to help you bear them—and I will."

"Never!"

"When you can think of it calmly you will see that I must. By no power can it be prevented. Send me away, I go; but the face of the woman blighted through me must move by my side forever. You can leave me, Nuella, but you can not take away that life-long pain."

"Do not talk so! Pity! What have I said? I never said you had any thing to do with it. Do not ask me questions; I don't know what I answer. I am in a place where one false step would—Father in heaven, help me!"

"Nuella, my wife that must be,—a voice within says it is through me you suffer. I stand by you. You will be vindicated by me. Your slanderers will be put to shame. We will scorn them, forget them, in our happiness."

"I am bewildered. You have come into my little life like a god, you overwhelm me with your greatness of soul, your gratitude where I have done nothing; I can return you nothing, but I will never tarnish your name; the nobler you are, the stronger I am to save you from that."

"Yield to me, darling; do not doom us both to inevitable life-long unhappiness. I pledge my honor to make you see with me that our fates are bound together. If when you have thought it all over you still have doubts, never dream that you are under any bond."

"What would you have me do?"

"Return with me to your old home; we will be married in the church you have attended——"

Nuella raised her eyes to the horizon, and a radiance was in them as if she had caught some celestial vision. She moved on swiftly, silently, then paused, and turned to her lover eyes full of dreamy wondering trust. But suddenly her ear caught a sound whose omen she understood better than the southerner—a sound as of bullets singing through the air, which began to freeze as if an iceberg were floating through it. "We must hurry," cried Nuella, and began to run; but it was too late, for the Arctic dragon was upon them with tornado coils, teeth of ice, and vomit of stinging blinding snow. The hurricane was against them; the snow did not fall to the ground but was held in the air, and it was like moving against a marble wall. Nuella began to stagger, and turned her back to the furious blows of the storm. Stirling, realizing the danger, implored her to keep moving, but at last she sank exhausted. He lifted her in his arms and struggled on until a horror shot through him—it was as if he were carrying a log. He called her by name, but there was no answer. Near the foot of a large oak he laid her down, covered her with her shawl, his overcoat, coat, waistcoat—placing a log beneath the folds so as to secure air should she be covered by a drift—and then ran toward the village, in the face of the storm. His burning heart alone kept Stirling from sinking until he fell on the threshold of the nearest house—that of Naboth Warriner, who was soon on his way with a wagon to rescue Nuella. Half-frozen as he was Stirling also returned, and they found a white mound where he had laid Nuella. Haggard with fear he tore away the snow, which, the hurricane having passed, had settled to a thickness of several inches over her. Nuella, perfectly comfortable under that white wool, rose up as from a happy slumber.

When they were talking over the adventure next day, Nuella said she remembered only his taking her in his arms, and then laying her down ; the rest was a pleasant dream.

"Let us resume our talk," said Stirling ; "you were about to say when our wedding should take place in West Lebanon Church"—

"Was I ?"

"I hope so. At any rate you didn't say no the last time, and silence is consent."

"Unless one's lips are frozen." Whereupon Randolph closed them otherwise.

## CHAPTER XXIV.

### A WREATH OF WINTER BLOSSOMS.

WHEN Stirling left White River Junction to seek Nuella, Manuel hastened to show Benton's confession to Mr. Grace. The minister was deeply moved, rose to his feet with a cry for justice, and started with Manuel to find a lawyer. At the parsonage door they met Benton coming, overwhelmed with fear, to ask the minister's intercession with Manuel. Layman, he said, had disappeared from the neighborhood. Benton declared that he did not know the innocence he was smirching, that Manuel would find him anxious to make what reparation he could, and that he was ready to leave home and search for Nuella. Manuel and the minister concluded to forego for the time appeal to the law. Mr. Grace demanded that the offender should be present in his congregation on the following Sunday morning. On that occasion he preached about "false witness," and caused great excitement as he spoke pointedly of "the vile and cruel slanders, now confessed, which had recently driven a pure and honorable young lady from the congregation she had adorned."

On New Year's Eve Ruth,—grown womanly under her responsibilities—sat with her father in his own room. The accounts of the passing year had been balanced, save the heaviest of them all. Manuel gazed into the fire with tearful eyes, and Ruth sat on the floor caressing his hand. She started up at a knock on the door, and the next moment gave a scream of delight: two letters were handed in, one bearing her sister's handwriting. They could hardly read, through happy tears, the sweet story told by Nuella. Manuel's letter was from Stirling. It begged him to arrange for the wedding to take place in church in six weeks, and desired that when Nuella came nothing should be told her of his late visit to the Junction, or of his encounter with her slanderers. She need only be informed that they had confessed. "Please be very careful on that point; it is important. The marriage should be announced from the congregational pulpit. We feel sure Mr. Grace will be glad to see justice done. We shall arrive February 10. We are happy."

Great was the sorrow of Bonheur at Nuella's departure. The school children assembled in the temple, where she was crowned with flowers, and sung to, and addressed by Maria with faltering voice. Mr. Alden read a poem written for the occasion. A procession of the whole village attended the lovers to the station.

The sorrow of Bonheur was the joy of White River Junction and West Lebanon. Sparkling was that wedding day which, after the long black night, dawned over the beautiful hills. The two rivers which, in immemorial time, joined their forces to break the high barriers, but preserved their white and brown colors, now with one sheen of ice united the towns they normally separate. When at twilight the bell sounded from the white spire of West Lebanon it evoked responsive sleigh-bells; along the bridges and the rivers they were heard, and lights as merry danced over the snow beneath the soft moonlight. The romance had been told from every pulpit, and at the Seminary, and the very elms and beeches around the pretty church seemed to have put on snow-pure veils to welcome the innocence so grievously wronged, and the crowds coming to witness her vindication and happiness.

When Nuella alighted at the church door a dazzling splendor burst from the interior. As the lovers advanced from the vestibule, the little girls Nuella had once taught there attended her, singing a chorus of welcome. Nuella had been told of the confession and flight of her slanderers, but she was not prepared for this scene. She could not repress her emotion, and stopped in the aisle to embrace these children who were as angels in white raiment welcoming her at the gate of heaven. Nor had Stirling any knowledge that such a reception awaited them. Proud and elated he pressed the trembling hand more firmly on his arm, as they were received by Ruth with the other bridesmaids and groomsmen. The girls of Tilden Seminary, where Nuella was educated, conspiring with conservatories far and near, had made the pulpit a pyramid of flowers; beneath an evergreen arch stood the bride and bridegroom,—fit frame for the tableau in which the scene centred. A choral antiphon had been arranged between male voices (a college choir from Dartmouth) near the organ, at the church entrance, and female voices (the Seminary choir) near the pulpit. Nuella in white bridal dress and veil was so beautiful that homage could be heard whispering through the crowded assembly. The singing gave time for her bewilderment to pass away; an infantine joy smiled in her eyes and the faded roses again bloomed on her cheek. As the chorus closed she turned her face to Randolph as if about to say something, but her eyes alone—he met them with a triumphant smile—spoke the fullness of her joy in that supreme moment.

When the ceremony was over the minister, in his brief address, said that during his long connection with the church he had never before known another occasion so fraught with general joy as this. By spontaneous good-will the community had united to offer this festivity to their young sister and her honored husband; nobody had to be urged, all were eager. By favor of Miss Ruth the wedding gifts had been sent to the church. At this moment the choir of maidens parted, a curtain was drawn back, and a table laden with presents was displayed.

"Could I only kneel to you!" whispered Nuella. Stirling's answer was a kiss.

The venerable minister held out his hand, but Nuella threw her arms around him and kissed him. Then followed Manuel and Ruth, with embraces, tears and laughter: then the children Nuella had taught, and suddenly the whole crowd surged forward to shake hands. Ruth led them to see the presents. A handsome piece of silver was engraved with the words: "Emanuella Rhodes. From the Sunday-school."

The Junction House ball-room was presently the scene of a dance and a supper of a magnificence hitherto unknown in that region. The night trains as they passed showed a head at every window, wondering at the illumination and the violins making the ear of night tingle. The rose of dawn was unfolding when the last departing sleigh-bells were heard.

A happy week at White River Junction followed the wedding, but the end of it brought sad tidings from Kansas. A package came from Alfred Rhodes, inclosing the title to his land claim there, with a bequest of it to his father, and a letter stating that he was wounded. The letter was written by himself. The package had been brought by hand to Tabor, Iowa, and there mailed by Captain John Brown, who also wrote to Manuel. Colonel Rhodes, he said, had been shot in the side by Missourians; he did not know how serious the wound might prove, but from what he had heard, thought it not necessarily fatal. Unfortunately, however, it was hardly possible for the sufferer to receive proper care. He expected to hear again about the colonel in a week's time and would forward any information he might receive to his father.

Nuella had long forgotten her notion of going to Kansas—it belonged to an oubliette closed and sealed with the year just dead. But now it rose again and Stirling, remembering her words in the wood at Bonheur, spoke to her silent thought, and said, " Where you wish to go, I will go."

" Alfred was always an affectionate brother," was her only reply.

"Suppose we should go to this Tabor—it sounds like the region of our Captain Gideon—and decide there whether we can, or need, attempt the further journey?" Stirling suggested.

This, after much consideration, was the course determined on. A week was given to preparation—on one day of which Nuella slipped off alone, and after a grievously long absence from her husband, privately confided to Manuel's care her signed and attested will. The next day Stirling and Nuella took their places on a westward train: the journey of their life was begun.

## CHAPTER XXV.

### A BY-WAY OF OLD VIRGINIA.

WENTWORTH left the northward train at Fredericksburg, where he bought a horse, having resolved to travel on horseback to The Palms. His baggage was intrusted to a grain-wagon returning to Fauquier, except what was packed in his ample saddle-bags. Thus equipped he started at daybreak. Reaching the edge of the town he paused on the brow of a hill to observe the picturesque scene. On his right the Rappahannock flowed peacefully through its meadows, bearing here and there a scow laden with grain and propelled by negroes with long poles. Forward, in the distance, the river disappeared beneath a long bridge, beyond which rose high green hills, on each height a mansion whose white walls gleamed through stately trees. On his left was the marble monument of the mother of Washington. As he rode on he met carts on their way to town laden with early summer fruit. On the bridge he moved slowly, looking at the rapids, the fish-traps, the islets, with here and there a troop of merry swimmers. It was all pretty and idyllic; but as he passed through the village beyond he reflected that in New England a river with such falls near its head of navigation would run golden sands. From the top of a hill beyond he surveyed again the beautiful vale, the shining river, and distant steeples mirrored in its peace. Little could he dream that where he paused artillery would presently be planted, the tranquil air tremble with shot and shell, that peaceful town on the horizon become historic in the annals of war.

As the rider traveled on, the sun began to burn, but, shaded by an umbrella, he was able to enjoy the novelties of a Virginia summer. Houses and people became rare; now and then negroes gazed at him from the fields of maize; occasionally he met one of the long white-bonneted wagons which railway transportation had not yet fossilized; but for the most part the wayside liveliness was contributed by shrill concerts of the cicadas, bright lizards, spotted snakes, striped ground-squirrels, the dove's cooing, the colin's call, *Ah, Bob White;* and once he stopped to listen to the melodies of a mocking-bird. The road was fringed with wild flowers, the Virginia creeper was decorating fence and field, and sometimes through a dark wood the voiceless "nightingale" flashed like a torch.

For seven or eight miles of the way, Wentworth felt as if he were getting beyond the human habitat; he could not hear even the lowing of a cow or baying of a dog, but only wild sounds; and a sense of loneliness oppressed him. He sank into a long reverie, from which he was recalled by a human voice. He looked up and saw a handsome dwelling-house, fifty rods from the road. There was another call, and he presently saw, within the road-side fence, a gentleman who was hailing him.

"Good morning, sir, are you traveling far?"

"To the neighborhood of Warrenton."

"Won't you alight for a time? You've a long ride before you."

"Thank you, but I think not."

"It's near dinner time, and you're welcome to food for yourself and horse. If you're a stranger to these parts I may warn you that you've passed the only tavern."

"Yes, I am a stranger, but I have some food."

"But your horse may suffer. You had better rest a little, sir. I don't know that we've much to offer, but I shouldn't like to think of your going on without any refreshment."

"I will not refuse your hospitality, so kindly offered."

"I'll meet you at the gate a little further on."

The Virginian gathered from his guest as they moved slowly to the door that he was on his way to The Palms.

"Ah, Judge Stirling's place! Very glad to meet you, sir. The judge hasn't his superior in Virginia. We have known each other many years, and I should never forgive myself if I'd let any relation of his pass my door without coming in."

"I'm not a relation, but one of his family is my best friend."

"I'll be bound it's Gisela. I'd have to challenge you, sir, if it's Gisela—no help for it but to eat my bread and salt.—Tom! see this gentleman's horse fed. You'll stop for the night, Mr.—?"

"Wentworth. No, thank you—I must get on."

"Welcome the coming, speed the parting, guest is our way here. My name is Eden—Marshall Eden."

Thus on the lonely high-road our traveler was way-laid and presently found himself captive in a circle of attractive people. The matron presided with grace at her board, and the sons and daughters around it were refined and affable. After they had learned that he was on his way to The Palms there were not wanting significant smiles, which the guest suspected might be due to a "reckon" that he was going there as a suitor. The young people ran on with enthusiasm about Gisela and Penelope, who had visited them, and gave him loving messages for them.

It was nearly three o'clock when he started on his way. He hoped to reach Warrenton that evening and ride over to The Palms—several miles away from that town—in the afternoon of next day, which was Sunday. But his plans were destined to be upset, and he was to have another experience of the hospitality of this region. At about five o'clock a sudden thunderstorm arose, the sky was palled, the thunder and lightning grew furious; and in the distance the rain was as a mighty wall moving toward the high-road. No umbrella could live in the hurricane, and Wentworth had resigned himself to a drenching, when he saw a negro running toward him, shouting and waving his arms. The man said his master had seen him, and hoped he wouldn't think of facing such a storm. Wentworth had no hesitation this time, and galloped to the house through pursuing hailstones.

"Come in, sir, come in!" said the sturdy old farmer who met him in the porch. "Lucky I caught sight of you, for it's going to be a mighty hard storm."

"You are watchful people in this region. This is the second time to-day I've enjoyed Virginia hospitality."

Entering the parlor they found the family gathered in the center of the darkened room, their feet on each other's chair-rounds—traditional securities against lightning. They greeted Wentworth and invited him to join their circle. It was too dark for faces to be distinguished, and the thunder was too loud and continuous to admit of much conversation; but even this terrific storm was not enough to paralyze curiosity.

"Are you on your way to the Camp Meeting, sir?—good gracious! wasn't that loud!"

"No, madam"—a venture—"I am going to The Palms."

"Oh, the Stirlings' place."

"We said"—farmer's voice—"we thought you might be one of the preachers."

"I never saw a Camp Meeting."

"Indeed!" (three female voices).

"It is an interesting——my! that *must* have struck something!"

"I wish I could never see another Camp Meeting" (youthful male voice).

"Nonsense, Bob, it's lots o' fun" (young female voice).

"I wonder you both are not afraid to talk so while the very lightnings of heaven are around you" (thin and elderly female voice).

"Well, Aunt Sarah, I'm in earnest" (Bob). "There's

more rascality Camp Meeting times than all the rest of the year, and no hand's fit for any thing."

"But people can't go on the year round without some little excite——oh, oh! wasn't that a crash!" (young but serious; female).

"I don't belong to any church" (farmer), "but respect them all. However, I can't say I think much of these Camp Meetings. I've seen a good many, and rather dread when they come round."

"The first time we met, Mr. Morton, was at a Camp Meeting" (soft matronly voice, followed by a chorus of laughter).

The thunder presently died away, the lightning flashed at longer intervals, but the rain continued, and Wentworth was persuaded not to go further that evening. He made himself agreeable, entered into the young people's games, taught them new ones, and the little ones included him in their good-night kiss. When the rest of the family had retired he joined the farmer and his eldest son in a smoke. In the course of their conversation he learned that the Stirlings had been in some trouble about the eldest son, who " was said to have become an abolitionist and got into some row about a runaway negro." As to which Robert said, "I've known Ran Stirling all my life, and I won't believe he ever did a mean thing unless he tells me so himself—and I don't know that I'd believe it then." To this sentiment Wentworth responded warmly; but he carried an anxious head to his pillow.

The Sunday dawned bright, and all the family were going to the Camp. Wentworth was glad to go with them; it was not much out of his way, and he did not wish to reach The Palms until after dinner. The Morton cavalcade started early. The sun was hot, but the rain had laid the dust and the ride was pleasant; Wentworth found it especially amusing, for he had a witty companion in the family reprobate—Julia—who sat her horse well, and gave him an anecdotical account of every body and every thing. As they approached the Camp the roads were massed with processions of wagons, gigs, buggies, sulkies, carioles, coaches, horses with two on most of them, and endless lines of negroes on foot. The Camp was in a forest. Tents and shanties, three deep, surrounded a vast horse-shoe space filled with plank seats. Outside the circle of tents were booths for cider and lemonade, the bars for strong drinks being farther off. Gay parties filled the tents and grounds. The early prayer-meeting was not quite over in the rude forest chancel when Wentworth arrived. He took his position at a point which commanded a near view of the congregation of negroes, whose benches were behind the platform-pulpit.

By ten o'clock the seats were crowded. There was much expectation from the preacher of the morning, a famous young revivalist from Washington. He was a handsome, unmarried (the fact was widely repeated) and rosy man, under thirty years. Appearing last among the score of preachers on the platform, his coming excited a sensation similar to that of a prima-donna's entrance among her chorus. He was dressed in newest broadcloth and starchest white cravat and linen; his hair concealed his ears with arabesque rolls;

a complacent smile was on his mouth, but his eyes were fixed and solemn.

He began his sermon with studied gesture and memorized rhetoric—spoke of "the star-fringed bosom of Night," and of "the cross, like the lightning-rod, drawing to itself the thunderbolt of Eternal Justice." Perhaps he would have been glad to go on exciting wonder by his imagery and knowledge; but that was not what he was brought there for. In front of him were several long benches which he had to fill with awakened and imploring "mourners." So after some fifteen minutes of ornamental discourse his voice grew loud, his form began to tremble, a pythonic rage dilated his eye, which seemed to behold the lost souls in their torment.

There were some scoffers just behind Wentworth who talked in half-whisper.

"You take your brimstone neat at this bar,—hey, Bill?"

"That's so. No hell-and-water here."

"He's been there and knows all about it."

"You ought to be ashamed of yourselves," said an excited woman to the young men; "you'd better be thinking of your poor perishing souls."

The preacher seemed to be conscious that he had a large mass of this contemptuous defiance before him. There was no word for the skeptic, none that implied the possibility of an intellectual doubt or negation; the preacher was concentrated upon the task of fanning the spark of fear or feeling in each soul till it caught fire, or rubbing the driest sticks of conscience till they burst into flame. His trained ingenuity sounded like the gust of inspiration. His arms now beat wildly, his face grew red, his heaving chest shot out agonized appeals. Suddenly from among the negroes a wild shriek was heard,—then another, a moaning yell. It only needed this signal: mingled shouts and cries broke forth behind the platform, and a large number were seized with convulsions—some rolling on the ground. Above these weird noises from behind him the preacher's voice climbed higher and higher, till the moanings began in front, among the whites. On he went, picturing the gay youth, the worldly girl, torn from the pious mother's arms to be cast into eternal billows of fire,—the father's cry for his beloved boy—in vain, in vain ! Into the burning lake they are plunged to be tossed forever and ever.

"Mercy! Mercy!"

"Oh, save me!"

The cries broke out here, there, as if arrows had sped at random and pierced hearts everywhere; one after another pale, terrified women—more rarely men—were led into the inclosure to kneel at the Mourners' Bench. As the orator's voice began to sink from exhaustion, preachers on the platform uttered exclamations—"Hallelujah!" "Praise the Lord! Another soul coming to the mercy-seat!" "Glory to God! Thirty souls seeking the Lord while he is near!" "Brethren, let us have that next bench for the pore sinners." Most of the preachers and several from the inclosure beneath them, now roamed through the crowd, bending to whisper persuasion wherever a down-dropped head or tearful eye was seen. Weeping women were entreating husbands or sons to go and be prayed for. Many were led forward, amid shouts of the already converted.

Most of the "mourners" were from the "poor white" class. then so-called; a few, however, were fashionably dressed, and over these the shouts were especially loud. Wentworth remarked the refined appearance of one girl, about fourteen years of age, led in by a coarse, red-faced man of middle age. Her face could not quite be seen—a handkerchief being held to her eyes—but the shapely figure and simple dress denoted a lady. Her approach to the altar excited much commotion; whispers went around, hundreds stood on benches to see her. Unusual importance was evidently attached to the surrender of this girl. But just then a young man dashed along the aisle, leaped like a leopard from bench to bench, rushed into the inclosure, parted the girl from her red-faced captor, whispered a word in her ear, and placing her hand in his arm led her away. The crowd made a path before the angry flash of his eye, but cries from the preachers followed him.

"There goes a soul dragged off to perdition!"

"God pity that pore soul!"

"It's hard for the rich to enter the kingdom!"

"Young man, you'll have to answer for her at the last day!"

Unheeding these wrathful cries the youth moved on, resolute and flushed, and disappeared from the grounds. The incident chilled the meeting and virtually ended it. The congregation broke up into groups; some followed the disappearing pair, others went to the tents and refreshment stalls; the orator's exciting pictures had been surpassed, and there were left only a few to pray and sing with the mourners. When Wentworth found the Mortons they were preparing dinner on the grass, and eagerly discussing the sensational scene. Some declared the youth was right, others that he was wrong. Wentworth listened with idle curiosity until a casually mentioned name smote his ear.

"Who were those two who made such a scene?" he asked of Julia Morton.

"Why, didn't you know? Penelope and Douglas Stirling."

## CHAPTER XXVI.

#### THE PALMS.

THE fine old mansion called The Palms was so named by its first owner, Bennett Randolph, after the paternal home of his wife in Louisiana. Madame Randolph, *neé* Regnault, justified the name of the home built for her in Virginia, though originating in sentiment, by nursing two palmettos of the hardy kind (*chamerops humilis*) in front of her door. Her children declared themselves jealous of these palms, which indeed were tucked in their coverlets as carefully as the rest of the family. But madame died a hundred years ago, and her palms followed her; the name only remained. Mrs. Richard Stirling had been her grand-daughter. Her husband, the judge, was descended from a gallant adherent of the Earl of Mar who had been among those imprisoned at Newgate while their chief was flying. At midnight he was taken out of prison by two men, carried to a ship in the Thames, given a thousand pounds, and warned that if he again set foot in that country he would be beheaded. Tradition explained that this young rebel was a natural son of the Duke of Argyle, against whom he fought. The next land seen by this exile, Douglas Stirling, was Virginia, where he bought piedmont lands from which his sons reaped fortunes.

It was about four of the Sunday afternoon when Wentworth tied his horse to the rack and walked up a long gravel path, fringed with flowers, to the door of The Palms. He was not without some trepidation lest he might obtrude upon a family scene, consequent on that at the Camp. The reverberant hammer of a huge brass knocker made him quake, but the face of a gentlemanly mulatto reassured him. The judge, he said, was not at home but he would see if his son was. Wentworth was ushered into a spacious parlor, richly supplied with old-fashioned furniture, and with portraits. In one of these he recognized the source of his friend's indescribable charm; it was the picture of a youthful lady in gauzy white drapery seated beneath an arch made by two palms. While waiting Wentworth heard voices from which he was separated only by folding-doors. Both of these voices were pleasant, but one was so rich, so cheerily sympathetic, that he was still as one who fears to frighten a bird of beautiful song.

"My poor Pen, how terrified you must have been to let that miserable Lawson hold your hand and take you among those people."

"I didn't know it was him; I never knew anything at all till Doug spoke, then I peeped up and saw the horrid man. If I'd dreamed it was him I'd 'a' took to my heels. My! wasn't I glad to get away!"

"But I can't understand your getting into it."

"Well, it was just awful the way that preacher preached. Doug left me a moment with Fanny Eden and the Wallers called Fanny off, and I hadn't any thing to do but listen, and oh—h, such things he said about Satan, and the burning lake of hot fiery brimstone, and all out of God's own Word ; and he said if I didn't believe it I was calling God a—oh, I wouldn't repeat it for any thing."

" Which shows you are better than he was ; he was talking of what he knows nothing."

" But he said almost the same as what Dr. Hunton read in the Lesson last Sunday ; only he was so anxious to make me feel it, and Dr. Hunton wasn't. He said the wicked shall be burned into hell and all the nations that forget God."

" You dear goosey, you are not a nation that forgets God."

" Yes, I am. You may laugh, Gisela, but I forgot God this morning when Fanny and I were saying where we were going to eat—she was to dine with the Wallers who were going to have ice-cream. I hadn't thought a bit about God until I saw that preacher watching me—yes, he looked right at me, and stretched out his hands to me, and said, 'O young and thoughtless girl, think how it will be when you are trying to reach your dear mother's arms in heaven to be dragged down by a mocking demon and plunged into burning hell! Turn, I beseech you, before it is too late ! Come to Jesus ! Close in with the overtures !' Gisela, what are ' overtures '? I thought you played 'em on pianos."

" My poor darling, I can't help laughing, but I'm sorry too; I should not have let you go to that Camp."

" He said it all straight at me—he cried so loud I thought his head would burst, he looked on fire, his arms seemed to reach over the people's heads and touch me, a chill shot down my back, I followed him, and then I waked up and found it was that horrid Lawson who used to sell whisky."

"I'm glad Douglas saw you before you knelt among those vulgar people."

"My! I *am* glad. But, Gisela, isn't it dreadful to roll in a sea just like melted lead forever and ever and ever?"

"My sweet good sister, do rid yourself of such foolish notions."

"But Dr. Hunton said one day——"

"No matter what any one says, such notions are false."

"Won't bad people be punished?"

"I suppose so, but we don't know how bad people are, or how much they ought to be punished. Jesus says they will go to prison but come out when their debt is paid; and Jesus who once paid the debts of sinful men can pay them again. The fire and brimstone spoken of in the Bible are metaphorical."

"Metawhat?"

"Metaphorical. That is they don't mean exactly what they say,—just as when you said the preacher looked on fire; you didn't mean he actually caught fire."

"Ah, I see,—that's what it means."

"That is what it means. And you mustn't think that you are forgetting God when you are not exactly thinking of him. Whenever you are doing your best in any thing you *are* thinking of him. You forget God only when you forget yourself, and do wrong, and that isn't often, dear Pen. So let this be your last worry of that kind, and don't believe every thing you hear from preachers. Good men are sometimes mistaken."

An exchange of kisses followed, and presently a third voice was audible.

"It's a gentleman I never saw before."

"Father will be back in an hour. I've made Douglas take a nap. I'll see the gentleman myself."

When the door opened Wentworth looked on the loveliest face he had ever seen. The tear-mist lingered on Gisela's eyelashes, and the laughter still played in her eyes. It was the dimpled mouth of infant innocency under a strong brow, upheld by a straight delicate nose; the ample cascades of auburn hair could not hide the wide forehead; the force in the face found its softening touches in the translucent skin, the rounded outlines, and the large candid eyes quick with intelligence and affection. The golden mean of nature was attained in this perfect form, less hid than expressed by the casual summer raiment investing her unconscious beauty.

"This must be Randolph's sister," he said, "I am his friend Wentworth."

"How glad, how glad I am that you have come! We feared the heat had made you migrate north, and pass us by."

The tears started to her eyes as she took his hand, for he revived thoughts of her wandering brother, and she turned quickly to throw open the folding-doors.

"Pen!" she cried, "Penelope, it is Mr. Wentworth!"

Flushed and sparkling Pen darted forward, then paused with a shy laugh, and Wentworth seized both of her hands.

"And this is Miss Penelope! of whom Randolph has talked a hundred,—no, a thousand times; but Miss Stirling mustn't be jealous, for he has talked of her a thousand and ten times."

"Run, Pen, and tell Douglas who is here."

"You'd better not disturb him." But Pen was gone.

"He'd disturb us if he wasn't told. Papa dined with a friend to-day, but will be here soon. Every day he wonders if you will come."

"I wrote from Richmond that I was on my way."

"We shall probably get the letter to-morrow, but the surprise is pleasant. There's Douglas."

The face which Wentworth had seen in the morning flashing wrath on the crowd around his sister, was now all sunshine.

"I'm glad to see you, sir. No man in the world, unless brother Randolph, could be welcomer here than you."

"And I am happy to be here. Have you heard from him lately?"

"I'm glad to say we have,—a short note to say he is well and happy."

"And we have received a more important one," said Gisela, "from an old friend of ours, a lady who knows his wife intimately, describing her as so lovely that we feel much easier about him."

"There's papa!" cried Penelope, darting out to the gate. All went to the hall to meet the judge, who greeted Wentworth with emotion. As the general conversation proceeded it became evident to the visitor that the judge's children had withheld from him what had occurred at the Camp, and he did not mention his presence there, while relating his adventures on the way, and delivering friendly messages from the Edens. After supper the judge, apologizing for his "selfishness," took Wentworth to his library, where the conversation soon turned on the subject uppermost in the thoughts of each.

"There," said the judge, pointing to a batch of letters yellow with age, "are some letters that passed between my great-grandfather and my grandfather. I had not read them for thirty years when I came across them last week. I remembered nothing very striking in them, but thirty years can give a man new eyes—as well as take away the old ones," he added, as he put on his spectacles.

"My grandfather," continued the judge, untying the letters, "was in Edinburgh studying medicine, and in his last term formed the acquaintance of a young lady to whom, in the free Virginian way, he paid a certain amount of attention, not intending any thing very serious. But gossips began to handle the lady's name injuriously on account of his visits, and this youth of twenty-one promptly proposes marriage and is accepted. He writes to his father about it; the old man protests; the son is determined; the father threatens to disown him; the youth maintains that his honor is involved as well as that of the young lady, claims a small inheritance once bequeathed to him, and in the end brings his young wife to Virginia,

His father saw and loved her. Poor thing! she died of her first confinement, the child also died, and nothing remains of her in our family but her name, Gisela, and the little romance recorded in these old letters. And now, Mr. Wentworth, it has all come round again—not all, either, I hope; for though Randolph has acted in the same spirit as his great-grandfather, I am thankful to say I never threatened to disown him. From that my faith in Randolph saved me. And now I have received a letter from a valued friend, a Mrs. Shelton of New York, saying that his wife is her intimate friend, and a woman we will all love."

"What was the name of Randolph's wife?"

"Emanuella Rhodes."

Wentworth had to search his memory a little, and then told the judge how Nuella had devoted herself to Randolph in his illness. He did not fail to make the most of her attractions, but he was full of wonder at this strange event.

There had been important consultations in the parlor on the subject of the visitor's entertainment, and next day, at breakfast, Gisela informed him that about midnight she had seen a ghost.

"A ghost!" cried Pen,—"Oh, do tell us, Gisela! I thought you didn't believe in ghosts."

"I didn't till last night, but after I had been in bed an hour—but I assure you perfectly awake—the door opened and a sheeted figure—it may have been a shroud or a nightgown——"

"I do declare, Gisela, you are too bad for any thing," said Pen, blushing and laughing.

"I assure you, Mr. Wentworth and Douglas, it is

perfectly true,—the white figure approached my bed, bent down—think what an awful moment!—and spake."

"What did it say?" cried Wentworth excitedly, "don't keep us in suspense!"

"You wicked, wicked sister!" said Pen, her hands tight over Gisela's mouth.

"The fi-fi-gure s-s-said, 'I know what to do, take him to the Tournament.' That's a warning, Mr. Wentworth."

"It was a good ghost," said he, "and I like her."

"How do you know that it was a *her*, Mr. Wentworth?" said Pen.

"A *him* wouldn't have been so considerate. If either of you know that ghost I would be obliged if you'd ask her to walk with me in the woods and show me wild flowers and things."

"Can't I?" asked Penelope.

"It ought to be that ghost that was so thoughtful for me."

"I reckon you'll have to take me," said Pen, "but Gisela was naughty."

Wentworth's walk with Pen, whom he found an accomplished naturalist in the butterfly-world, was the first of almost daily expeditions. His horseback excursions were with Gisela or Douglas. His first week at The Palms glided with hours too unconscious of their serenity to be recorded.

Blessed are the days that have no history! But these, alas, too often lead on the day to which the heart vainly cries, "Stay, thou art fair!" Around pretty, but somewhat sleepy, Warrenton there is no imposing scenery; it is a land of gentle slopes and languid rivulets, of deep woods, green lanes, and many flowers; a land of fair ladies, of whom one was fair enough to make our Bostonian write to a northern friend—" This is the most picturesque country I have ever seen." The words came from one wandering in an enchanted land, his brief southern life rounded with a dream.

## CHAPTER XXVII.

#### FAIR DAYS AND A FEARSOME NIGHT.

BUT dreams pass,—the happier the swifter. Wentworth realized it with a heavy heart when, after a fortnight of happy days, he awoke one morning with the vision of a beloved face receding from him and vanishing away. The great tender eyes which had kindled a new warm life in his soul might mislead the morn with their beautiful light, but they could not stay the advance of that stern day whose remorseless voice said, "Thy repose must end : the task of life is waiting."

Gisela also had her dreams; they were fair but haunted by the like stern presence which said, "Yes, he must go: resign yourself to the inevitable ; and remember, if by any appeal to this man's weakness— a word, a look—you withdraw him from the vocation that waits, you smite him to fruitlessness."

The main stem of friendship between Wentworth and the family at The Palms was grown before his arrival ; his presence had carried it to leaf and flower. Brief as his visit seemed, on that sad day that warned him it must end, the intimacy formed registered years instead of weeks. Penelope met him that morning with a shining face, and a copy of *The Flag* containing an announcement that the tournament at the Springs would take place in three weeks.

"Won't it be nice for us all to go! There's to be a masquerade in the evening. I know what I'd like to go as. Please beg Gisela to let me go!"

"Certainly you must go; but don't you remember the ghost? You'll have to go as a ghost."

"And what will you go as?"

"I think I'll have to be present as another ghost."

"What fun!"

In the afternoon all of them rode farther than usual, and they reached the Rappahannock, halting there in a grassy glade shaded by sycamores. There was visible only a small frame house, at the end of the riverside grove, to qualify the solitude.

"An old white witch lives in that cabin," said Gisela,—"a lucky witch, who casts on you the good instead of the evil eye. She makes her living by telling happy fortunes. Our swimming shore is near there, and she keeps our costumes."

Wentworth desired to visit this "Mother Collamer," and they found her at her door smoking—a shriveled crone in cotton gown.

"Come for yer fortens or a swim?" said the delighted old woman.

"Let's have our fortunes told," said Wentworth.

"I'll fetch the cards in a minute, Miss Gisela. I seed two of ye on them cards this blessed mornin'; ses I, thar's a pair a-comin' of pertickler luck. Come in!"

The interior of the cabin was surprisingly neat. The black cat—the regulation familiar of witches—met them with glassy eyes and leaped on Penelope's lap, whereon Gisela winked and nodded to Mother Collamer in a way to signify that Pen was their new friend's favorite. This rather confused the cards in their prognostications.

"Water's fusrate this arternoon," said Mother Collamer, "clean and wholesome, and yer purty gowns ready fur ye, ladies."

The bath was at first declined, but when they were all presently strolling beside the silvery river its erlking peered up at Gisela, and she could not resist his fascination. From childhood she had passionately loved the water, and equaled her brothers as a swimmer; now her soul, which had become feverish, cried for baptism in this pure flood. Douglas gave his costume to Wentworth, while for himself the witch had to conjure a dress out of her mysterious universe, —somewhat grotesque, but clean. Mother Collamer's house had two rooms for their preparations, and they soon had their swim. They had a grand match across the river and back, which Gisela won.

Another victory she might have won had it not been already hers. If there were coquetry in Gisela—and she did not come out of a pious tract—it was left behind when she entered the water. There the beautiful arms, embracing waves pure as her liquid eyes, the dimpled chin kissing dimples of the stream, the radiant face, were charmed from all self-consciousness; in ecstasy of a love as yet faintly dreaming, Gisela became part of the sunshine, and of the snowy cloudlets to which she looked up as they too floated in their azure depth; in that hour she was a self-forgetting child again, and Penelope appeared the elder. In this southern solitude Wentworth for the first time beheld in one maiden the form of Innocence and face of her sister, Freedom. No last shreds from monastic ages, no thought for past or future more than the lily is haunted by, clung to this naiad of the Rappahannock, on whom no eyes looked but those of purest love.

The sun was nearly set when they mounted their horses; a great flame overspread the West to light them home; the note of the whippoorwill was already heard. Wentworth and Gisela rode quietly, but the others dashed on ahead.

"We shall be late," said Wentworth.

"Fortunately I am an irresponsible creature about tea-time, and only looked for when I arrive."

"You are fortunate. My idea of happiness is to roam without any string tugging to pull me back at this time or that."

"I have snapped several such strings, and advise you to snap yours. The last I snapped was early tea. I haven't managed supper yet, for papa is woe-begone if we are not all at supper."

"I'm suffering a severe pull from my string just now."

"What is it?"

"I must leave and go to work."

Gisela was grave and silent. Several times she seemed about to speak, and Wentworth waited.

"Let's have a gallop!" she presently cried, at the same time touching her horse sharply with the whip.

It began as a canter, but Gisela again and again touched her horse, which became excited and dashed forward at full speed. At last a gate had to be entered and the freak ended. While Wentworth was holding open the gate for Gisela to ride through, a young man passed by on a fine horse, touched his hat to Gisela, cast a vexed look at her companion, and rode forward on a canter.

"It is George Pinwell," said Gisela, "son of a mill-owner."

"And your admirer."

"What made you think that?"

"He told me so as he passed."

"He didn't say a word."

"Except with his eyes."

"So you really think of leaving us?"

"Yes. It is a question of duty or pleasure, and pleasure must give way."

"Duty or pleasure. Those words have a sort of foreign sound to me. For me life divides itself into happiness and necessity. Happiness is my religion; necessity a dark unconscious demon which I propitiate. As for 'duty,' our departed parson made it mean every thing disagreeable, our poor Aunt Dabney made it out what other folks wanted us to do, whether we thought it wrong or right; between them they scratched the word out of my dictionary."

"May not Duty be better described as moral necessity,—what one is compelled to, not from without but from within?"

"You know we shall be sorry to part with you; you can not be mistaken about that; but a judge's daughter can understand the *noblesse oblige* of a professional man. Are you fond of the law?"

"I haven't had a case yet."

"Since I've grown old enough to be interested in papa's decisions I do not think quite so highly as once of the legal profession. Papa lately read me something about the ancient wager of combat out of which duelling arose; it was supposed that in the combat God would protect the right, but was abandoned because he did not seem to attend duels regularly. But now there is a wager of wits. It depends on a trial of wits between Mr. This and Mr. That whether Mr. The-other shall be strangled, or some baby's estate be devoured by a cormorant."

"One of these days we may have female lawyers, and then—"

"The legal devices will be more—more devicious than ever (a pun! I'll tell Doug that). Portia used to be my goddess, but I've lived to discover that her law was as bad as the sneak she pleaded for, and the fortune-hunter she married."

"If you are ever admitted to the Bar I hope you'll be my—that you will be on my side of every case."

"Ah, that will be far away in Boston. Well, you must go—I know that—and make your career among your people. That is both your necessity and happiness; things rarely one in this big world, though we sometimes unite them in our small sphere at The Palms."

As the conversation continued, this fair lady somehow appeared to Wentworth as one eluding him, or passing into reservations of thought and feeling where her personality was intrenched. The fortress might seem to be air, but to his touch it was adamant.

On the day following Judge Stirling requested an interview with his guest in his library.

"Mr. Wentworth," he said, "you are my elder son's friend. As we get older we use that word 'friend' more rarely. You are his friend. I feel certain you would be glad to do Randolph a service."

"You do me characteristic justice. Randolph is rarely absent from my thoughts, and it would be my happiness to serve him."

"It happens that he is far away, and his position here under a cloud, at a time when his interests require legal attention. A valuable property, bequeathed him on arrival at majority, has become involved in disputes, at certain points. Randolph's titles are clear to my own mind, but of course can not be decided on by his father. The case will come on in October. The papers are numerous and require careful sifting; there must be examinations in Fairfax clerk's office and elsewhere. Randolph is here only by power of attorney, which I can confer. There is no attorney at our Bar who could or would do for Randolph, even for the heavy sum he would require to act at all, what a friend can do for him, in conjunction with his father."

"You can not know," cried Wentworth, grasping the judge's hand, "what happiness you open before me. I fear I'm hardly sorry enough that Randolph's interests are questioned, so glad am I at the prospect of working for him, and of making myself useful to you and your family."

"It will bring you little money or glory."

"That makes me happier. To think that my first law-work should be for him!"

"Then it is agreed that you will work for us. If you have other affairs you had better look after them, for this work will not end till the middle of October."

"I am without parents, and have not begun practice. I live on an income left by my father. I need not leave this neighborhood. No doubt I can procure lodgings near you."

"Near me! you must live beneath this roof; your work must be in this room."

The old man rose up and walked to the window, where he stood for a few moments, looking as if at the sky; at length he came slowly back and stood before Wentworth, to whom he spoke in a low tone.

"You have no father,—take me!"

Never before had Wentworth been so moved; he managed presently to lift his eyes to the benignant face bent over him, to hold out his hand, and for the first time in his conscious life to say—father!

Wentworth would have uttered the word with yet deeper emotion had he known that, after he had retired the night before, another ghost had moved softly through the house, a more mature ghost than Penelope, and had whispered to the judge that his guest was about to leave.

"We should all be sorry; we have our summer schemes for his amusement; but he is not the man to remain unless it could be made a favor to you. Can't you get him to do something for you, papa? He's a lawyer, can't you find some documents requiring arrangement—or something?"

"Gisela, this man is stealing your heart."

"How preposterous, papa! I am only grateful to him for Randolph's sake. Why, I'm two years older than he is. I feel sure he has his love affair cut and dried long ago. Never fear! So long as my dear old dad lives, I live at his side."

"Well, child, I will tell you—to go no further—that there are some serious legal questions affecting Randolph's property about which I had resolved to consult his friend, and if he will remain he may render important assistance."

"Oh, papa, the very thing!"

A soft kiss, and the ghost vanished. Of this Wentworth never knew. On the other hand there were certain things Gisela did not know: for instance, her northern friend's eccentric views on the advantages of a wife being somewhat older than her husband. Had she known this she might not have been so free with their guest. Whatever feeling may have been in her secret heart she did not draw out for analysis: she arranged her theory of a right relation between Randolph's friend and herself with the possibility of marriage left out; had such contingency as his falling in love with her suggested itself, she would even have secured his departure. When it was arranged that he should remain, it was the natural outcome of her theory that she could harmlessly enjoy his friendship, even if she must pay the cost in sighs when he had gone.

"Now then you are our brother," she said, giving him her hand; "you take Randolph's room, attend to his affairs, adopt us, but without replacing him in our hearts—you bring him nearer. But remember, you are my younger brother—Randolph told us your age,—and elder sisters are tyrannical."

"I unhesitatingly submit," said Wentworth, with a courtly bow, kissing her hand.

"I declare!" exclaimed Pen, just entering; "if you oughtn't to do that at the Tournament ball, Gisela as Queen Elizabeth and you as Sir Walter Raleigh!"

"Excellent!" cried Gisela; "Pen, you shall go to the ball for saying that."

They chattered on, and when Douglas came in every thing was chattered over again. To crown their joy a letter came from Randolph, written in a cabin in Kansas, saying that he hoped to be within reach of a Christmas dinner at The Palms. When the judge brought in this letter Pen began to caper, and Wentworth seizing her waltzed until they were exhausted.

It may have occurred to the reader that the attention given by this abolitionist to the subject that brought him South had not been absorbing, during his stay at The Palms. The estate consisted of over a thousand acres, on which were nearly a hundred and fifty negroes,—considerably more than were needed, but Judge Stirling would not sell a negro. Wentworth had roamed a good deal about the farm—often with Pen, pet of the servants—had talked with them in the melon-patches, and eaten whitest heath-peaches selected by them; he had remarked their contentment, and understood why Randolph had resented accusations against slaveholders. His general views of slavery had not been consciously changed, but the subject was daily becoming more remote. His ideas of the method of dealing with the institution, with master and slave, had been affected more than he knew by residence on Leroy Island: his mental attitude had altered too; instead of dwelling on shades of the picture he was detecting its lights. One anti-slavery superstition of his had utterly perished,— that the negroes of the South, as a race, were pining for freedom. Judge Stirling, unwilling to part families or countenance slavedealers, had to feed and clothe many more negroes than could repay him by labor, and once Wentworth heard him say that if he should hear some morning that fifty had run away he should feel as if an estate had been left him.

One day a brother judge visited him at The Palms, and several eminent lawyers were invited to dinner, which was an hour later than usual and prepared with much care. Penelope was not present, and Gisela was the only lady at the table. The guests expressed satisfaction at meeting a member of the Boston Bar, and the conversation steered clear of the perilous issue between North and South until toward the close of the dinner. Gisela had taken care that no " fire-eaters " should be invited, but only old-school Virginians, whose sentiments concerning " slavery in the abstract " were inherited from Washington and Jefferson,—though they had developed a comfortable *modus vivendi* with the actual institution, and resisted all interference with it. Gisela was a little nervous when the subject was raised, and made an ineffectual attempt to give the conversation another turn. It proceeded affably enough, however, and Wentworth received from the head of the table a grateful glance for the tact he displayed. He hardly deserved it, for he felt but languid interest in the conversation, being held by the vision of that superb being in her faultless costume,—the grandly simple architecture of the woman, not cold enough to be classic but rather of mystical beauty. At length, at the close of the dinner, it became necessary for the Bostonian to say something on the subject.

"Yes, sir," said Judge Stirling, addressing the table through his brother judge, "we can not wonder that people exaggerate distant evils: northern people hear of a few instances of cruelty to negroes and multiply them a millionfold, whereas if they lived among us they would realize that such things are exceptional. My Boston friend here has just passed nearly a year in the South, and, though we have not conferred on the matter, I doubt if he has observed many instances of such inhumanity."

"I have witnessed few indeed," said Wentworth; "on the contrary I have seen enough kindness toward that race, and comfort among them, and enough justice among their masters, to modify my——"

"Papa and gentlemen, will you excuse me if I now retire?"

As Gisela suddenly rose with these words all present stood and bowed. Wentworth, whose words had been interrupted, looked straight at her and saw lightning in her eye; superb still, but coldly statuesque, her neck and shoulders turned to marble, she bowed and moved out of the room. What could have occurred? It was indeed a custom at The Palms for ladies to retire from the table, leaving gentlemen to enjoy their coffee and cigars, but Gisela had gone prematurely, and while a guest was speaking. Wentworth cast a sharp glance at the gentlemen who had sat next her, having a suspicion that one of them had taken too much wine and forgotten himself.

When the guests were leaving, Gisela, now with Pen at her side, parted from them in the parlor. She was still pale and worried. When all had gone Wentworth expressed a fear that she was not feeling well; but she only answered. "Forgive me, I can not speak now," and with a strange look—was it pity or anger, or both?—she passed wearily out of the room and did not appear during the evening.

A weight was on Wentworth's heart; a dull incomprehensible care sat beside him through the evening, and lay beside him on his bed. He ascribed his sleeplessness to the heat, but his pain warned him it was not that.

Was it in a dream? He thought he heard a low knock at his door. It was past midnight; he had been the last to retire and could not imagine that any other in the house was awake. Gisela might be ill—in danger! He sat up in bed and listened, breathlessly. The knock came again, gentle but unmistakable; it sounded as if requesting quietness, and he stepped softly to the door, opened it a little way and peered out. It was Gisela,—her eyes red with weeping and expanding with painful agitation.

"Put on clothes," she whispered, "but no shoes. Take this candle. I will wait for you."

Wentworth quickly reappeared, and Gisela, barefoot, moved softly before him along the corridor, down little flights of steps and up others, without uttering a word, until she reached her own room. She noiselessly opened the door and closed it after they had entered.

"You said you had not witnessed the cruelties of slavery—look there!"

She pointed with one hand, holding forward the candle with the other, and Wentworth saw on the floor what at first seemed a heap of clothing; but as he gazed a head was raised from the dusky mass, a young and handsome but now haggard quadroon face was uplifted, and large plaintive eyes stared wonderingly at him.

"Look there!" said Gisela, her bare arm pointing like that of an avenger; "you may see what you have not seen—slavery. There are no polite gentlemen here to hoodwink you: look! It is no worse than what these eyes have seen many a time. That woman, Alice Ross, has some education, I taught her myself —in secret, because it is unlawful: she has a heart; she was married a few months ago to a man she loves as much as your Boston girl can love; he and she are to be sold at the Woodward auction to-morrow, and parted forever."

The poor woman began to sob, and Wentworth gazed on her; then he looked up to Gisela, whose eyes were fixed upon him—in them, visible through her tears, pity and anger.

"Can nothing be done to stop this business?" he asked.

"Nothing. I only brought you to see one of the victims you are deserting. I could only weep for your weakness, but God has rebuked it. I lay sleepless with sorrow that a man should bend from his cause ; and that woman was groping through the dark woods by midnight, and called beneath my window. I am her only friend. Now that you have seen her you can return to your repose."

"I accept your reproach and scorn," said Wentworth, utterly humiliated, "but I am not worth a minute's notice in the presence of this woman's distress. I will go."

He bowed low, his face on fire, but when, at the door, he turned a last look on the two women, he was pale as death. That piteous look of his smote Gisela with a horror at what she had done which for a moment paralyzed her. She presently followed him hurriedly, but it was too late. She could only pause before his door—the commonplace wooden door—and reflect what forces must be locking it fast, for her to return without rushing in to shed her fast-falling tears at the feet of the man she had so cruelly treated.

Gisela sat for a few moments on a step in the corridor, then returned to her room, where for some time she was occupied in making up a bundle of clothing for Alice. The day was faintly breaking when, with a last kiss, she parted with her humble friend at the kitchen door, and watched till, with a despairing wave of the hand, she blended with shadows.

## CHAPTER XXVIII.

**A GOOD DEED SHINES FAR IN A NAUGHTY WORLD.**

BEHIND a barn, which supplied shade for a "shady" scene, a score of men gathered to bid for the human stock of the Woodward estate, in chancery for payment of its late owner's debts. These bidders were not southern gentry, but its agents, its left hand doing sinister work which its fair right must not know. The company looked askance at one man who joined them; he was not of them or known to them.

The silent trembling chattels were successively sold, at prices ranging from five hundred to a thousand dollars—until Alice Ross was brought forward. She did not look her best, being haggard from causes known to but one of the company. The bidding languidly reached six hundred and there stopped.

"A fine healthy young woman, gentlemen—a little peeky just now but worth a good deal more than is bid. Speak up, gentlemen! Six hundred bid."

"And ten," said the stranger, bringing all eyes on him.

"Twenty."

"Thirty."

"Forty."

There were whispers and murmurs among the

dealers. Angry glances were cast at the interloper, who perceived that they were not competitors, but a ring for dividing the negroes among them at pre-arranged prices. He had to fight a combination, and the bidding for Alice mounted to a thousand. This was the stranger's bid, and then the dealers began to sneer.

"A thousand and ten."

"What are you a-bidding for, Snellings, when a gent's got his eye on a fancy lot?"

"Ha-ha, he-he!"

"And twenty."

"And thirty," cried a bidder angrily.

"There's Bob now. Don't interfere with the course o' true love, Bob!"

"Mr. Auctioneer," said the stranger, "I desire to make my bids without remark. If not, I can only leave, and report to the court that the sale was not fair."

"Quite right, sir! Gentlemen, I must insist that no offensive—"

"Who is the fellow, anyhow?" cried an enraged bidder.

"None of your business, Mr. Sands!" shouted the frightened auctioneer, "and if you can't behave you can go!"

The bidding now proceeded quietly, the dealers making their bids spitefully, till the stranger made a bid of thirteen hundred and turned to go. A bidder had added "and twenty," but when the previous bidder still moved away he became alarmed.

"Are you all done, gentlemen? Once—twice—"

"Stop! I take back my last bid—the man may have her."

"Can't be done, Mr. Crupps, you've bid and must stand to it. Once—twice—"

"I'll take the bid off Mr. Crupps's hands if he wants," said the stranger.

"Then it's your bid, sir. Is any more bid for this lot? Going—once—twice—thrice—gone!"

After the sale of Alice, the dealers got off a little way and held an excited consultation, causing some delay.

"Gentlemen," called the auctioneer loudly,—"let me have your attention, if you please! I have to announce that the next lot, 97 in the catalogue, is withdrawn. There was some question about the man's ownership by the estate, and it was agreed he should pass by private arrangement to Mrs. Woodward's brother, Colonel Lewis, of Harper's Ferry. So we'll now take lot 98."

Alas, the omitted "lot" was Darnley Ross. After all Wentworth had not saved poor Alice's husband. He waited till the sale ended, paid for his purchase with a check on the Warrenton Bank, and started out to prepare his buggy. As he did so, he observed the man Crupps, who had withdrawn his bid, talking excitedly with another, whose face he remembered—George Pinwell. When presently alone with Alice she informed him that she had friends with whom she could stay for a time,—Uncle Josh Williams and his wife, belonging to Judge Stirling and living at a remote part of the estate, to which she could direct him. They had driven a few hundred yards when

Mr. Crupps stepped out of some bushes and asked for a few words.

"I'm sorry I let that bid go now," he said with a smirk, "and wouldn't mind giving you twenty or thirty dollars for your bargain. Fact is, there's a gent considibly set on getting the gal, and—"

"He'll not get her," said Wentworth, with a vicious lash on his horse.

Alice said her husband had been taken to Harper's Ferry the night before without her seeing him. Wentworth consoled her with a promise that she should follow him to that neighborhood.

"I didn't know there was but one angel in the world," said Alice, "but now I know there's two."

"There's but one, my girl, and that is the lady we saw last night."

Uncle Josh Williams—who with his family received their friend Alice with great delight,—after consultation about Darnley, drove with Wentworth to see a free negro, who, he said, could discover any thing about distant negroes. This was Caleb Stone,—squatter on a bit of 'No-man's-land,'—who was instructed to learn whether the new owner of Darnley would part with him, or, if not, whether a place could be found near him for his wife; who would be given freedom and a few hundred dollars. Having advised caution and given the men money, Wentworth left them too much dazed to thank this providence which had surprised them, and drove his buggy back to its livery-stable in Warrenton.

Meanwhile consternation had prevailed at The Palms. Gisela, having over-slept the breakfast hour, hastened to the library with her carefully prepared apology, only to find her father mystified by Wentworth's non-appearance at his urgent work. When he did not return for dinner, wildest fears took possession of her. He had apparently taken nothing from his room, and had gone off after a hurried breakfast without speaking to any one. Gisela watched at her window through the long, long afternoon; and when, at dusk, she saw him walk in at the front gate, hastened to his room and awaited him there. With confused look and agitated voice she began her petition for forgiveness, but when he took her hand and said: "I have bought Alice," she sank on her knees, silently clasping his hand, which was wet with her tears.

Caleb's negro-telegraph soon brought tidings that Darnley's master would not sell him—"there's some of the family blood in the boy,"—that he had a good home, that Alice could find a residence at Harper's Ferry by calling on a free negro named Dory Curtis. Darnley, it was added, was in great joy about the news from his wife, and prayed God's blessing on the gentleman and Miss Gisela. He hoped to thank them in heaven if he never had a chance to do it in this world. Some days later, Alice, with well-filled trunk and money enough to make her feel like a princess, was on her way to Harper's Ferry, with a pass from her purchaser.

This matter happily settled, the young people at The Palms gave their attention to preparation for the festivities at Fauquier Springs. For some time, indeed, quaint pieces of brocade and other relics of grand-maternal finery had been visible about the house, and one day Wentworth found a Walter Raleigh suit in his room, beside an ordinary one, which had disappeared for a time from his wardrobe. Rooms had been engaged for them at the Sulphur Springs Hotel, and a more cheerful party could not be imagined than the four who drove from The Palms on the eve of Tournament-day. Pen darted about like quicksilver, till Douglas threatened to put her with the driver. He was answered with a hug and kiss; then she kissed Gisela, and when Wentworth wept bitterly because he wasn't kissed, called him her " poor 'ittle darling—he sall have a kiss "—while Gisela cried " Oh, shocking," and hid her face. Then they stopped for Wentworth and Pen to gather chinquepins, and farewell-to-summer, or other flowers. Pen was standing up in the open carriage and twining Wentworth's hat with flowers, when two men on horseback made way for the carriage, after passing whom the Stirlings broke into laughter. One was a colporteur and had thrown some tracts into the carriage, the other was red-faced Mr. Lawson who had once led Pen to the Mourners' Bench. Wentworth pretended to be mystified by the laughter and Pen's blushes; but when presently the others got out for pawpaws he confided to Gisela his knowledge of the Camp-meeting scene.

On occasion of its midsummer festival the Fauquier resort was very gay. The hotel dinners and suppers were banquets. The companies promenading along the colonnade, or distributing themselves through the embowered walks in front, made a fairylike scene under glimpses of the moon through a canopy of foliage. Pen was the first to grow somnolent, but she found a bat in her bedroom, which Wentworth and Douglas were both required to expel. When Wentworth was returning from this exploit to the veranda, where he had left Gisela alone, he saw a gentleman beside her. The two were at the end of the veranda, where it was rather dark, and Wentworth loitered. He did not recognize Gisela's companion till he suddenly left her and presently passed him with an angry scowl. He saw that it was George Pinwell, pallid and furious, and a certain sympathy shot from his heart to the poor fellow who was leaving such a prize as Gisela. Had he answered the scowl at the moment it would have been to say—" we are in the same sinking boat, so let us not quarrel." For Wentworth now felt certain that Gisela could never be his wife; she had built up her whole relation with him on a different basis; she was elder-sisterly at times, at others a child at his knee, but always so free in his presence, so businesslike, so careless of the impression she might make, that the possibility of any nearer relation between them had plainly never entered her mind.

"Poor fellow," said Wentworth, resuming his seat beside Gisela.

"Did you kill him?" she asked calmly—it was too dark for her expression to be seen.

"Kill him! why do you jest?"

"I didn't know you had so much sensibility."

"Yes, I have. Any man in love moves my sympathy."

"Gracious! who are you talking about?"

"Mr. Pinwell."

"Oh dear, I was thinking about the bat!"

Having received satisfactory assurance that she and Pen were secure from bats for the night, Gisela asked Wentworth the cause of his compassion for Mr. Pinwell.

"He loves you and you do not love him," said Wentworth.

"You do not know him; he would like to put a brass collar round my neck with his name in full on it, he would like to use our connexion to rise higher in society than the Pinwells soar; but he is incapable of love, because inherently mean. Your girl, Alice Ross, could tell you a story about him which would prevent your ever associating his name with mine."

"Our connexion!" The words were proud, and Wentworth's heart trembled. Had not the half-darkness veiled her expression he might have recognized that infinite contempt for Pinwell's motives was consistent with utmost humility. In fact, Gisela's fault was deficiency of self-esteem. Before Wentworth, to whom she knelt when he bought Alice Ross, she remained kneeling; had she seen into his heart as they now sat on the veranda she might have felt some pain at finding a lover in place of a demigod.

"Associating his name with mine!" These too were proud words, and Wentworth's heart sank; but it was with self-reproach. He remembered that he had seen Pinwell with Crupps just before that slave-dealer had tried to buy Alice from him for "a gent set on getting the gal," the brutality of the offer in the girl's presence having angered him. He did not know, however, that Pinwell had dogged his buggy that day until he saw him enter the house of a free negro suspected of connivance with escaping slaves. Another thing Wentworth did not know—that jealous rage had just impelled Pinwell to inform Gisela that he had seen her " Boston friend" driving about the country with a pretty colored girl; being thereupon ordered by the lady to leave her instantly and never dare approach her again. The dusk had enabled Gisela to conceal her agitation and meet Wentworth after the bat exploit in the merry vein that sounded inconsiderate. But even in the darkness he saw the flash of her eye as she uttered those final words. An oppressive silence followed. He felt that the incident had removed Gisela further from him. He had, in thought, associated her with a base fellow; it was an indignity from which, she must feel, a fine instinct would have saved her. He longed to do her justice—and himself.

"Gisela," he said, "your life with such a father, and such brothers, has raised your standard of male humanity so high that other mortals toil after it in vain."

"I am not conscious of it; but whatever my standard, it matters little to Fauquier mortals. Douglas would fight any man under sixty who came too close to us, and my affections are lavished on the grandfathers of the neighborhood."

"What! Do you mean you never had a lover?"

"Walter, the dim moonshine invites confidences sometimes, but at others, as Bottom found, it causes an exposition of sleep, and makes one a donkey: that is my case now; I am yawning, and shall presently bray."

"Gisela, I never contradict a lady, but you were never wider awake in your life."

"Oh-ah-h. What was that last remark? I was just dozing off."

"Actress!"

"Sweet dreams, Walter!" she cried, leaping up with a burst of laughter.

Gone! A moonlit cloudlet of white, with infantine face laughing through it, flitted to the nearest of the little porches bordering the grounds, and vanished, leaving the puzzled youth alone with the waning light, the dreamy nocturne of the frogs, and unanswered *who* of an owl. He wandered beneath the trees till the last window of the hotel was darkened, then passed to his room. "I can not sleep," he said, but listened to the serenade of a whippoorwill, and sank into slumber so profound that breakfast gongs failed to break it. At nine he ate the remnants of a past meal with sauce of suggestions from Pen, abetted by Gisela, that he should appear at the ball as one of the Seven Sleepers.

The Tournament, despite an occasional tendency to the grotesque, was a brilliant scene. The young men rode fine horses, tilted at ring pendent over grassy lane, and when successful bowed with pride before the queen and her court on platform of purple and gold. The victorious Ivanhoe of the occasion was no other than George Pinwell, who was crowned amid acclamations by the queen—a stately belle fron Staunton. This conquering hero was escorted to the hotel in grand procession of knights and ladies, and the rest of the afternoon was given up to the promenade, and the strains of a military band.

The grounds were brilliantly lighted for the *fête* of the evening; arches of many-colored lanterns stretched between the trees and the hotel columns. The lower rooms were decorated and thrown open for the dance. All their picturesque characters had stepped from the pages of Scott and Byron. Douglas was a Corsair, Penelope a piquant Pocahontas. When Gisela, as a naiad, her white dress shimmering with silver threads, entered the room leaning on the arm of Sir Walter Raleigh in his courtly velvet, the noisy room became still. Two handsomer figures never appeared even at the Springs, so famous for summer beaux and beauties. They stopped to greet the Edens, and Wentworth was introduced to several agreeable ladies with them. His intimacy with the great family of Stirlings, fabulous rumors of his wealth, his fine looks and manners, made Wentworth a lion,—not to the entire satisfaction of all gallant Southrons present, and, as we may easily guess, decidedly to the dissatisfaction of victorious Ivanhoe. Gisela danced with many gentlemen, and evidently enjoyed her dances,—floating in the waltz as if her naiad dress were again in eddies of the Rappahannock. She was swiftly surrounded by admirers. A "rising young professor" from Charlotteville was "devoted," and managed to secure two dances and a promenade in the portico with her. Sir Walter had then only got one, and consoled himself by galloping with Pocahontas till he was exhausted, and wondered she wasn't.

"I only get tired standing still," said Pocahontas,

—"but I do wish somebody would be about to kill somebody with a tomahawk, so that I could save him."

"Well, whom shall I kill?" asked Sir Walter.

"Not him," said Pen, indignantly, as Pinwell passed—"I wouldn't save *him*."

"What have you against him?"

"I never could bear him, and I just now heard him say something horrid about—somebody I—know. He didn't know I was behind him. After that he had the impudence to ask me to dance."

The masquerade meant to last through the night. Conspiring mammas and chaperons understood it, and slipped off for naps, watching each other's charges by relays. At about one o'clock Sir Walter had a glorious waltz with the naiad, after which they strolled out under the starlight, for the moon had gone down and the lanterns were flickering into extinction. They strolled as far as the great stone basin in which the fountain splashes, and seated themselves there.

"You have been happy to-night, Gisela."

"Perfectly. I am happy. Are not you?"

"I haven't inquired of myself yet."

"I've had several things to make me happy—I've met people I'm interested in, I love to dance, and— but no matter for more."

"Tell me the third thing,—that's the postscript, always the best part."

"If you will have it, I was glad to have these Southern gentlemen meet a gentleman from the North, and understand—that's all. I'm glad to have you meet some of our best people. What do you think of the costumes? Isn't Pen beautiful?"

"Indeed she is, and she has danced me like an elf. A good many costumes are beautiful,—Fair Rosamond's, Rowena's, the Maid of Orleans, a dozen others."

"And not a word for the poor naiad!"

"I heard hers admired on all sides, but I remember her in a more beautiful costume."

"And pray when and where was that?"

"Once, near this hour, on a sacred night."

"What did naiad have on then?"

"I don't know. Her character was, a Madonna."

"What a memory you've got! Now, I'm cultivating a faculty for forgetting things, still I can't forget my frantic behavior and injustice the night poor Alice came, though I have never asked your forgiveness."

"You were right, and needed no forgiveness. I was not perhaps so yielding to those gentlemen at the table as my tone implied, but I might have given way before this if you had not—sprung to my side. It had begun to seem so unimportant to any human being what I might think or say, especially down here among men doing their best, that my conscience was getting silent. Then another conscience rose to remind me of my duty."

"Duty—Boston word for happiness, I suppose. I never saw a happier man than you when you sent to Harper's Ferry two thousand dollars to be seen no more."

"It would be obtaining credit on false pretenses to let you suppose my happiness came only from helping those negroes. I might have done that in any case, but my chief happiness came otherwise."

There was something ominous in these slow words and low tones; Gisela became uneasy; she went to the fountain, drank a mouthful of the water, and stood there a moment, then glanced toward the hotel.

"You do not ask what caused my happiness," said Wentworth, "but I will try and tell you—it isn't easy."

"It's never easy to analyze our happiness," said Gisela, catching at a straw, and ran on volubly—"so many things enter into it—a mood, a bit of news, a friend's smile, a—"

"That's it—a friend's smile. I lost a friend's smile one day and it returned the next. It gave me happiness; and my heart whispered—what if that smile were always on you!"

"How beautifully this water flows in the soft starlight! Listen—it is musical too. But Pen will need me."

"She is not the only one that needs you."

"How a half-light transfigures things! That Hygeia is poor plaster by day, but now she is ideal; to-morrow she will be mere plaster again."

"Then it were a pity the day should dawn."

"But it must dawn, and the goddess be commonplace again. Glamour would be sweet if it could last; but it fades, and only the hard reality remains. Come!"

"No, Gisela, stay with me and bear with me."

"I have engagements to dance, and really must go."

"Not till you have decided where I am to go in this world, and for life. Gisela, you once saved me—"

"Walter, I mean to save you now. Please take me to the hotel."

"What can you mean, Gisela? There is but one

word that can save me, and you must speak it. Dear Gisela, you have my whole heart; say only—take my hand for life!"

Gisela sank on the stone seat, and sat still as if a carven part of it, her face bent and hidden in her hands. Wentworth tried to take one of her hands, but she shook her head, and a great sob came from her heart.

"O my friend," she said at last, laying her hand on his shoulder, "how fearful is all this! My true and dear friend, what a heavy wrong have I done you!"

"No wrong, Gisela, but every good except the last and greatest; now complete your work. Gisela—take me to your heart forever!"

"O Walter! There are mountains between us. I know you—I see your future—a leader among your people, by your side the wife now waiting for you in that great world. Hasten away—to-morrow. What! tie yourself to an old woman, in this little corner of the world which she can not leave! It is out of the question. Oh, this is terrible!"

Gisela threw up her arms as if bewildered, and trembled violently. Wentworth placed his arm around her and pressed her head on his shoulder.

"My own, my love, I do not know the cause of this grief," he said, as he stroked her hair.

"I have done you great wrong," she said, starting to her feet—"I ought to have persuaded you to leave us instead of contriving to keep you. Now I must strike the best heart that ever beat. It will not do. My age—my father whom I can not leave—your career—think!"

"Gisela, you say you are the older. A year or two perhaps. It is but a superstition that the wife must be the younger. Your father? He is mine—the only one I have—and I do not mean to part from him. You reason against me, but there is only one reason which can send me from you. If you can not return my love, I am hereafter dumb."

Gisela tried to answer, but silently sank again on the stone seat and clutched it as if about to fall.

"Say it now, Gisela, if my sentence must come—I will wait till day-break. If you can not love me—and I know I am not worthy of it—I will strive no more."

"Be strong, Walter—and let all this be as a dream."

"A dream indeed, if my love is unanswered. But is that so? Something is making me bold. Is it truly so?"

"Ah, if I were only dead! But I am determined—I say no!"

"Because you have no love, Gisela?"

A burst of tears was Gisela's answer.

"Yes!" cried Wentworth, "I am loved by the woman I love, and nothing shall part her from me. Now you may struggle, but it is from love, and in vain. If there be any mountain between us I will wear it down if it take many years. But it shall be done. You see I am calm, Gisela. This is no sudden passion."

"You are trying to put on a chain."

"No—I am gaining a wing. It has lifted me over the mire before this, and I hold on to it."

Wentworth with a great passionate power clasped

her in his arms and kissed her again and again; she struggled a little, then her head lay still on his breast, and he heard the low tones of a prayer.

There was a silence in that seclusion as if the surrounding world had ceased to exist, though they might have heard the music and dance at the end of the grove had not diviner harmonies held them. But presently a closer sound startled Gisela, and she leaned forward. There were approaching steps, and low voices—distinguishable as three when they came near. The speakers were close to the basin of the fountain.

"The mere fact that a man's a Yankee is not enough, Pinwell, unless he says or does something against us."

"I tell you I watched him, and saw him enter Caleb's house with a nigger."

"That does look suspicious, fellows."

"What I say is this; just get him by himself and tell him he's got to leave this state."

"That's easy to say, Pinwell, but suppose he won't."

"I know he will, if he thinks he may get the Stirlings into trouble."

"That shows, Pinwell, that you think he's a gentleman."

"There's reason why he ought to like the Stirlings, he's living on them."

"But they say he's rich."

"The fact is, fellows, you must excuse me. I can't see that the man's done any harm, and to tell the truth, Pinwell, I'm afraid you are thinking more about Miss Gisela than southern rights."

"I feel the same way, Pinwell. The man might have been talking to the negroes about fishing or shooting. I'm off."

"Damn him, I'll tackle him myself."

This was Pinwell's soliloquy, as the others walked off. Wentworth listened until his enemy also moved away, muttering oaths, then laughed aloud; but Gisela said "hush," and was in more anxiety than she cared to express. She was silent on their way to the hotel, and felt that Pinwell's eyes were watching them,—her shining dress could be seen from the furthest covert. They entered the ball-room just in time for a Sir Roger, and the masquerade came to an end.

"Where is Walter?" asked Gisela, as she entered the breakfast-room next morning, where she found Douglas and Pen.

"I don't know," answered both.

"Douglas, please go and find him—now, without finishing breakfast—and," she added, in his ear, "whatever you do, keep near him all the time till we leave this afternoon. I'll tell you why when you come back—it's important."

Douglas walked over towards the fountain, and quickened his steps when he saw Wentworth confronting Pinwell and two others. As he was approaching he saw there was a quarrel.

"I am ready to give account of myself to any gentleman who has a right to ask it," said Wentworth, "but have nothing to say to this ill-bred spy——"

At this Pinwell struck Wentworth, who, with a swift blow, sent his antagonist reeling against a tree. Douglas reached the spot just in time to catch Pinwell's hand as it was drawing a pistol.

"No, you don't—no murder!" cried Douglas, firing the pistol in the air, and so drawing a number of people to the spot, while Pinwell's two comrades slipped off.

"Damn you and your abolition friends," cried Pinwell, "you and your brother are no better."

"Stop, George Pinwell! if you say another word about my brother I'll thrash you right off—you sneak!"

"Well, you're two against one, but I'm ready for you."

"Clear out, you cur!" said Douglas, taking Wentworth's arm and turning toward the hotel.

So ended the Pinwell incident. He and his two companions—strangers to Douglas—disappeared from the Springs before dinner, and Wentworth never saw Pinwell again. Gisela and Pen knew nothing of what had occurred until, as they were about to start for The Palms, a young man, whose voice Gisela had recognized as that of an acquaintance when he repudiated Pinwell at the fountain, came to the carriage and asked to be introduced to her friend.

"Mr. Burroughs, Mr. Wentworth."

"I congratulate you, sir, on having given the conquering hero a lesson he needed. I hope you'll not believe many southerners capable of assassination. The feeling about here is entirely with you, and the fellow has had to run."

Wentworth answered graciously, and took off his hat to the company in the veranda, who all bowed smilingly as the carriage drove off. Gisela was aghast, Pen bewildered, at what they had heard. The whole story had to come out when they were on the road, and Gisela, forgetting herself, put her arm round her lover and leaned her head on his shoulder. To Pen this seemed so natural that she did the like, her tears streaming. Poor Douglas was blushing for his sisters' exceeding affectionateness, when Gisela caught sight of his face and burst into a laugh.

"Dear Doug doesn't know what to make of us; give your old sister a kiss, boy, and say who you'd like best for a new brother!"

"Gisela, are you daft?"

"Quite, Doug."

"She's only daft enough to become my wife."

A tremendous crack of a whip in the air reminded these demoralized travelers that they had a negro driver; a scream from Penelope, who seemed to be fainting, happily gave them something to do.

"Are you going away?" cried the child, throwing her arms around her sister's neck with a burst of tears.

"She'll never part from you, dear Pen, nor I either," said Wentworth, who was rewarded with kisses so soon as the little mouth could straighten again. Douglas grasped Wentworth's hand, in evident agitation.

In the evening Wentworth was giving reassurances to the father, declaring that they would never part from him.

The venerable face grew pale, but the just judge answered, albeit with quivering lip.

"Gisela is near to my heart, but she will forsake all others and cleave to her husband when that is the right thing to be done. You and I know what a heart you have found, my son: there is only one man on earth to whom I would yield her with joy. He now has her. I would say to her, where he goes go you! though my life departed with her."

For some days the judge was caressed by Gisela and charmed by her confidences from his feeling of loneliness. Douglas too required comforting treatment. Wentworth was unremitting in affectionate attentions to father and son; he made Douglas go with him to Prince William Court-house and to Fairfax, where records had to be examined in Randolph's interest, and their friendship gained daily in depth and fullness.

How wonderfully a happy man can work! Wentworth seemed always to have leisure enough; he could ride with Gisela, capture butterflies with Pen, shoot wild turkeys with Douglas, play whist with the judge; but, the while, masses of documents were digested, a ream of paper covered with notes, and, six weeks after the excursion to the Springs, a clear statement by this Boston lawyer in the Fauquier court secured all the claims of Randolph Stirling. The Palms now needed but the return of the wandering son and his bride to complete the happiness of its circle. This was promised. Another note came saying they had started on their eastward journey, and hoped, on reaching Washington, to learn that no trouble need be apprehended if they should come to The Palms.

About this time occurred that event at Harper's Ferry which shook Virginia like an earthquake, and was felt throughout the land. Wild rumors spread through the neighboring counties, in which white invasions and black insurrections were confused, and the panic was universal. When the raid on Harper's Ferry occurred Wentworth was on a visit to Boston; this was perhaps fortunate, for the Pinwell element in most southern towns was raised to the surface by that tempest, and a Yankee in Warrenton streets might have proved a tempting victim for the sins of his section. At any rate Douglas returned from town one day much excited by something he had heard; also Uncle Josh Williams reported to Gisela that he and Caleb Stone had been questioned by a small company of men, including Pinwell, as to the subject of Wentworth's interview with them in the early summer. Under menaces the negroes had confessed that the gentleman wanted Caleb to tell him the whole story of his mother's ghost which appeared the fourth of July and told Caleb she died of poison in Tennessee. It would not have done to mention Harper's Ferry, where Alice had gone.

Wentworth suspected something of this when he received in Boston a letter from Gisela more cheerful than usual about his absence, and expressing the hope that he would accept an invitation, of which he had written, to visit the Minotts. But little did any of these happy young people imagine that amid the stormy events of that time a special thunderbolt was making its way toward them, under their rosy sky, where all the morning stars were singing.

# CHAPTER XXIX.

### INTO THE JAWS OF DEATH.

IN a small room at Tabor—whose only furniture was a stove, a cot, and a pine table on which lay a large map of Virginia—Captain Brown (*alias* Gideon), sat in eager conversation with Randolph Stirling through the small hours of night. A purpose had formed in the captain's mind for which co-operation of a Virginian were worth more than an army corps; for indeed this puritan wool-grower turned warrior, what time the dew of a mission to smite slaveholding Midianites settled on his fleece, heard his heavenly Man of War warn him against too many soldiers, lest Freedom should vaunt itself, and say, Mine own hand hath saved me. He wanted a few only, but above all he desired a Virginian: he had never met with another man from that state so friendly to freedom as Stirling, and with characteristic superstition leaped to the conclusion that here was his heaven-sent Purah, his spy, to help him discover the secrets of the spoilers. This belief led him to speak with Stirling about the mountains of Virginia, declaring that they had been built by Jehovah to be the refuge and fastness of a race defending its freedom. It needed only that trumpet should answer trumpet along those heights, for all the oppressed to flee to the mountains and find the shield of Almighty God about them. Stirling had lost his early faith in slavery; he felt strong sympathy with fugitives from oppression; but he recognized in Brown's notions, so far as he could think what he was driving at, not only fanaticism but a great and dangerous fallacy, namely, that the slaves were a race groaning for liberty. The slaves, he urged, are now evangelized; they believe in the command " servants obey your masters," and that they will offend God by disobeying it ; they dread the northern climate; too many of them have comfortable homes to seek uncertainties elsewhere.

"What is a comfortable home without the God-given right to freedom !" cried the captain.

" But they do not find it God-given, and have long been taught to resign themselves to affliction for the greater glory hereafter. But whatever their motives, I am convinced, by long intimacy with that race, that the fugitives fly from special hardships, and that the majority would stay where they are even if you could open the gates of liberty before them—as you can not."

" Young man, is there a God? His arm will be laid bare. And when you shall see it, will you stand on his side? Should I be able some day to show you these oppressed people you think so contented coming by thousands from the house of bondage, would you then stand at my side to help them ?"

" Wherever I shall see man or woman whom I can save from wrong and suffering I trust my help will not be found wanting."

" Young man, for the moment your eyes are held in

some things, but I feel that the Lord of Hosts has an appointed work for you, because of which he has opened your eyes to the evils of slavery, though you were born in the house of the taskmaster. Before long I may remind you of your promise to help those fleeing from oppression, and call on you to see the salvation of God."

With this the Captain gave the mystified Virginian his hand, cast on him a strange sorrowful look, and gave him an envelope containing directions for a journey into Kansas with letters of introduction to one or two friends there. For on the arrival at Tabor they had heard that Nuella's brother was still alive, and resolved to try and reach him. They carried with them many things which might be of service to the suffering man.

A strange wedding journey! Severe as it was, this pilgrimage of love had compensations; it was through sublime scenery, it was healthful, and it gave Stirling and his wife the intimacy of years while developing the character of both into greater strength.

They reached the cabin of Major Felzen, to whom Captain Brown had directed them, only to hear that Colonel Rhodes had been removed from the neighborhood. He had nearly recovered from every trouble except a fractured right arm, when it was discovered that a party of raiders, hearing he was disabled, had resolved to capture him and some things of importance believed to be in his possession. Under the circumstances it was thought best that Colonel Rhodes should leave the territory for a time, and he had gone off with friends; but whither, Major Felzen could not say. The major gave them hearty welcome. He had no wife, but there were in his house a Swedish woman and her daughter, who had immigrated with Mormons but refused to join their community, and found asylum with this countryman. There were also in the house a negro woman and her husband, escaped from Missouri, and in much dread of pursuit.

It was soon proved that the fears of these negroes were well-grounded. On the third morning after the arrival of the Stirlings the tramp of Missourian horses was heard. Felzen's door was barricaded, the men all armed themselves, and a siege was awaited. At length a voice at the door demanded admittance, at hearing which the terrified negro wife whispered—"It is my master; he will kill Charley." Hardly had she spoken when the door was broken in and Felzen shot dead. The rush of the six Missourians was too sudden for resistance. The negroes were first bound and Stirling held fast. He had managed to knock an assailant down, but that was all.

"Shoot the white man," cried one of the raiders, "but keep the gals. Gals is skeerce."

"Shooting's too good, we'll hang him up as a skeercrow for nigger-stealers."

Stirling and Nuella could only exchange looks of silent despair. This then was the end of their sweet romance!

Though in those days there was no escaping negro without a slave-hunter on his track, there was also no such hunter without a free-state avenger on his track. These six Missourians had been pursued for two days and their triumph was brief. The free-state men crept up velvet-footed, nine men, and the raiders were overpowered a few minutes after they had broken in the door. They fought with tooth and claw—their weapons being instantly seized,—but had to yield. One ruffian, just tying Nuella's hands behind her, had leaped in front of her and grappled with fury a man who came to her rescue, and they rolled on the floor. Stirling, whose hands were tightly bound behind him, bounded to the assistance of the free-state man, though he could only use his feet. In another moment his cords were cut.

While the two men were presently engaged in binding this huge ruffian, they did not look at each other. As they rose up their eyes met : once more Stirling and Layman stood face to face. Layman hardly recognized the man who had struck him down in the street at White River Junction ; but at sight of Nuella he was stupefied. There was an ugly gash on his forehead, received from the man at his feet, and his men, who spoke of him as " Colonel Layman," now pressed around to know if he was much hurt. Nuella could not see at once the man who had fought her ruffian, but knowing he was wounded brought handkerchiefs. At her approach Layman hung down his head, but she recognized him. As she was tying a handkerchief around his forehead she spoke to him gently. In her happiness she had already forgiven and forgotten him.

" How glad I am it is you. Randolph, this is an old acquaintance of mine from West Lebanon,—Mr. Layman, this is my husband Mr. Stirling."

Stirling had already spoken warmly and now again poured out his gratitude. Layman looked at him steadily, and perceived that he did not wish the fact of their having met before to be mentioned.

"Your wife is forgiving, Mr. Stirling," said Colonel Layman, "after the evil I once done her."

"All was over-ruled for the best," said Nuella; "you have risen to be a rescuer, and have saved me and my husband."

"Henceforth we are all friends," said Stirling; "whatever is unhappy in the past is blotted out with this blood of yours."

Poor Felzen was silently buried in the forest. The raiders were brought out bound, to surround the grave of the man they had slain. When the shallow grave was nearly filled the Swedish girl planted an evergreen in it, and said, "He was a good man and very kind to us." While she and her mother were shedding tears on the grave of their friend, a strange cry was heard.

"Let us pray!"

A bareheaded young man, apparently deranged, made his way to the grave, and was recognized by the free-state men,—also by two of the Missourians, who had once driven this poor youth trotting before their horses nine miles under a fierce sun. The sunstroke had not yet lifted from the brain of Captain Brown's son, who now gave a glance of pity at the bound men, then fell on his knees beside the grave.

"O God," he cried, with uplifted face, "bless the poor men who are tied and dragged and trampled under horses, and bless their mothers who are crying for them at home. Save them from being hunted with bloodhounds!—Poor men, I will undo your ropes," he added, springing up and moving towards the Missourians.

"Oh, don't hurt them," he cried, as Layman's men restrained him, "they have mothers and wives and children."

The prisoners were released, their horses and money given to the two negroes. The valuables in Felzen's house were collected, the Swedish women taking their own with them. They all then made for a point twenty miles away. Colonel Layman told the Stirlings that he had helped Colonel Rhodes to get off, that he had gone northward with a wagon party, and no doubt would find his way to White River Junction. On the day following there was another funeral; the Swedish mother could not recover from the shock of the struggle at the cabin, Felzen's death, and the fatigue of traveling. She confided to Stirling her daughter, to be taken to a relative in Detroit, and her little treasure of money and jewelry. At the small free-state camp which they reached at length, they found four more fugitive negroes, just arrived with two wagons, in which they were about starting for Iowa, with the hope of making their way to Canada. After consultation it was determined that Stirling should undertake the conveyance of the six negroes, two of which were men, to Canada. Colonel Layman took care that they should all, even the women, be armed, as pursuit of the negroes was probable.

Their itinerary included a small German settlement near the south-west corner of Iowa, and on their approach to this place occurred the first incident of importance to our story in this weary journey. Stirling was told that he could rely on these Germans for assistance. While yet a mile distant he was hailed while passing a saw-mill. Two Germans, having observed the negroes, came out to warn them of danger: a strong party of Missourians had been prowling about there for twenty-four hours, professedly to arrest a murderer, but really, it was believed, to overtake fugitive slaves. The leader of the Missouri party had stated that the murdered man was a worthy German named Felzen, whose valuables had been carried off by the assassin and his confederates. After consultation it was arranged that the wagons should be left at the saw-mill, to be driven into the village by the Germans a few hours later. The party led by Stirling was to break up into groups of two, and go on foot to the village at different times and by different directions. On arrival there they must all find their way to the house of a man named Henermann.

This plan brought Stirling's party safely to Henermann's house, where a consultation was held. The eastward road being certainly watched, the escaping party were advised to leave as they had entered, on foot, and in separate groups, but in a southerly direction. The wagons were to be driven out by Germans and to await the gathering of the party at a point two miles south, from which they were to veer eastward again by an unusual route. They were to start that night—there was moonlight—and at the same time a decoy wagon would start on the watched road. All this was perilously complex. There was little danger of their not reaching the wagons, but the route after that was obscure and a mistake might carry them into Missouri. Stirling inquired if there could be found some German who, if handsomely paid, might be willing to go out with the wagons and accompany them as a guide till they should reach a more certain road.

And now occurred one of those coincidences whose marvelousness grows with their frequency. While Henermann and his friends were suggesting persons possibly available for this task, Stirling caught one name—Hartmann—which had a familiar sound. He could not at once remember where he had heard it, and asked Hartmann's first name. "Franz!" The man was at once sent for, and proved indeed to be the Fraülein's lover. Nothing could exceed the young man's amazement and delight on hearing tidings of his sweetheart, and Stirling told enough of his own services to her to engage his gratitude for their assistance. The lover was a new-comer, and swiftly made his arrangements to travel with the party to the east, having resolved not to rest until he had found his bride.

It was near daybreak when this glad impatient Franz sat waiting with the wagons for the arrival of the fugitive company. They came, group after group, by their devious ways. Stirling, his wife, and the Swedish girl were alone waited for. They had started across a field for a road that passed along the edge of a thicket, and all eyes were now strained in that direction. At length in the far dusk the shadowy form of a woman was seen bounding, as if winged, toward them. It was the Swede, her face ghastly, who rushed to them and sank with exhaustion and terror, gasping out her fearful tidings.

"She is shot! she is dying! her husband may get killed too!"

Alas, it was but too true. A sharp report in the thicket, and Nuella, who was next it, fell,—just as Stirling fired back into the covert.

"Randolph, O my husband," she said, as he took her head in his lap, "fly, fly, they will kill you!"

"My wife, my darling, where are you hurt?"

"I am sinking,—hurry, don't stop," whispered the failing voice, "you can not help me, I am dying."

"And for me, for me—O my God, if I had only been on that side!"

"Would it have struck you?" whispered Nuella; "then I'm happy. You made my life beautiful."

"Nuella, live, live, live! O my sweet——oh!"

She had expired with her last kiss. A great cry of horror came from his heart, he sank back; the little head was pillowed in peace on his prostrate form.

Had his own life only been at stake, Stirling could not have parted from the lifeless form of Nuella, who had twined herself about all his heart-strings, and before whose nobleness he had bowed more reverently every day since their marriage. But when they had laid her on the ground beneath an oak—just as the rising sun ushered in the darkest of nights—and the negroes began a wailing hymn, Franz Hartmann said—"Hush! you must not sing; there is danger around us!" Then Nuella's brave face appealed to him whom her heart had once more shielded, that he should forget self, and even leave her dear slain self to fulfill his trust. Her remembrance should be the safety of those hunted human beings. So Nuella was buried under the oak, and the sorrowful fugitives and their deliverers moved on.

Wherefore, from whom, came this stroke out of the dark was never known. As they drove on Franz strained his eyes toward the wood where the tragedy occurred, but Stirling when he next raised his head looked in another direction: he stood up in the wagon, gazed on the southern horizon, then stretched his hands toward it and said—" Pitiless, pitiless!" If there had lingered in his mind any doubt concerning the spirit of slavery it was left buried in the grave of Nuella. But no feeling of vengeance rose in him; and when, a few hours later, as they were driving over a bridge, a negro handed him his revolver, picked up on the scene of the tragedy, Stirling calmly hurled it into the stream, saying, " I have fired my last shot."

In the evening Stirling conversed with the Swede in German, and she told him a strange history of her life; the negroes also had stories to relate which he found instructive; and had Nuella been there the journey might have proved one of thrilling interest. But the ever-recurring horror permitted nothing to beguile him; it seemed a weary life-time before they reached Detroit. There the Swede was consigned to her friend, and the rest passed on to Canada, where they were received with welcome. Franz, of course, by this time was well on his way to Peacefield and his Mathilde. Stirling told him the address in Canada where he could be reached by a letter for a week or two, and begged him to write.

Stirling, his charge fulfilled, desired only to hide himself and pass silently through his ordeal of grief. He found a little hotel in the neighborhood of the negroes, whose experiences he heard and studied a good deal. He wrote the story of his brief married life, from its happy opening to its heart-breaking end, to send to Manuel when he could summon courage to do so. He wrote long letters to his dearest friends— to Wentworth, Judge Minott, Maria Shelton—keeping them, however, beside him, adding a little from day to day. He was loth to send them; perhaps he dreaded to reveal yet the hermitage of his sorrow. But on an early day in October his solitude was penetrated. He had given a somewhat vague address to Franz, but a letter from Hilda, after some delay, found him out.

"Franz Hartmann," it said, "has found his Mathilde at last, but in their joy are mingled tears for their benefactor. Alas, for the heavy tidings he brings concerning you. We had heard through Judge Minott something of the touching circumstances of your marriage, and he promised to send us your address if he could discover it, for we longed to have you more than fulfill your promise to visit us again, by bringing your wife. Before the fearfulness of your bereavement words sink into lifeless things. But we can not think without concern of your lonely stay in Canada, nor forget that a deed of humanity, similar to that which has now made the tragedy of your life, deprives you of the solace of your father's home. May we not claim the privilege of friends, and beg you to come to us here—at once? We had hoped for your promised return under happy circumstances, but under none could have desired it so much as now. Come, dear Mr. Stirling, and make our house your home. You shall have what seclusion you may desire. The world shall not obtrude on your sorrow. It seems longer than one brief year since we walked together in our grove, but the Indian Summer is again here to soothe your trouble. And there are hearts here that sympathize with you. My father is absent this week, but my mother sends expression of her deep sympathy, and trusts, with me, that you will answer this note with your presence."

Stirling sat holding this letter for a long time; then he wrote a grateful note declining the invitation, and started with it for the post-office. But it was some distance, and as he walked his steps became slower; a gentle sympathizing face, with some of Gisela's look, rose with friendly persuasion before him; the dingy tenements around were hid by vision of a quiet grove; he turned upon his steps, and in the evening wrote to Hilda that he hoped to be at Peacefield Pines before the middle of the month.

But in the following week this plan was changed, and Stirling's mind much disturbed by two letters brought him by a negro.

DEAR SIR,—I hear from friends in Canada of your safe arrival there, under the providence of God, with six souls delivered from the house of bondage. This shows that what you said at Tabor was not mere words. I have also been informed of the murder of your wife by slave-hunting assassins. Terrible as is this blow, I feel assured that the Lord has chosen this means of bringing home to you the condition of the millions of wives and husbands who are in the power of such murderous oppressors. I pray and believe that your eyes must be now fully open. You said to me at Tabor, that if you should see human beings escaping from bondage you would help them. The time has come for me to remind you of that promise and require, in the name of God, its fulfillment. If you will meet me on the bridge at Harper's Ferry on Sabbath evening, the 23d inst., your doubts (if they remain), of the slaves' desire to rise, will disperse; you will see the outstretched arm of Almighty God, and the deliverance of those who cry to him day and night. Private. Yours faithfully,—BROWN.

DEAR SIR,—Captain John Brown has been much excited the last few days by a letter received from Canada concerning you. He read it to us, and says that he knows you, and has reason to believe that you will be at his side when his long-meditated blow is struck. Though I am writing this by another hand, and do not give my name, you and I have met, and I am anxious to save you from danger. Captain Brown has mustered here (at a place called Kennedy's Farm, Maryland, about two hours march from Harper's Ferry) about twenty men, with whom he means to attack that town, seize the arms there, distribute them among the slaves and overthrow slavery. This scheme could only succeed by a miracle; but the captain fully believes that miracle will occur—literally. He believes that he has been appointed by certain signs to deliver the slaves, and that, if necessary, the Potomac would open for him and his people to walk through dry-shod.  He has received in the north large sums of money from persons who can hardly know that it is intended to lead a handful of young men like sheep to the slaughter.  Some of our number are in ignorance of the doom that is over them.  We are all bound to him by solemn oaths.  I am willing to die, but I feel bound to warn you not to be induced by any thing he may write to join us, unless, indeed, you have such influence over Captain Brown as to be able to stop his insane project.  In this case you might save lives by coming here.  He told me he meant to take a look at Harper's Ferry on the 16th.  You might see him if you were there, or could easily inquire your way to this farm-house.  But unless you are certain of such influence over him, I implore you do not be misled into joining us.  We are doomed men.—A FRIEND.

Stirling resolved to try and stop this wild business.  He would secure an interview with Brown in some hotel or hostelry, and there if he could not be dissuaded he should be detained, quietly.  But there was no time to be lost.  By going through Cleveland and Columbus he believed he could just make Harper's Ferry by October sixteenth.  He traveled night and day.

But the anonymous correspondent and Brown himself had not rightly indicated the time when the attack was made.  On such small wires hang great weights.  Stirling was asleep in his berth, after midnight of the Sunday he had hoped to pass at Harper's Ferry, when he was aroused with the other passengers by a loud cry—"Wake up! wake up! there's trouble going on!" All started up in panic, and heard with dismay that the train had been seized by robbers. The bewildered passengers were marched off under guards to a railway hotel. There they were told that robbers had taken possession of the town. While Stirling was making inquiries of servants in the kitchen, the train moved off—about sunrise. He remained a prisoner in the hotel all day, but felt that perhaps this was best, for he had now little doubt that Captain Brown had struck his blow. On the morning of the day following, the guards having disappeared from the hotel doors, he walked out toward the armory. There he beheld Captain Brown seated on the ground, covered with blood, with several officers around him, while frantic men were rushing to and fro, and shots were heard in every direction. Stirling was standing on the opposite side of the street, and when Brown looked toward him, incautiously waved his hand in token of recognition and pity. The next moment he was struck by a bullet and fell.

"You are shooting your own citizens," cried Brown, "that man is not with me—he is a Virginian."

The man who had fired on Stirling hurried away. Brown was at once carried off. Stirling lay unnoticed, and gradually recovered sufficient consciousness to crawl through a rude gate that stood open in palings near him, and to close it. Beyond this was a small stable which he managed to reach and enter. There he lay on straw and lost consciousness again. After some time a negro brought a horse into the stable, and Stirling was aroused as if from sleep.

"My man," he said to the trembling negro, "I am shot and will probably die, but try and bring me water."

The man crept softly away and presently returned with water, and accompanied by another negro. "He is one of the men that came here to die for us," said one of the negroes. The two bore him to a vacant stall, nearly covered him with hay, and placing bread and water beside him, said they would remove him as soon as it could be done without their being observed. Then Stirling again sank into unconsciousness.

## CHAPTER XXX.

### THE WANDERER'S REST.

ENCOURAGED, as we have seen, by Gisela, Wentworth postponed his return to Virginia and accepted the invitation to visit the Minotts, who were eager to hear about his experiences in the South.

One morning, while they were lingering at the breakfast-table, a letter was opened by Judge Minott which extorted from him a cry of horror. It was from a negro man, and rudely written, a letter from Stirling being inclosed. This, the negro wrote, had been found in the pocket of a gentleman wounded in the fight at Harper's Ferry, and now lying there in the house of a free negro. He seemed to be nearly senseless. "We are doing all we can but are afraid to say any thing about him to the white people, who are furious. The only doctor who has seen him is myself, but I don't know much about a thing like this, and only doctor colored people in little things. His wound is in the head, and I'm afraid he won't live. He ought to have help. If anybody comes after him let them ask the sexton of the Baptist meeting-house. I will send this to be put in the letter-box at Baltimore."

The letter of Stirling inclosed told the tragical story of his wife's death. A penciled postscript added:

"Although I have written this letter I dread sending it. I am now on a train bound for Harper's Ferry, where I hope to prevent the fanatical scheme of a good but misguided abolitionist, fraught with danger and evil. I then hope to reach my dear old home in Virginia."

The first southward train bore Wentworth and Dr. Jeffries Wyman. Cautious inquiries at Harper's Ferry brought them by midnight to the bedside of the sufferer. He was lying in the best room of the free negro's house, where his constant attendant was Alice Ross. For it had speedily become known among the colored people of the neighborhood that a man wounded in the John Brown fray was hidden in this house, and Alice had at length identified him. She lived in a house near by, where Darnley came every evening.

The bullet had not entered the brain, but had plowed deep and driven a portion of the skull upon it, with what extent of lesion could not yet be known. Trephining was required, and having removed the bits of bone pressed into the brain, the surgeon could do no more. Before leaving he went with Wentworth to a physician connected with the United States service, who agreed to take charge of the case, evidence being given that Stirling was a Virginian who had come to prevent the Brown raid. They all agreed, nevertheless, that secrecy was desirable on account of the prevailing excitement.

Meanwhile that negro-telegraph, which we have once before known in operation between Harper's Ferry and The Palms, had borne the tidings to

Gisela. Her father had just gone on circuit, so she could easily leave, and was soon on her way to Harper's Ferry. She was there guided by a friend of Caleb Stone to the house where her brother lay. Into an inner room she passed without knocking, and found there a young man, whom she supposed to be a physician, and a colored woman, who was kneeling at the foot of the cot. Gisela's step was so soft that the woman did not raise her head. At a low moan from the sufferer, Alice Ross, for it was she, lifted her face and saw her beloved friend seated beside the bed.

"I have prayed for you and you have come," she said, coming close to Gisela. "Master has gone for medicine but will soon be here. This gentleman has just arrived."

Gisela looked upon the wasted form of her brother, then closed her eyes for a few moments. Presently she glanced at the stranger with an expression of inquiry, and he came forward to whisper the explanation of his presence.

"You are a near acquaintance of his?" he said.

"I am his sister."

"I come from her he lifted out of grief."

"From his wife?"

"Ah, you do not know—his wife is dead."

"Heavens! Oh, Ran, my poor brother, what have you been suffering, all alone—your sister so far away!"

"My name is Hartmann," said the stranger, when the inquiring eyes were again turned on him; "she was helped by him in need who is now my wife. I am here to help."

When Wentworth and Gisela presently met they felt less surprise than might have been expected, neither having heard from the other since Stirling was wounded. How could either be absent at such a time? The negro who owned the house now gave it up to the friends of the wounded man. Gisela, Wentworth, and Hartmann took up their abode in it, Alice Darnley preparing their food in her house near by. Thus they entered upon their sorrowful watch. Franz was unwearied in his services, and seemed none the less fresh for sitting up all night. Franz told them of Stirling's adventures at Spindleton and Peacefield, as Frau Hartmann had related them; and the evenings he beguiled from some of their heaviness with the romance of his own life. Gisela did not fail to write to Mathilde of her husband's devoted services to them, and of their attachment to him.

The physician did not appear hopeful. The patient's eyes, even when open, gave no sign of recognition, and though he sometimes muttered words they could not be understood. The symptoms indicated a severe lesion, attention to which had been too long delayed, and when at length a crisis was foreseen it was with apprehension. During one day he had been especially restless, and had made repeated efforts to speak. The doctor then resolved to pass the night at the bedside. There was nothing that the watchers could do but sit with folded hands, their hearts filled with forebodings, while the sufferer tossed feverishly on his cot. A little before daybreak he uttered some words and the physician drew close to listen, the others standing around the bed. A little later his eyes were fixed on Franz who was at the foot of his bed, and a few feeble words came,—"Nuella, you have come . . . I am glad you have come . . . I thought you would not leave me."

"Wandering still," said the doctor, "we must be prepared for the—ah!"

"No . . . It is not Nuella . . . I saw her die." His eyes closed, and tears fell on his cheeks.

"Who is this he speaks of?" asked the doctor quickly.

"His wife, Nuella, lately dead."

"Then if he can rally, I believe he is saved."

The doctor waved them all out of the room. The greatest caution had to be taken that the patient should have as little emotional agitation as possible. But the improvement was maintained, and one after the other Gisela and Wentworth were allowed to greet him. Stirling's first smile answered the information that his sister and friend were betrothed.

"I thought I could never again be happy, but all is not lost," he said.

"Right, Ran," said Gisela—"don't lose courage. Soon you will be at home again. Your suffering in trying to save others, will make father feel prouder of you than ever."

"Ought you not to be with him?"

"Yes, Ran, he will soon return from circuit, and I must be there, but Walter will remain, and this kind gentleman who has come to assist us."

"Why!" exclaimed Stirling, as Hartmann came forward. "It is my comrade Franz. Have you come all this way for me?"

"Miss Hilda and my Mathilde can not rest, mein Herr, while you were in trouble. At their home they some time looked for you, but always you did not come, and Miss Hilda from the frau richterrin Minott got the schrecklich news. I must be here. Daily I send them one telegraphisch word. First it was, 'alas.' Forgestern it was, 'hope.' To-day it was, 'joy.' Their eyes will drip with much fun. When you may travel, at Peacefield Pines find you your welcome."

"When you return," said Gisela to Franz, laying her arm on the pillow around her brother's head, "carry to those kind ladies our love, but say that his first welcome will be in his father's house."

After Stirling's severe trials and disappointments, it is satisfactory to record the fulfillment of one of his hopes : he passed his Christmas at The Palms. It was some weeks more before he could be removed even by stages, but at last the wanderer returned to his father's house and embrace. What Christmas tales were told, day and night, to beguile him from sorrowful memories—tales of Leroy Island, of Wentworth's man-and-woman purchases, of the Tournament, and Sir Walter's combat with Ivanhoe ; also a sweet lovetale ; and the story of one securing the interests of his distant friend by his first law-case.

Before the year was out, Stirling also did a bit of professional work. Manuel and Ruth had several times written to him—Colonel Rhodes, also, who told him that poor Layman perished at Harper's Ferry. One of these letters contained a copy of Nuella's will. She had bequeathed her farm and homestead to her husband ; if he should not survive her, it should go to

Ruth. To Ruth was at once transferred the settlement, and she went to live on it after her marriage with Rev. Arthur Farwell, Mr. Grace's successor.

But Wentworth and Stirling, as partners, argued their first case in the library at The Palms. A judgment at once paternal and judicial had to be given on the conduct of Randolph in the fugitive-slave cases, at Peacefield and in Kansas. After it had been argued by the young men, the case was after all gained by Gisela who, in a Portia-like argument, pleaded that in such situation—a human being flying from a cruel master—the master must be held technically to his pound of flesh. The fugitives helped by Randolph were not covered by legal process; he could not assume that they were slaves at all; and so forth. The judge might have sifted these positions somewhat more severely, had it not been for a very serious event that happened about that time in his personal affairs. It was, indeed, an event that placed him in a situation not unlike that of his son.

Judge Stirling's legal career had from the first been singular. He had resolutely declined cases in whose justice he did not strictly believe. Lawyers laughed at the youth, and predicted that he would soon outgrow his scrupulosity; but he did not; and then friends remonstrated, for he was known to be refusing large retainers. But the young lawyer adhered to his principle, and in the end gained such a hold on the confidence of jurors and judges that his mere appearance in a case was almost equivalent to its being won. The common run of lawyers could not stand against his moral and intellectual power combined, and had him put on the bench to get him away from the bar. On the bench Judge Stirling's reputation for integrity and learning spread beyond his own circuit ; and on the day before this memorable Christmas, he received an appointment to the Court of Appeals. High as the honor was, the judge had taken it under consideration, for he was getting on in years, and he did not like the prospect of passing so much of his time in Richmond. But, before the time requested for advisement had elapsed, he had to decide a case concerning which pro-slavery feeling was much excited. A hundred slaves gained freedom by the decision. The family interested was influential, the agitation attending the raid and execution of John Brown had not yet subsided, and the manumission of these slaves caused so much feeling against Judge Stirling that his appointment to the Court of Appeals was revoked. The probabilities were already against his acceptance of the unsought honor ; but this incident struck deep in the judge's mind. For the first time he awakened to the fact that he had fallen upon a new generation. The day he well remembered, when his relative Judge Leigh had formally renounced his vast bequest under John Randolph's last will, in order to overthrow it in favor of another, written in sound mind, liberating the Randolph slaves. That day was gone. The Old Dominion had fallen under control of smaller men. The judge concluded that the new elements by which they were surrounded were not much more congenial to himself than to his son Randolph ; and one morning he surprised his family by announcing his retirement from the bench altogether.

The judge's resolution was received by his children with sympathetic expressions, with indignation at the causes which had led to it, but not with exclamations of regret. When he had spoken, quick glances were exchanged across the table, and eyes grew brighter. A curtain that had long hung motionless before a future of happy scenes, now visibly swayed and might possibly—even probably—rise.

From this time Gisela, Wentworth, and Randolph held daily and prolonged consultations, and in the end brought before the judge certain revolutionary proposals. The Palms to be let, after the celebration therein of a marriage; the family to reside together in Washington; an office there to bear on its door the words, "Stirling & Wentworth, Attorneys at Law."

"I thought," said the judge, "that I had retired from the bench, but you have brought me the heaviest docket I ever had to deal with in my life; and you must not be surprised if judgments are reserved for a considerable time."

One case in this last calendar of the judge was adjudicated very soon. He desired that the marriage should not be delayed. That step taken, more light might rise on the next. So it came that the first warm breath of spring clothed The Palms with rare and wondrous blossomings. It was Gisela's choice, somewhat to the surprise of the others, that this wedding should be translated from a fairy-tale. Whether it was that she desired all neighbors to know that they of The Palms bore no grudge for bygones, nor were any whit less happy for provincial inappreciation of the Three Greatest Men on Earth; or whether her historic sense required that the last festival of the Stirlings in their old mansion should be the culmination of its traditional hospitalities; so it was, that no care or cost was spared in the preparations for this wedding. Its magnificence now belongs to the folk-lore of Fauquier. Mammas whose hearts are yet ruddy, though their heads may be a little white, still tell their daughters of that enchanted day when the mocking-bird's magical music, and eye-chimes of the gopher and the Judas-tree, led on to a warm full moon, and lawns aglow with colored lights, amid which Gisela moved as a goddess, loves and graces dancing around her and her happy bridegroom through the charmed night, while the baronial banquet ceased not till sunrise. (For some phrases in this last sentence the author acknowledges his indebtedness to certain "Lines on a Scene at The Palms," which appeared in "The Flag of '98" just after the wedding.)

# CHAPTER XXXI.

### FLOWER O' THE PINE AND PALM.

CATS cling to houses, dogs to their inmates. Like man's faithful friend, our interest will follow those who have founded their new home in Washington. Twenty-seven years ago a picturesque old mansion on Capitol Hill was still defending its acre of homestead from siege of brick and mortar; and though, to-day, the inclosure contains a villa residence, also a two-storeyed office between that and the old mansion, these buildings represent some years' history of friendly invaders from The Pines and The Palms, who have brought these names with them.

The office of the young law-partners in Indiana Avenue soon became a center of prosperous business. The only anxiety of the family now was about Randolph, who could not easily recover from the effects of his tragical experiences. He worked with painful eagerness, and even the inexhaustible wit of Pen won but faint smiles to his face. An occasional cough caught the quick ear of Gisela. She remembered a tradition that some great-grand-uncle Randolph had died of consumption, and poor Ran had to make the acquaintance of cod-liver oil. One day Wentworth suggested that they should fulfill their college dream of a tour in Europe, but Randolph said he desired nothing so much as constant occupation.

"I'm going on a little journey in the opposite direction," he added. Two weeks later he sat beneath the oak in Iowa, where he last looked on the face of Nuella, while a workman was setting a marble memorial on her grave.

But it pleased dame Clotho to knit again the thread she once began spinning at Peacefield, which was so rudely cut by her sister Atropos. On a May afternoon, Randolph, just from the West, was walking through the Capitol grounds, his eyes bent on the earth, when he came close on an old friend, moving listlessly before him, with eyes following the birds, or perhaps the cloudlets.

" Hilda Leigh ! " burst from his lips.

Hilda seemed to wake up at sound of her name, and her face was filled with glad surprise. Her father, summoned to Washington by the government for consultation on a financial scheme, was then in the capitol, and she had accepted the invitation of Spring for a stroll. Randolph heard all about their ideal lovers, the Hartmanns—now officially established on the Leigh estate, the happiest herr and frau in Peacefield. Even Hilda's eyes betrayed some curiosity on learning that she was only a few hundred yards from Gisela and other members of a family whose wraiths had sometimes flitted about the Peacefield grove. Reciprocal informations past, there ensued a pleasant silence, at length broken by Hilda.

"Mr. Stirling, we are waiting for your promised return to Peacefield."

The half-closed eyes were on him once more ; the face that had appeared in vision, hovering near him in hours of anxiety and anguish, was again before him —beaming from its heaven of repose. The leaden cloud which no zephyr, no bloom, no roundelay of the Spring, could lift from his heart, now waned and receded before visible harmony, which carried all subtle-sweet meanings of zephyr, bloom and song. Had Randolph replied to her last remark with what floated through his mind, he might have startled this serenest of maidens out of her Nirvana of unconsciousness. He walked on in smiling but silent reverie.

"When is it to be, Mr. Stirling?"

"Do you know, Miss Hilda, that if you keep on, I shall go?"

"When is it to be, Mr. Stirling?"

"When you return."

"The first of June."

Mr. Derby Leigh discovered that his daughter was a rather perilous person to introduce to Washington society. She had not the remotest consciousness of her peculiar charm. On the bachelor congressmen, and others who buzzed around this beauty of unfamiliar type, Hilda's glowing nature shone with such equal uninquiring warmth that each was in danger of feeling himself the immediate jewel of her soul. She was so unconscious of the spell she was weaving around Randolph that she was ready to accept Gisela's invitation to stay with her. Mr. Derby Leigh, however, had read his young friend's face, and said he could not leave his hotel, and he could not spare Hilda. But she saw a good deal of the Stirlings and Wentworths, and they contributed much to the pleasure of her month in Washington. When her mother sent her a paragraph from a Peacefield paper saying she was the "belle" of Washington just then, Hilda only said "how silly," but she was glad when the time came to return to The Pines.

And there, sure enough, Randolph again walked with her in the grove,—in growing forgetfulness of the cruel winter that lay between the Indian summer of their parting and this June, flowering beyond all Junes since creation. Mr. Leigh introduced him to the old romance of Peacefield, to haunts of famous witches and gabled homes of ancient gentry; Hilda made him acquainted with the several pines, their needles, the varied wild-flowers, the choir of birds and their vestments. Stirling saw all these as root, stem, leaf, leading to one immortal flower. Droll that he should have groped about to explore New England, when all its history, meaning, genius, were gathered up in this one product—Hilda. Gradually there was formed in the mind of this Virginian an oration which would have thrilled Dane Hall, but there was no audience for it here, unless he should utter it to all New England as represented in Hilda amid the pines. One afternoon, indeed, the new inspiration did break forth, but poured itself in one word.

"Hilda!"

She stood still, but no other word followed: this one soft plaintive cry out of a heart longing to recover its early dream, two hands stretched out to her for rescue,—this was what Hilda heard and saw in that solitude. Her hands met Randolph's silently; where her heart had gone her life followed.

\* \* \* \* \* \*

Some twenty years ago, the Wentworths, leaving their little Pen with her Auntie Pen (Mrs. Basil Stirling) at The Palms, Warrenton, visited the Leroys and Rev. Mr. and Mrs. (Eleanor Ravenel) Stringfield in South Carolina. On their return they brought two selectest palmettos, (one presented by Mrs. Bertha Ravenel, and the other by Mrs. Charlotte Leroy), which, in warm season, stand at their door on Capitol Hill to justify the name of their house. Hilda, not to be out-done, has two evergreens from Peacefield for sentinels at The Pines. The gardens are the realm of Wesley Hampton, who found out his master and demanded the right to serve out the time between his flight from Savannah and the proclamation of emancipation, and remains as master of most people about the place. Under his especial sway are two venerable widowers, Judge Stirling and Derby Leigh, who, in the home built for them, are sometimes visited by their old friend Minott. The three venerable heads, crowned with white blossoms, laugh together as they see clouds that once covered them floating as tinted islets in their evening sky. The last time Judge Minott—dreamer to the last —parted from his old friends, he paused to observe Gisela's palms and Hilda's pines: as he looked the small trees climbed high, and intertwined their branches; and through their green arch shone a fair vista,—northward, southward.

**THE END.**

www.ingramcontent.com/pod-product-compliance
Lightning Source LLC
Chambersburg PA
CBHW031432230426
43668CB00007B/506